THE EMPOWERED LOVER

The astounding science of how you can elevate your relationship even without depending on your partner to change.

ARNO KOCH

IMAGINE EVOLUTION

This book is designed to provide general information regarding the subject matter covered.
However, laws and practices often vary from state to state and are subject to change. Because each factual situation is different, specific advice should be tailored to the particular circumstances. For this reason, the reader is advised to consult with his or her own advisor regarding their specific situation.

The author and publisher have taken reasonable precautions in the preparation of this book and believe the facts presented in the book are accurate as of the date it was written. However, neither the author nor the publisher assume any responsibility for any errors or omissions. The author and publisher specifically disclaim any liability resulting from the use or application of the information contained in this book, and the information is not intended to serve as legal, financial, or other professional advice related to individual situations.

ISBN: 979-8-9886137-2-5
ISBN: 979-8-9886137-0-1 (pbk)
ISBN: 979-8-9886137-1-8 (ebook)

Contact the author:
Email: service@imagine-evolution.com
Web: www.imagine-evolution.com

For Felix and Lara

CONTENTS

INTRODUCTION

It's a warm summer night in July 2020 in suburban Los Angeles. The pandemic is in full swing. People are confined to their homes for... how much longer? Nobody knows.

Frank grabs his camera, puts a collar on their dog, Sam, walks over to his wife Janine, and tells her that he is heading out to take a photograph of the Neowise comet.

"That's unusual," she says, looking at him skeptically. "You don't usually leave the house at 9 p.m."
"It's unusual to be able to see a comet in the night sky," Frank mansplains.
"Are you sure you're not seeing someone?"
"100% sure," Frank replies and heads out without asking Janine if she wants to join him.

Two hours later, Frank walks back into the house. Janine greets him at the door, but her face is not happy.
"Where did you go?!"
"I tried to take a picture of the comet, remember?"
She squints, comes up close, and smells his collar. Frank chuckles.
"Why did you switch your phone off, Frank?"
"I didn't."
"I tried to call you, but it went straight to voicemail!"
"I drove through the Santa Monica Mountains, trying to find a spot with no light pollution. I guess you called me while I had no service."

Janine gives Frank a long glare. Frank kisses her goodnight and makes his way upstairs to go to bed. Fifteen minutes later, as Frank is dozing off, the bedroom door opens.

"Where's your phone?"
"It's charging in the office as usual."

A minute later, Janine comes into the bedroom with Frank's phone, sits down on the bed next to him, and starts to operate his phone. Frank leans over to see what she is doing.

"Are you afraid I may find something?"

Frank's head drops heavily back onto his pillow. Thoughts racing. What the heck! How DARE she! SHE is going through MY phone and acts as if I had done something wrong! But what is she looking at? An overwhelming feeling of being completely out of control spreads through Frank's body.

"What can I do to relax the situation?" Frank asks himself, gathering his thoughts. "Focus on what you can control," he answers himself.

So, Frank focuses on his breath. Box breathing is a breathing technique that the Navy SEALs practice and use to stay calm in combat situations when bullets fly over their heads.

Box breathing, Frank does, until Janine gets up without saying a word, leaves the bedroom, shuts the door behind her, and is gone. It's over. Had she seen something that she found suspicious? Had she not?

Running out and checking the phone could fan the flames...

As Frank has a pure conscience, he decides to have faith, turns around, and falls asleep quickly. The next morning, he wakes up with his wife next to him. No sign of irritation, no word about the evening.

Later that morning, Frank steps out of the shower and feels the need to say something.

"I am sorry that I made you feel like I was hiding something yesterday. I know that you have been cheated on in the past, and I can only imagine how that must have felt. But you thinking I could have done such a horrible thing to you was a little hurtful to me as well."

"Oh, was it?" comes the sarcastic reply.
"It was," he says and leaves it at that.

Ten minutes later, Janine apologizes. "I am sorry. I trust you, and I know that you did not do anything bad." As Frank gets to his office, he opens his phone and is curious about what content she had checked. The last app that was opened was the navigation app. Apparently, Frank passed the test.

A test that Frank could have avoided. Although he mastered his emotions and his response well that night when the conflict ensued, Frank was still unaware of how he could have prevented hurting Janine. It didn't occur to him how simply asking her if she wanted to join him could have changed her perception from "Why does he want to leave me at night?" to "He wants to do something that I am invited to, and I have a choice to join or not." Looking through the lens of his innocence, Frank missed his contribution to the situation. The question "What can I do to relax the situation?" occurred to Frank early enough to prevent an escalation but too late to prevent the hurt and the conflict in the first place, while Janine displayed another cornerstone of healthy relationships: The power of apologies.

You sometimes find yourself in very hurtful situations with the person you love the most. You know that you are also the person who they love the most, but it still hurts, or rather, because of it. No matter how clear the responsibility for a conflict may seem to you in the moment, you've played your part just like Frank did here and only realized much later. Often the contribution is just showing a lack of awareness or empathy.

As one partner interprets what they see through the lens of their past experiences and the evidence of the other partner's disregard for their feelings, they feel anger, sadness, fear. Their body releases stress hormones, cortisol, adrenaline, which then occupy their body, shifting their focus to be hypersensitive to any sign of confirmation of their suspicion, any sign of danger. Trying to match any behavior they perceive with their expectation. Anxiety is an expectation. An expectation of danger. The conscious mind sets the expectation, the unconscious mind strives to fulfill it.

Suddenly you're in the middle of a conflict, and it is absolutely justified and normal to be frustrated when you get accused of something you did not do. Your body releases stress hormones as well, and it is justifiable to express that frustration and get angry with your partner. But how will that be perceived? Be it justifiable or not, an expression of anger or frustration must be interpreted by them as an attempt to hide guilt, a smokescreen to hide evidence. So does defending yourself. That way, you can't win.

This book is about winning. Winning the relationship game, you and your beloved. Creating win-wins. It's about your communication with yourself and your partner. Effective communication. Love-Based Language that gets you the results you want and helps you prevent conflict or at least fix it in the inevitable moments when you find yourself in it. Not only in your intimate relationship, but also with your family members, your coworkers, your employees, your boss, with yourself, and any person you ever talk with. So that you can be your best self in the most challenging of moments and speak with your partner, not only with loving intentions but so that they feel your love, your empathy, and your compassion as an empowered lover.

Why does the world need yet another book on relationships? Hasn't John Gottman figured everything out in his over four decades of scientific research? Hasn't the Bible provided all the answers we need 2000 years ago?

I believe diving into and incorporating John Gottman's research into your marriage is a very powerful thing to do. I have enjoyed relationship literature from experts like him and from people coming from scripture who distilled a great chunk of relationship advice out of the book of books and helped thousands of people that way.

They just miss one piece. As you read those books, it becomes too easy to drop into the fallacy of recognizing what you are doing right and what your partner is doing wrong.

As I was struggling in my own relationships, I read relationship advice and thought ever so often, "Yes! My partner needs to hear THIS!" And then I'd go to them and try to mansplain my new insights. Their response? They would either not be open to hear it in the first place, or they would and then I would observe closely if they put it into action and in most cases found that they didn't.

In fact, they probably even tried, but I didn't see it, while I was oblivious to my own failure to make the new behavior a habit instantly. Then I resented them for their lack of implementation and ever so often stopped implementing the wise advice myself. Yes, I was a toxic person in my relationships.

A relationship is the co-creation of two human beings. No interaction is ever only one partner's fault. This book is for you and only for you. If your partner chooses to read it too, or wants to hear about it, you can appreciate that, but it's not my intention.

Every piece of advice in this book is presented from two angles so you can use it to improve your communication no matter what side you are on. You will become the change that you want to see in your relationship, to become an empowered lover who takes full responsibility for the part you play in your relationship.

You will find some concepts repeatedly in this book for two reasons.

1. Who has the time to read books multiple times these days? Reading things multiple times helps remember them.
2. You may choose to revisit certain chapters later on, and I want each chapter to stand well on its own. Reading this book cover to cover is one option, but you may also read the chapters in the order of importance they have for you.

There is no magic trick to elevate your relationship, but there are ways to shift the odds, to increase the likelihood that you and your partner will fulfill each other's needs better than ever before, and it's at your fingertips.

PART ONE

IT'S ALL IN YOUR HEAD, BUT IS IT?

"When you share emotional baggage, you don't release it. You multiply it."

— Chapter 1 —

STRUGGLES

"What comes out of you when you're squeezed is what is inside of you."

I am sitting in the living room, shaking. I have a knot in my throat. Somehow, I am able to speak.

"Can you let Mom finish?"

I am 13 years old, and my parents are having one of their regular arguments. It's chaos around me, and I don't know how my younger brother and sister manage to sleep through this. Maybe it's because it's their normal, our normal. A normal that should not be normal for any child, but it sure is for these three kids.

I am mediating an argument between my parents that is not going anywhere. It never does. And I am just hoping that it won't get to the point that I am so afraid of: "I am done! I'm getting a divorce!"

What is the topic about? I can't remember. But I remember how I felt. No, I am feeling it viscerally. My body is flooded with stress hormones – cortisol, adrenaline – and I am trying to keep my composure. The 13-year-old is alive and well but in the body of a 30-year-old who is experiencing the situation for the nth time.

I am having a fight with my girlfriend, and we're having an argument. About nothing. But I'm done. I know this relationship won't last. How can I ever marry this woman? On my drive home, all I am thinking about are her imperfections that I am projecting out and convincing myself how they make a life together impossible. This is not Mrs. Right.

Things escalate quickly in my relationships. As soon as I perceive a shortcoming in my partner, voice it, and receive pushback, the 13-year-old wakes up inside of me. The fear from years ago creeps up, and my body does what bodies do when dangers loom: release that cocktail of stress hormones that make your fingers tingle and switch my brain activity from consciously processing information to a millions-of-years-old part of my brain that provides quick reflexes and is always ready to fight. You don't rise to the level of your expectations (I will stay calm next time), you fall to the level of your training. And training I had in my childhood. My emotions blown out of proportion, I catastrophize and try to explain to the poor girl in front of me how her behavior is detrimental to herself and our relationship. Mansplain how her ways are not serving her nor us. Did she do anything wrong? Not at all. She just didn't meet my preferences in the moment. But I am sitting there once again with that knot in my throat, sabotaging a relationship that could and should be sweet and loving. And I have no idea that I am.

I am sitting in a toxic trap in which I am the toxic person. The yelling, blaming, shaming, guilting, and labeling that I saw my parents expose each other to, that my siblings and I were exposed to, is what I am now projecting onto my partner. And I have no idea that I am. By virtue of exposure, I have learned how to handle conflicts, and it is not working very well. But I feel all righteous about myself. In addition, I don't know about the emotional baggage that I brought from my upbringing and empty out over my partner every time I am displeased with what I see. I just feel the results of the automatically released stress hormones. It's all I know, and I can't help it. My thoughts are hijacked, and I sulk in them and mull them over for days, believing that if I stay distant, it will teach her a lesson and emphasize her wrongdoing.

How did I get into that toxic trap? How did I get out? The obvious culprits were my parents. As they never had a concept of handling conflicts in an amicable fashion—always blaming, shaming, guilting, labeling each other and confessing the other person's sins to them—that's how I learned to handle conflicts. Us kids were physically disciplined, and the word "divorce" was ever on the table.

Don't get me wrong, I am looking back to a very happy childhood. My parents are wonderful people who love their children with every fiber of their being. The many happy times outweighed the unhappy ones by far. My parents would drop everything when we kids were in trouble and fought as deliberately with any outside force that threatened the family as they fought with themselves. They somehow managed to get through their emotional turmoil. I love them deeply, we talk every week, but I had to go through a forgiveness process and release my trauma from the intense experiences described above. In the case of my dad, it took me 38 years.

As I was physically disciplined, I passed it on to my sister. When she did something that I did not approve of and I was angry enough, I'd do what my dad did to me and hit her.

They say that the first act of war is an act of defense, and you don't have to look far into the past to find how a situation you need to defend yourself can be crafted. It doesn't matter if it's a country (Germany "shooting back" at Poland or fabricated weapons of mass destruction...) or an individual.

Sometimes I wouldn't even care. My sister would be watching TV and minding her own business, I'd come home from school and decide I wanted to watch something else, and well... she better comply. Looking back, it didn't even matter what she was watching. Maybe it was even something that I enjoyed the previous day. I just wanted to watch something else, aka I was looking for a reason to vent a frustration that I brought home from school.

At some point, it must have been around age 14, I realized that this was not okay. Yet, it took a while to change my ways and overcome my toxic habit. At the same time, shame and guilt crept up. I knew I had done wrong. A lot.

I tried to soothe my feelings by telling myself how I was a different person now, how the individual doing those things had been a child that didn't know better, and it kind of helped. Kind of.

I was able to talk myself out of those bouts of guilt, but they returned on a regular basis. Rationalizing them did not release them.

I realized and had to confront an undeniable truth: My mind may have developed and changed, but it had still been these hands at the ends of my arms who did what they had done, and there was no undoing it. Just like my father's hands did what they had done, and it couldn't be undone.

I was looking for something that I couldn't quite pinpoint for a long time until it dawned on me. I wanted him to apologize. I wanted him to take full responsibility and tell me that he was sorry. I wanted him to ask me for forgiveness. I needed him to.

My dad and I had a lot of great times and experiences together, but the way I was treated when my behavior didn't meet his expectations left scars. I don't even think that how my dad responded to my misbehaviors was a great exception. Many dads did the same or worse. But I do believe that it is an experience that requires healing for one's own sake and to not pass it down to future generations.

When my dad hit me, he never apologized. He was always 100% certain that it was the right and appropriate thing to do. "I was a difficult child."

Did he love me? Absolutely, there was no doubt about it.

What is love? How do we learn what love is, or is love a universal thing, the same for every human on the planet?

Each and every one of us has a natural, unconscious understanding, perception, and expression of love that is so self-explanatory that it can be hard to grasp that different people may have a different understanding. The book *The Five Love Languages* by Gary Chapman illustrates how we express and perceive love in different ways. The question remains: How are those differences formed?

There are many factors, but one is how our parents behave towards us. What our parents do is love. It can be altered and molded, but we drop out of childhood with a solid blueprint.

My father was hit, too. And thankfully, he already applied a few changes to how he had been treated. His dad beat him with a stick, and not only as an immediate punishment, but I remember my dad telling me how my grandfather would announce a beating, then they could go about their merry ways, have fun and laugh, and then my grandfather would remember the promised beating, produce the stick, and go about his painful business. Talk about building distrust and uncertainty. Compared to that, I was well off.

I reasoned how my dad had improved and acknowledged it, but that didn't mean that it left me unscarred. It was something to be grateful for in an odd, distorted way, but nothing to be grateful for in the grand scheme of things. I was hurt and traumatized. And I hurt and traumatized my sister or added to the trauma inflicted by our dad.

Traumatized? Really? I use the word trauma liberally. I believe there are different degrees of trauma on a scale from one to ten. One may be an argument that still makes you feel angry, sad, or embarrassed years later, level ten may be the result of being raped or from military experiences like witnessing gruesome deaths of a person you're emotionally connected to. Then again, same words heard from an important person over and over again can be just as traumatizing.

I was about 23 years old when I gave my sister a call and invited her over to my apartment. At that point, our relationship was not good. We coexisted and met on a regular basis, supported each other when necessary, but I remember our conversations as rather shallow, disconnected, and quick to become annoyed or even hostile. She had no idea what was coming.

We sat together and chit-chatted for a bit when I brought up our childhood. I apologized and took full responsibility for everything I had done and made it clear that I had no excuses. My hands were the ones who did what happened, and I deeply regret it.

I also made it clear that this is not one of those "sibling apologies" where you apologize a few times and when the topic comes up again, you say, "Come on, how much more often do I have to apologize? When will you get it?"

This was a forever apology. I vowed that whenever the topic came up until the end of our lives, all there would ever be is the repetition of my apology. We ended up in each other's arms crying, and I remember this moment as one of the most intense feelings of love that I have ever felt towards another person. That moment is now pretty exactly 20 years ago, and whenever the topic comes up, I only repeat my apology, and I hope that my apologies were able to help my sister experience some healing and that I may be forgiven someday.

I am deeply grateful and humbled that the relationship with my sister has flourished ever since, and I am very grateful to be able to call her my best friend today and someone whom I can share everything with.

As the relationship with my sister improved in the wake of our conversation, my need to hear the same from my father grew. I visited my parents as often as necessary and kept the conversations with my dad to a minimum. Why could he not show up the way I did? Even worse, he still applied an amount of force towards my brother that I couldn't bear being around.

Which was one reason I stayed out of the way, as I wanted to avoid any looming escalation that I didn't feel would change anything, anyway, besides possibly tearing the family apart.

Even worse: the nightmares. Every few months, I would dream about beating up my dad.

About seven years after the apology to my sister, my mom called me and told me that she would be on a business trip over my brother's birthday and asked if I wanted to take the drive with my dad. It would mean so much to him. "Hell no!" was my answer. In a car with my father for two and a half hours? Twice in one day? To say that I was repulsed would have been an understatement.

But as that phone call sunk in, I realized what a golden opportunity it was. Two and a half hours of him being forced to fucking listen to me. Twice. And I had a few months of preparation. I called my dad and told him we would drive together. Honestly, I can't even remember if I called him or if I called my mother and asked her to tell him.

The day came, and Papa was happy. His son spent time with him for once. Usually, I would only call him up when I needed something, like borrowing tools or needed help repairing my car. Now I was just there to keep him company. And company I kept him. He had no idea what was coming.

After a bit of chit-chat, I got to the meat and potatoes. I explained to him how I felt about certain things during my childhood. I told him that I could rationalize what he did. I told him about my apology to my sister. To say that we had a deep conversation would have been an understatement. He asked me questions, seemed to try to understand my perspective, and at some point, I received what I had thought was almost impossible: a half-assed apology from a man who doesn't apologize. I was happy as a pig in shit. I felt like a bit of healing had taken place. I opened up, and our relationship got better. Until Christmas three years later.

Childhood stuff came up, and my father said he had never apologized; he had done nothing that required an apology as I had been a very difficult child. I got up and left. I was back at square one.

Meanwhile, my relationship life was following a continuous, ever-repeating cycle. I found a girlfriend, was head over heels, the in-love feeling wore off, I started to focus on her shortcomings, we had insane arguments about how she was not living up to my expectations, I would start nagging, chastising, criticizing, mansplaining, get all contemptuous, and call it quits. I even held positive traits against them and declared them weaknesses. Like if they were generous towards someone other than me, I'd tell them how they were being taken advantage of.

At age 36, I hit relationship-rock bottom. I married, and at that point, I already had a really bad feeling about it. How bad?

I remember sitting in the car with her on a rainy winter night in front of the Oaks Mall in Thousand Oaks, telling her that I was only going in there to buy wedding bands because I knew I had a bit of time to give them back. I could not believe that she still wanted to proceed.

Why did I do this? We had moved from Germany to the US together, and if we didn't get married, she would have had to go back, and I felt an excruciating guilt for pulling her out of her environment and job, relocating her to the US, and now dropping her like a hot potato. At least, that's how I saw it.

I remember taking a long walk the night before the wedding and thinking if I should call it off and pondering if I was just "getting cold feet" or if I was about to make the biggest mistake of my life. My best man voted for "cold feet," and when I picked him up the morning of the wedding, I nicked the car in his driveway. A bad omen? Maybe. Certainly, a sign of my distress.

Almost a year later, my ex-wife and I came back from our honeymoon vacation, and upon arrival, we had an insane fight about nothing, stopped talking for a month, and I came to the realization that it was time to end the marriage after only one year and made my biggest childhood fear come true. I filed for divorce. At that point, I was still not aware of the toxic trap that I was sitting in. I felt all righteous about my decision and ruminated about how this relationship had been my worst decision ever and even made me a lesser person.

Two weeks after filing for divorce, something unexpected happened.

I met my beautiful wife and mother of my children. Within days (literally), I noticed the good things my horror relationship had taught me. I started to notice, value, and appreciate things that I had looked down on in the past, and I was over the moon. This is the woman of my dreams. The kindest and gentlest person I had ever met. But shortly after, it dawned on me... what if my pattern kicked in again? It always had. Yes, I felt in love, and it felt different, but hadn't it felt different every time? I became deathly afraid of sabotaging this precious relationship as well.

I remembered one of my favorite lessons:

Once is an incident.
Twice is a coincidence.
Three or more times is a pattern, and you play a part in it.
Every. Single. Time.

This is the story about how I stepped out of my toxic trap and helped others to do the same. I will touch on neuroscience where it is helpful and share all the tools and strategies that I use myself whenever opportune and explain how you can do it too, to create a change in your relationship without involving your partner or *making them change*. You don't want to use tools and strategies for the rest of your life? Good. Me neither.

A "tool" is just a label for a behavior. Whatever behaviors you repeatedly express eventually become a habit, and instead of *doing something*, it becomes part of who you *are*. The new autopilot that unconsciously navigates you through the difficult situations that life inevitably throws at you.

In this book, you will find a lot of anecdotal evidence of things that have gotten results for me and for people who I have worked with. This anecdotal evidence is backed by science where helpful. Don't believe a word you read. You're invited to try out what makes sense to you and adopt what serves you.

That day in the parking lot, I did the wrong thing out of compassion instead of the right thing with compassion. A mistake that may have led to the amazing life and family that I am enjoying today, but one that I never want to repeat and see people do over and over again. <u>Do the right thing with compassion instead of the wrong thing out of compassion</u>. Because if you don't, then you forget to show compassion for yourself. I have no regrets when I think of that day, but I learned for the future.

Chapter 2

INTELLECTUAL AND EMOTIONAL RESOURCES

"You have always done the best you could with the resources you had available at the time" – NLP presupposition.

I found myself in many stressful relationship situations and thought to myself afterwards, "Why did I say that?" or "Why did I not say that?" or, either way, "I should have been smarter than that!" Sound familiar?

It's not that I lacked the intelligence to come up with the right answer or that I am a slow thinker, and chances are, you're neither (even if you think you are because you're always slow when put on the spot).

The reason is that we not only rely on our intellectual resources. Those are only 50% of the equation, if even that much. The other 50% is our emotional resources. And when something triggers our stress response, we divert processing power to a very old part of the brain, sometimes referred to as the lizard brain or crocodile brain. This part of the brain sends a signal to the adrenal glands to release the stress hormones cortisol and adrenaline, and scans every signal (visual, auditory, kinesthetic) from the environment for hints of danger.

Cortisol and adrenaline not only make us feel stressed but are also neurotransmitters that fulfill important tasks in our bodies.

Blood vessels respond to the presence of cortisol in one of two ways: They either expand or contract. Those blood vessels that expand let more blood through, while those that contract let less blood through. Now, guess which blood vessels do what?

Blood vessels that support, for example, the digestive system, the immune system, and sexual organs contract. You don't need those when you have to fight, run from, or hide from a wolf.

Depending on the severity of the danger and your level of fear, the digestive system can respond in really crazy ways. You can literally be afraid enough to shit yourself. During my military service, I heard a story of a soldier who crapped himself during an exercise when a tank jumped out of the brushwork and drove right over the hole he dug himself. You can imagine the overwhelming amount of fear that guy must have felt.

Then again, some people use food to emotionally regulate and start eating when stressed...

Stress reduces the desire for sexual activity. Even animals that are kept in stressful conditions in a zoo don't mate, no matter how long you keep a male and a female in the same enclosure. A married couple living in the same house won't mate if they are stressed. Now, what's stressful for one animal species can be cool for another. What's stressful for one person can be cool for their partner, and now you have a couple where one person wants sex and the other one doesn't.

Then again, there are people who use sex to emotionally regulate and want even more sex when stressed...

Stress affects the immune system. I remember an argument, or rather a shouting match, with my ex-wife that left me sick for three days. My immune system was clearly affected. There is also more and more evidence that points to stress as a factor for developing immunodeficiency diseases over time.

And lastly, a stressed body has a hard time falling asleep. Lack of sleep deprives you of the ability to tap into your intellectual and emotional resources and sets you up for a stressful day ahead.

What about the blood vessels that expand? Blood vessels in the arms and legs expand, for example. Those are the body parts we need to fight, flee, or hide. You may have experienced the expansion of the blood vessels in your hands following a scary situation in your car.

When a car next to you swerves and for a moment it seems it may hit your car, you can feel a tingling in your arms, hands, legs, or feet. That's your blood vessels responding to the danger and your body getting ready to react.

Instead of consciously assessing the situation and responding thoughtfully with sophisticated logic, that crocodile brain uses very simple mechanisms and falls back on our earliest learned behaviors. Have you experienced people who, or have you even yourself reacted to negative news with a response that looked more like the tantrum of a three-year-old than the response of a sophisticated adult? The good news is it's neither your fault nor their fault. Any person who would have had the exact same experiences in their life as the person with the tantrum would have reacted in the exact same way. I know a person, for example, who grunts or scoffs every time they disapprove of something I do or say. Here's what they don't think: "Arno did something that I disapprove of, what would be a smart and impactful way to show that? – Ah, I'll grunt!" No, it's an immediate unconscious response. And so is the snarky comment you get from your spouse, the sarcastic remark, the eye rolling, the cynical, snarky reply.

Or those interviews where a camera team stops a person on the streets and asks what the name of the president is, and they say the name of the last president, some weird name, or just give a blank stare. Then we laugh at the "stupid" person.

The truth is, most of those people know the name of their president, but being startled by three people and a giant camera, with a microphone held to their face, guess which part of the brain talks to the camera? It's the crocodile brain, and it's not concerned with the names of presidents. It processes how to get out of the situation, and the processing power of the conscious mind, with the irrelevant information about president names, is reduced to a minimum.

In situations like that, you have always done the best you could with the resources you had available at the time.

You see, the resources of your conscious mind are limited and can get hijacked by the emotional mind, that old crocodile. You were not in your right mind.

Here's the good news: There are ways to shift processing power from the crocodile brain back to your conscious mind inside those situations, and there are even ways to overcome the triggers that activate the crocodile brain in the first place. You will learn about these in part two of this book.

Learn these? Not quite. You will learn *about* these. You will gain the knowledge of what you can do, but at that point, you will not have learned anything. Because...

1. Learning is not the accumulation of knowledge, but learning is the change of behavior.
2. All learning is unconscious. Learning is the process of programming your unconscious mind so that it knows what to do in the state that you're typically in when the learning needs to be applied. You don't rise to the level of your hopes, but you fall to the level of your training. Or, in other words, you fall to the level of what's programmed into your unconscious mind.

You will have the opportunity to learn by following the instructions in this book.

But wait a minute, didn't you just say that the conscious mind knows the presidents and the crocodile mind does not? – That's right, but if you were approached on the street multiple times every day and got the question every time, then you would not get triggered anymore. Your crocodile would stay out of the picture, and you'd have your memory available. And that's the difference between those who give blank stares and those who know the right answer in a stressful situation.

Stress is a matter of perception: What's stressful for person A can be a piece of cake to person B. Experiencing stress means being in dissonance with reality, needing the world to be different, and not being okay with how it is right now. One person may make peace with the world instantly, while someone else may need years.

You see, in many cases, you don't even need to learn what to do, you just need to learn how to master your state of being so that you can draw from the information you already know. You will learn new things that you can do or say. You will learn how to master your state of being so that things you already know and the new things become available to you in moments where it really counts: stressful situations like crucial conversations in your relationship.

Before we get into it, I would like to bring your attention to a pitfall that I hope you will gracefully circumvent in a wide circle.

I used to learn things that could have made a significant difference in my relationships, and then I would feel frustrated that I only learned them today and not five years ago. This not only led me to engage in thoughts that kept me stuck and hindered my ability to make positive changes, but it also triggered the release of stress hormones that impaired my creative thinking, overall well-being, and hindered further learning. As a stressed state is a state in which you utilize your (unconscious) learnings without effectively adding to them, I found myself merely repeating my toxic patterns instead of discovering or implementing fresh solutions.

When you discover things, tools, and strategies that could have served you in the past, get excited about putting them into action, practice them and think about how they will elevate your relationship in the future. If you sulk in the sadness around not having learned them earlier and how much time you wasted… you just waste more time.

It's kind of like the person who finally buys a car after walking to work for ten years. There is no value in ruminating about how life would have been if they had bought that car earlier. It's about appreciating and enjoying the car now, along with the saved time in the mornings and afternoons.

Your default thought patterns, such as the one I just described, are ingrained in your unconscious mind. The good news is that you can reprogram it with new default thought patterns.

Chapter 3

A MODEL OF THE UNCONSCIOUS MIND

"All learning is unconscious."

We've touched on the unconscious mind already, but what is it? It's kind of a vague entity that is easy to use as an excuse and hard to grasp. It is somewhere inside of us and doing things like beating our heart and breathing our lungs. Except now that you read it and breathe consciously. And in a minute, you'll be breathing unconsciously again.

You may have heard the claim that humans use only 10 percent of their brain. If that were true, what's the rest for? Nature is impressively efficient. Why equip an organism with 90 percent more brain capacity than it needs? Or is it just fatty blubber that keeps the thinky-thinky parts safe? Some sources attribute the claim to Albert Einstein, and it's only part of the whole quote. We use only 10 percent of our brains consciously; 90 percent is attributed to the unconscious mind. In my search for further evidence, I came across the work of Dr. Joe Dispenza, who quotes that, according to some cognitive neuroscientists, we are conscious of only about 5 percent of our cognitive activity. So, most of our decisions, actions, emotions, and behaviors depend on the 95 percent of brain activity that goes on beneath our conscious awareness. An even greater discrepancy.

Others say 10 percent refers to the potential we're using. Looking at how many people have a goal of acquiring riches and how few amass billions of dollars, that seems true. Or how many aspire to live a fulfilled relationship life and the few who do, although the percentages look a bit friendlier here. At least I choose to believe that.

Other scientists say that it is entirely unclear what is conscious and what isn't...

What is clear is that we do things while being unconscious of them. That means we can perform actions that can be videotaped but we either have no recollection of them, may be surprised when we become conscious of them afterwards or even just rationalize them later.

I want to illustrate that using a few examples of behaviors that are unconscious, inside and outside of relationships.

Who is driving your car? If you're not quite sure, then you can take a stretch of road with no car in front of you or behind you (that's important to stay safe) and operate the pedals with your left foot. You will find that you need to focus very carefully on the pressure you put on the pedals; still, the result will be choppy at least, if not outright dangerous in case another car is following you too closely.

When you use your right foot as you normally do, you can drive, eat a burger, and talk on the phone at the same time. Instead of carefully focusing your foot to get it right, you only set an intention, and your body unconsciously adjusts the angle of the steering wheel and the pressure on the pedals.

I had my favorite epiphany of an unconscious thing I was doing about three weeks after my LASIK eye surgery. I had to blow my nose, took a tissue and – took invisible glasses off my face and put them down on the table. For decades, I would have sworn taking off my glasses before blowing my nose was something I did consciously. Yet, I stood corrected.

Bringing it back to relationships, what makes you react to a snarky remark from your partner in split seconds, like rolling your eyes, scoffing, or even uttering that snappy response? One doesn't think, "I did not like what I just heard. What would be a sophisticated and intelligent response that will make him/her alter his/her behavior? – I'll scoff! That'll cut it!" *scoffs*

Or, what initiates the stress hormone production upon receipt of an unpleasant text message or seeing the obscene gesture of the driver in front of you? It's the unconscious mind.

If all of those things are unconscious, how did they become unconscious? You "programmed" them into your unconscious mind by virtue of doing them. When you started driving at age 16 or 18 (depending on what country and circumstances you lived in), you drove with your right foot then just like you drive with your left foot today. If you continue to use your left foot, the process will become smoother and smoother until you drive your car as well with your left foot as you do with your right foot. When you're done, you exercise the task from your unconscious mind.

I was riding snowboard for 15 years but only with my right foot in front. I could never do it with my left foot in front. I had not taken the opportunity to learn it because it was so difficult for me and inconvenient, while riding with my right foot in front was fast and fun. Two things swayed me to practice riding with my left foot in front. First, after a while, my neck started hurting as I constantly turned my head to my right. Second, good snowboarders can ride both ways and even do fancy tricks like switching during a jump.

I decided to take a few days and learn to ride with my left foot in front. It was like relearning snowboarding. I had to go back to the bunny hill and gradually progress to more difficult slopes. I had to program it into my unconscious mind.

You can divide that programming process into four steps: the four levels of competence.

1. Unconsciously incompetent
2. Consciously incompetent
3. Consciously competent
4. Unconsciously competent

This is what that looks like:

Justin drives to the ski resort, rents the equipment, walks over to the bunny hill, sees the four-year-olds dashing down, and thinks, "that doesn't seem that hard!" He then walks up the bunny hill, puts his skis on, gives himself a firm push with his ski sticks... aaaand transitions in split seconds to the next phase. Justin is now consciously incompetent, collects his stuff, and decides to take ski lessons. He learns the pizza wedge and manages to get down the bunny hill in one piece. Justin is now consciously competent. A few more lessons, lots of practice, transitioning from the bunny hill to the blue slope, to the red slope, to the black slope, and one day he finds himself skiing with a friend, pulls out his phone, and takes a video of his friend skiing. As he is focusing on recording the video, Justin notices that his feet are skiing by themselves and know what to do – he has become unconsciously competent.

You may have heard that multitasking is impossible and that it's only possible to alternate tasks. So how can we do several other things while driving, like eating and taking a phone call? Or ski and record a video? It's because we can only alternate conscious tasks (like writing an email and speaking on the phone or frying an egg and painting a picture), but it seems like we can add as many unconscious tasks as we like. The unconscious mind appears to be much faster than the conscious mind.

How fast? If you remember high school math or go back to your school notes, in case you still have them, you will be able to calculate the trajectory and velocity that a ball of a certain weight needs to have to hit a target that is five feet away. That calculation may take you 15 to 30 minutes. You can also pick up an object on your desk and throw it into the trash can. Your unconscious mind just made all those calculations in a split second. It took you years to program it into your unconscious mind. My 4-year-old son is in the process of doing just that at this time, mostly with things that are not supposed to become airborne...

As you witnessed your parents arguing or argued with siblings or friends on the playground, at and after school, you programmed your conflict-solving behaviors into your unconscious mind. Or, if your parents followed the philosophy of never having a conflict in front of you, you missed a great portion of that. By the way, I believe it is absolutely crucial to exercise conflicts in front of our children, to help them learn how to solve them. I believe it is just as crucial to avoid having yelling matches in front of children because it teaches them disempowering behaviors that then impair relationships they later have in life.

How does that programming of conflict-solving strategies take place? How long does it take? If we find the questions to those answers, creating new habits or changing old ones becomes readily accessible. We already found one component – repetition. But there is another component: emotion. The more emotion we connect to something we do, the faster it sticks and the more readily it becomes available. A sad example of this is traumas and phobias. When Lionel was 7 years old, he walked into the house of a new friend and neighbor. Instead of finding his friend, to his surprise, the neighbor's German Shepherd found him, pushed him over, stood over him, and barked in his face. Lionel was shaken to the core and feared for his life until the dog was recalled by his friend's dad.

Those few seconds left a deep imprint in Lionel's unconscious mind, and for the next 60 years, his unconscious mind thrust him into a fear response every time he saw a German Shepherd. He had to change the side of the road he was walking on if someone with a German Shepherd came his way. German Shepherds would sense his fear, notice that something was off, and growl at only him, confirming his fear. Lionel had developed a phobia. Thankfully, his fear was only connected to German Shepherd dogs and never extended to other breeds.

Sexual assault or horrible experiences during military service or witnessing gruesome accidents can lead to similar responses. While a certain extent of an experience may traumatize anyone, it is known that two people can go through the same experience side by side, and one leaves traumatized while the other leaves unfazed.

What all kinds of trauma have in common are the persistent negative emotions that are being created in the moment that then flood the body again when triggered. On the contrary, persistent negative emotions can also be released and not get triggered anymore. In that case, one remembers how they felt at a certain moment in time, but they don't start feeling that way again when they think of that moment. An example can be the death of a relative where one was overwhelmingly sad when they received the news, cried for days, but remembering the situation today feels either neutral or even brings back positive emotions like love, gratitude, and wonderful memories that were shared.

In my case, I remember when my grandfather died at age 96 in 2014. I remember exactly where I was when I heard the news: I was on a business trip, sitting alone in an office in my custom-tailored suit – and cried and cried when my mother called and broke the news.

Yet, as I write this paragraph, I tap into memories that my grandpa and I shared, things that he taught me, and that my son carries his name, Felix. The negative emotions that I felt at the time have been processed and were released in the grieving process.

Thinking of those moments in my childhood where I mediated arguments between my parents, it wasn't so for a long time. For decades, the emotions that I felt at the time resurfaced in every conflict I had with partners and added to the appropriate negative emotions in the moment. And that's how emotional baggage impairs today's well-being; you may (and should) have appropriate negative emotions during conflicts: frustration, sadness, fear, guilt, and so on—normal, healthy emotions that contain information and generate movement towards solving a challenge. But when the experience of those emotions triggers emotional baggage, then it's as if those emotions get stacked on top of the appropriate emotions and blow the whole emotional response out of proportion and thus the physical response as well. The result: a blowup, yelling, cursing, catastrophizing thoughts like "maybe this relationship is not meant to be" or "I KNOW s/he is cheating!"

The emotional baggage can even get triggered by random experiences that, for most people, have no negative emotions connected at all.

Felicia is washing the dishes with her husband, Justin. As Felicia watches him dry a bowl, she notices that he does it the exact same way her ex did it. The thought of her ex reminds her of when she walked in on him having sex with her best friend. The feeling of betrayal creeps back up. "Why did that asshole Jake even ask me to marry him two months before he did that?" She feels the anger returning. Does Justin have it in him as well?

Later that evening, Justin asks her what movie they should watch, and she snaps back that she just wants to read a bit and go to bed. His offer to massage her back is brushed off. He has no idea what is going on and wonders what he may have done wrong. Felicia feels like she can't tell him. She consciously *knows* that Justin is a great guy who never gave her any indication whatsoever that he may do something like that, but the emotions she experiences right now are there and real, the hormones of stress are gushing through her body. They exist and can't be rationalized or explained away.

If she tried to suppress them and pretended everything was okay and spent the next time close to him, chances are she'd initiate a fight and say things she can't take back. Justin is suddenly in the kitchen with a crocodile that at least knows to crawl into its den for (temporary) healing.

We'll explore later what Felicia can do to overcome the shadows of her past that cast that impair her relationship, but let's first understand what happens inside.

Chapter 4

THE MIND-BODY CONNECTION

"Beauty is in the eye of the beholder."

Let's face it: I'm a meatbag, and you're a meatbag. Of course, each one of us is a very different, very individual, and very, very special meatbag – some more, some less. Some skinnier, some stockier. Some are very proud of their fancy attachments, have surgery or train to make them bulkier, while some of us don't bother. Some of us add stuff like pictures, metal, hair, and implants, covering it with more or less fabric, and so on, see *Figure 1*.

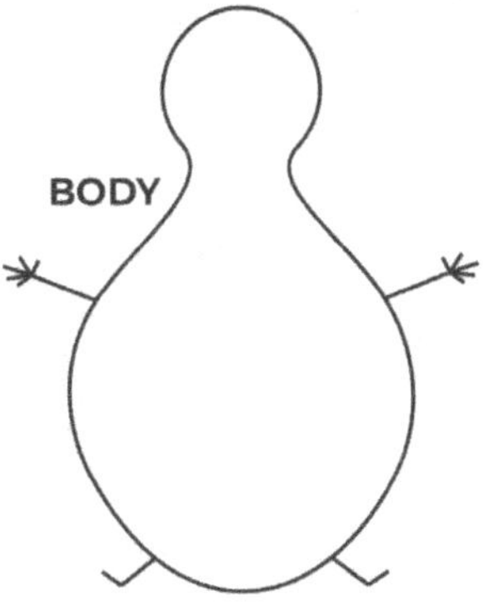

Figure 1

Trillions of cells make up the meatbag, with the most abundant molecule being water. Most tissue is muscle, fat, or bone, kept dry and safe from most environmental influences by a more or less thick layer of skin.

You do want to let select parts of the environment in – particles to keep that meatbag alive and kicking, information that helps you know how and where to arrange your special meatbag in space. The meatbag is how we appear in the 3D world, how others see us, how we appear in the mirror, and also how we interact with the outside world – our movements, behaviors, and voice. As most people call it their body, let's stick with that moving forward.

Inside each of our bodies is a mind. Where is that mind? "In the brain" comes to mind immediately. But is it? Sure, most neurons are inside our head, but neurons – which evidently make up our mind – are spread throughout the body. Every cell in our body is capable of responding to information and sending information to neighboring cells, and then there are millions of nerve cells that deliver information to our mind. Or at least to a part of it: the unconscious mind.

As we find accumulations of nerve cells in certain parts of our body outside the head, limiting our mind to the neurons in our brain doesn't do it justice. It's kind of everywhere. Something like *Figure 2*. What we're building here is a model that helps us understand and use the unconscious mind more effectively.

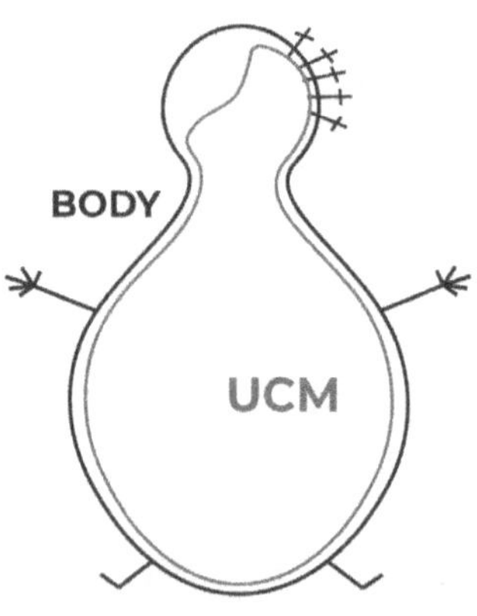

Figure 2

In this model, the little antennae sticking out of the head symbolize our five senses. In reality, they are represented by millions of sensory neurons that make us see, hear, feel, taste, and smell. These senses are connected to the unconscious mind, not the conscious mind.

You may ask, "But I am conscious of what I feel?!" That can be true, but while your unconscious mind knows everything that is going on in all those nerve cells all the time, your conscious mind does not.

For example, your unconscious mind knows the moisture level of your feet, but your conscious mind is only aware of it now that the letters on this page have brought it to your attention.

Your unconscious mind also knows how your butt feels on your seat, while your conscious mind just wonders about it right now. Depending on the quality of the surface you are sitting on, your unconscious mind may bring it to your attention at some time in the future if your sitting position becomes uncomfortable. As you're thinking about the comfort level of your sitting position and may or may not have used the opportunity to make adjustments, the moisture level of your feet has drifted back into unconsciousness – until now.

You see, your senses are hardwired to your unconscious mind but only get passed through to your conscious mind when opportune.

A study published in 1990 called *Human Photoreceptor Topography* by a team around Christine Curcio found that an average human eye contains about 96.6 million photoreceptor cells. Add the millions of olfactory receptor cells in the nose, gustatory receptor cells on the tongue, the mechanical receptors, thermal receptors, and pain receptors of the skin, hair cells in our ears, and the spatial receptors in the muscles, tendons, and joints that provide information about the body's position, movement, and spatial orientation, and you get an idea of how much information our unconscious mind processes every second.

Mihaly Robert Csikszentmihalyi, professor of Psychology and Management at Claremont Graduate University and author of the book *flow*, estimates that the conscious mind can process up to 120 bits of information per second.

It's kind of like standing in a dark room with a flashlight and believing that what you see in that spot is all there is. Pickpockets and magicians base their professions on this.

To be able to process that flood of information, the mind generalizes, distorts, and deletes incoming information into comprehensible chunks. Looking at those numbers, it becomes obvious how two individuals can experience the same scenario side by side and tell stories about it that sound as different as if they had spent the time in different locations.

One person may see things that the other person does not see, or even weirder, one person sees things that don't even exist. We even have a word for it: hallucination. When most people read the word "hallucination," they think of a mirage in the desert. But that is only one option – a visual hallucination. Hallucinations can pertain to any of our five senses.

Ever thought your phone vibrated but it didn't? That's a kinesthetic hallucination. Ever heard someone call your name, but nobody did? That's an auditory hallucination. I remember driving in the car with my wife when our son was just born, and we talked about poopy diapers. She said, "Does our son need a diaper change? I think I smell something." I thought so, too but it turend out that he did not. That's an olfactory hallucination. It's as if, besides the actual five senses, we had five virtual senses plugged into our conscious mind as well, that we can consciously tap into or that can send us signals that add to or even replace the "real ones."

When you dream, your virtual senses take over completely, and you can have full-on sensory experiences of crazy adventures involving all your senses – you can eat, drink, and even have orgasms.

We also use these virtual sensory faculties to fill in information that is not given, to create a conclusive representation of reality. This is also how you recall memories. When you read the word "apple," you see an apple in front of your mind's eye. Sometimes, I speak with people who tell me they don't "see" the apple when they talk about it. But even if they believe that they can't "see" the apple, they do have an "inner representation" of one. This representation helps them describe to me what constitutes an apple and helps them distinguish it from an orange when they find one in front of them.

I want to invite you to play along with me for a minute.
Imagine you are walking on a path in the countryside. It is a

beautiful summer day, you feel the sun on your skin, the sky is blue with a few small clouds, and the birds are singing. On one side of you is a meadow with a horse. You decide to walk up to the fence and pluck some grass. You see the horse trotting over to you in all its elegant beauty. You feed the juicy grass to the horse and pet its soft nose and strong neck. Then, you return to the path, leaving the meadow with the horse behind the fence, and continue your walk. On one side of you is the meadow, and on the other side of you is a forest. As you enjoy your walk, the bees and butterflies, the warm sun on your skin, and the birds singing, you slowly return from the beautiful scene, placing your attention back into the environment you're sitting in. Now, I have a few questions for you:

- What color was the horse?
- What material was the fence made of, and what color was it?
- On which side of you was the horse?
- On which side of you was the forest?
- What kind of path was it?

I did not share any of this information in the story, but your mind made up some – if not all – of it. I have asked audiences these questions, and some people insisted that I had said on which side the horse was, except all the other people in the group remembered that I didn't.

I remember one person who told me that she could not "see" things in her mind's eye. She described her horse as colorless, more like a sketch of a horse – but it was located to her right.

I also had a person in an audience once who claimed she had no mental picture of her car. She saw nothing, only black. But after hearing the story, she could clearly remember that the horse was brown.

Just like that, we fill in the gaps of any kind of information we ever receive and create an inner representation that makes sense to us.

Now, imagine you and your spouse, coworker, or friend read the story and talked about it three weeks from now. Can you imagine the discussion going on if one of you saw a white horse and one of you saw a brown horse? Can you remember a situation where such a discussion ended up in an argument or even a serious fight in a relationship of yours?

To make things worse, we not only fill in parts of stories or information with objects, colors, sounds, or other information, but our memory of things can even change.

There are a few extraordinary (often negative) events that took place over our lifetimes that millions of people remember and we can exactly recall where we were when we received the information or saw the pictures. Depending on your age, do you remember where you were when you heard that the Challenger space shuttle exploded? Where you were on 9/11? Where you were when you heard of Michael Jackson's death? Or Kobe Bryant's death?

The psychologist Ulric Neisser researched the evolution of memory. He asked a group of 44 Emory University students right after the Challenger explosion to write down how they experienced the moment when they heard of the tragedy. He went back to those students about three years later and had them write down the story once again. Not a single story was entirely correct; many had changed significantly, and about a quarter were completely wrong.

One student initially heard the news while chatting with friends. Three years later, she said some girl came running down the hall screaming, "The Challenger exploded!"

Confronted with their original stories, some people even said, "Yes, that is my handwriting, but I don't know why I wrote that. It is not true."

Maybe there are way fewer gaslighters out there than we think...

The vast majority of neurons are located in the brain, about 85 billion. The conscious mind is known to reside in the neocortex. It makes up about 40 percent of our brain mass. (Trivia for dog lovers: In dogs, it makes up 7 percent of the brain mass, and in cats, about 4 percent)

There are also clusters of neurons in other parts of our body. We have about 40,000 neurons in our heart and 100 million neurons in our gut. Have you ever followed your heart? Or listened to your gut? Those were intelligent decisions (even if they turned out to be wrong), and you can tune into that part of your mind whenever you choose to. Figure 3.

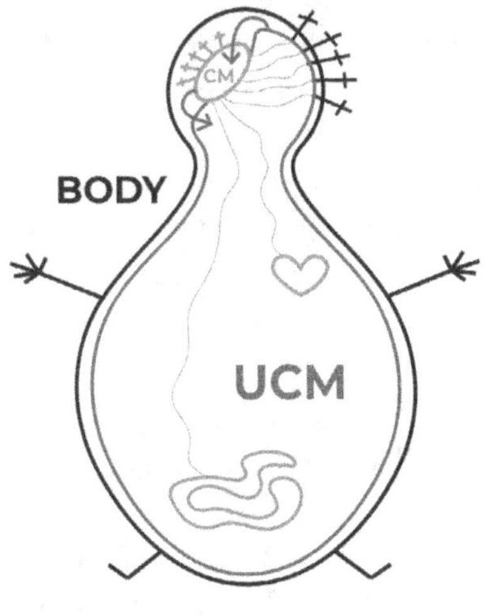

Figure 3

Memories can be triggered in different ways. Someone can ask you about a situation in the past, a sound, or something you see, feel, smell, or taste may remind you of a situation in the past. You may be facing a task and search your memories for insight into how to solve it, or a memory may even pop into your mind randomly.

Just like memories, the awareness of sensory input also becomes conscious at times. As your unconscious mind harbors all of this information, how do the conscious and the unconscious mind communicate?

You can say that the conscious mind is the goal-setter, and the unconscious mind is the goal-achiever. The conscious mind creates a goal in the form of a picture or inner representation, like, for example, the goal of reaching a certain destination, and your unconscious mind then gets you there by operating the gas pedal, brake, and adjusting the steering wheel while you may consciously listen to a podcast, an audiobook, or take a phone call.

Let's look at the specifics of a situation we all experience on a regular basis:

Your bladder is filled to a level that presents discomfort to your body.*

*The reason I pick this example is that stories about sex, pee, and poop trigger strong emotions and, as they do, are likely to be remembered. You're welcome.

Your unconscious mind is plugged into its sensors and detects that you need to pee. It brings the respective sensory input to your attention and asks your conscious mind, "What shall we do?!"

Your conscious mind may respond, "Let's head to the toilet in the master bathroom!" It does that by sending your unconscious mind a picture of the respective toilet that it would like to use. Then, the unconscious mind walks you there, pulls down your pants, and so on.

Now, why does your unconscious mind check in with your conscious mind in the first place? Because you may not be in your bed but in a hotel room, and activating the same program you usually run will let you bump into a hotel wall. Which may have even happened to you in case you wake up in hotels often and sometimes your conscious mind believes you are at home.

You could also be on a campsite, and activating the same program would lead you to pee in someone else's tent.

As you make your way to the latrine, your unconscious mind will still monitor your surroundings and interrupt the pattern if something unusual or dangerous happens. If, for example, you step out of your tent and there is a bear between you and the latrine, your unconscious mind will stop you in your tracks and let you consciously find a solution instead of walking you right into the shaggy plantigrade.

What happens if the communication between the unconscious mind and the conscious mind gets confused?

The other day, I wanted to put some dirty laundry into the hamper in the bathroom. My conscious mind gave clear instructions to my unconscious mind, and as it executed, I was already deep in conscious thoughts about a different topic. Then, my unconscious mind checked in and noticed that something was off.

I had just dropped my dirty underwear in the toilet. After laughing out loud, I tried to understand what had happened.

Our hamper at the time was a white basket with a white lid, located next to the toilet. Normally, the lid of the hamper was closed; this time it was open.

I pieced the situation and my unconscious program together: The conscious mind instructed the unconscious mind with a picture of the hamper, and my unconscious mind activated the program "walk to the bathroom, open the lid of the white thing, then put your clothes in." As the "lid of the white thing" was already open, but there was another "white thing with a lid," it just chose to open that lid instead.

So close.

Just as close as the other black Jeep was to our car when my wife called and told me that she just sat in the wrong car. There was another black Jeep parked close to ours in the big Target parking lot, and either it was left unlocked, or our key worked with that car as well, which is known to be possible. Either way, my wife got into the car when she noticed that something was off until it dawned on her that it was not our car.

As mentioned earlier, our brain deletes, distorts, and adds information to make quick sense of our surroundings. And that's a good thing because it saves us a tremendous amount of time. Seeing a car in the approximate place of where your car is parked, that is of the same make and color, is sufficient information 99.99% of the time. Until it isn't. Would it make sense to closely observe the license plate of your car every time before you get in? Probably not. Anyway, which information we choose to delete is not even a conscious choice.

Your unconscious mind reacts just as readily to a bump in the road with an automatic steering movement as it pulls up a response pattern when your spouse triggers you...

The question is, what can you do to access your unconscious mind and make it serve you best?

Just like in the previous examples, you set your life and health goals consciously, and your unconscious mind does what it takes to achieve them. When you visualize a goal and connect it with elevated emotions:

- It opens your perception filters, so that you will now recognize opportunities that get you towards your goal.
- It makes you feel uncomfortable if you do things that contradict your goal or your values or beliefs.
- Strenuous tasks that help reach your goal may come to you easily and effortlessly, and bystanders may tell you that they would never have been able to do them.
- Doing so may even create an "energy field" that draws the realization of your goals to you, as the law of attraction suggests.

How does a perception filter open? Years ago, I drove the same way to work every day to my engineering job in Germany. After two years of driving the same way every day, I needed to drop off a letter. In Germany, you drop outgoing letters off in public mailboxes, which are bright yellow, about one foot by one foot by one foot in size, and usually attached to dark house walls. I could not recall having seen a single one along my way to work in two years. So, I decided to pay attention and see if I may be able to locate one. As I drove the same way with open perception filters, I found not one but seven mailboxes along the way.

Similarly, when you feed your unconscious mind an inner representation of your goal, you will open your perception filters and may see opportunities that you have been blind to before those filters were opened. Examples could be recognizing YouTube videos that may offer crucial information, bumping into people who can help you get where you want to go, seeing ads for the seminar you need, or noticing that there is an open spot next to the parking spots for people with disabilities. Maybe even seeing how your partner is trying to do something kind even in a situation when you are frustrated and may usually default to defensive responses.

When you set a goal and commit to it, maybe even obsess over it, you create a force that is stronger than TV, social media, partying late nights with friends, and other activities that move you away from your goal. A force that drives you to the gym while others are still in bed or watching TV already. A force that keeps you in the office, going the famous extra mile while others are already at home, but you're not stressed about it, you are excited. A force that makes you read books on relationships or hire a coach to really make a change while others are busy liking posts on Facebook or just ranting about their spouse in Facebook groups or to their friends.

How do you set your unconscious mind up for success in that manner? There are few ways to do it:

1. Set the goal and connect it to a very powerful emotion. Falling in love would be an example. Or the death of a loved one due to a certain disease, which makes a person dedicate their life to helping humanity overcome it.
2. Steady repetition.
3. Refocus on the goal over and over and over again. Visualize it, pretend it has happened already, and imagine a strong sensory and emotional experience. Even feel grateful for having achieved it before the fact.
4. Focus on the pain that comes from not achieving that goal and the satisfaction you will feel when you have achieved it.
5. Hang up pictures that remind you of the goal.

Chapter 5

THE HUMAN ENERGY FIELD

"That you can't see anything doesn't mean there is nothing."

When I say that we are beings of light, I sometimes lose a good part of my audience. When you and I go into a dark room, we will not see each other. But if we change the wavelength and look at each other through infrared cameras, we will see that we're glowing pretty bright, and photons are shooting out of us left and right and all around. So, the question is not if we're emitting something, but what are we emitting and what effect does it have?

Are we emitting other kinds of "energy" as well? Let's say we had only one neuron in our head and one in our butt. In biology class in high school, we learned that neurons communicate through electric charges. At the same time, we learned in physics class that an electric charge creates a magnetic field around it. So even if there were only two neurons in our body, we would create an electromagnetic field. It would be a weak field, but it would already exist and be detectable. So, the question is not if we have an electromagnetic field, the question is how strong is this field and what does it do? See *Figure 4*

With every thought, hundreds or thousands of neurons fire, so it makes sense that every thought has its distinct electromagnetic field. The question is not if it's there, the question is how strong it is.

Isn't it amazing when you're deep in conversation, and suddenly your conversation partner says the exact word that you were about to say? Have you ever pulled your phone out of your pocket to call someone, and that person called you in that very second? Or you think of someone, and that person interacts with you shortly after? You could hypothesize that those are not coincidences but that we do emit some kind of information that may be received by others. If we do, then it should be possible to measure or even read it.

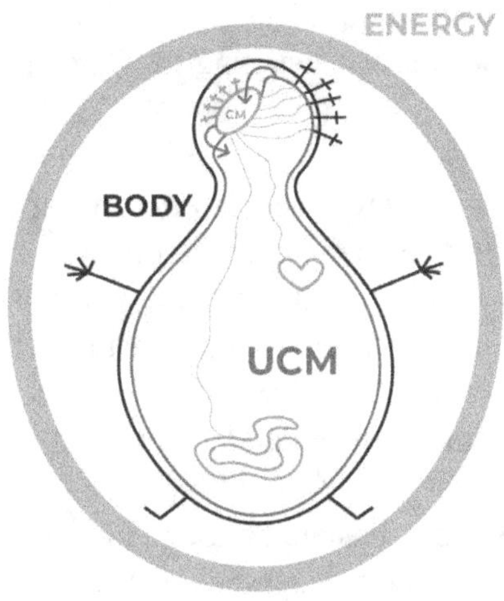

Figure 4

In 2009, Thomas Naselaris et al. conducted a study called *Bayesian reconstruction of natural images from human brain activity* in which test subjects were shown photographs while their brain activity was measured with an fMRI, a contactless way of measuring the magnetic field of the brain. Later, the subjects were asked to recall the pictures, and a computer was able to reconstruct the picture the subject was recalling. In other words, they proved that the electromagnetic emissions of the brain are distinct enough to be read and transcribed into the image that the person is thinking of, just like a radio wave is translated back into music by your car radio.

In 2023, researchers from the University of Texas, Austin, led by Dr. Alexander Huth, assistant professor of neuroscience, and Jerry Tang, a doctoral student of computer science, published a study titled *Semantic reconstruction of continuous language from non-invasive brain recordings* where they connected an artificial intelligence language decoder to the fMRI scanner. They first trained the decoder by letting the individual listen to 16 hours of podcasts, and later used the trained decoder to analyze the readings of the thoughts of the participant. The accuracy of the readings was stunning. When participants listened to another story, imagined telling a story, or watched a silent movie, the AI decoder could describe what the person was listening to, watching, or even only thinking about.

With every thought, different neurons fire in a specific sequence, so every thought has its own electromagnetic signature and creates a unique electromagnetic field. Like every word has its own electromagnetic signature as it is being broadcast by a radio station, so that the radio receiver can decipher it and translate it back into the unique audio waves that you can understand.

The same word will be translated into the identical frequency and will be translated back into the same word every time. You can say every radio signal carries a chunk of information. So does every thought signal. As it gets translated into an electromagnetic signal, this signal now carries the exact same information and then... how can this information be received and into what can it be translated? How far does it travel? Receivers could be:

- The cells inside our body
- Other life forms (humans, animals, plants)
- A hypothesized, unified, intelligent field that we may be able to communicate with and tap into. You may call it God, the universe, or whatever your faith suggests, and you feel comfortable with. And, of course, you're free to not believe in its existence.

You may have heard of the law of attraction, a mysterious "law" that has yet to be proven, although many say it has been proven already through countless examples. The law of attraction says that every thought you send out attracts its material equivalent back to you. A practice that is also known as manifestation. I cannot prove that the law of attraction is real, but there is anecdotal evidence of experiences that seem to be too concerted and too well-coordinated to be explained as luck or accident. At the end of the chapter on the spiritual state, you will find more about this, as well as an explanation that will satisfy skeptics just as much as believers.

Putting It All Together

Your and my existence is comprised of four layers or bodies:

1. The Meatbag, or physical layer, comprises everything physical about us, including the neurons and sensory receptor cells. It follows the instructions of our Unconscious Mind and, indirectly, follows the instructions of our Conscious Mind. It reacts to instructions from our energy field and energy fields around us. Electric (thought) signals get translated into chemical substances, like hormones and neurotransmitters, that set other biological processes, like movements, in motion.
2. The Unconscious Mind is plugged into the physical layer and knows in all detail what is going on. It is the realm of emotions that set the body in motion, the bridge between the body and the conscious mind, and the achiever of our goals. It contributes to the creation of our energy field and distinguishes only between normal (=good) and not normal (=bad).
3. The Conscious Mind is the realm of our thoughts and the creator of our goals. It influences the creation of the energy field around us.
4. The Energy field inside of us and around us interacts with energy fields around us like the energy fields of other people. It may even attract realities to us.

The thoughts of your Conscious Mind and the thoughts of your Unconscious Mind create emotions that set your body in motion. The activity of the neurons in your body creates energy fields inside of your body that interact with each other and create energy fields that interact with the outer world.

When you take charge of your thoughts and create thoughts of a future that you desire, and when you combine those thoughts with elevated emotions, those emotions may set your body in motion in different ways and create new results. Gratitude, for example, is not only the result of receiving something you appreciate but makes it more likely that you receive something good in the future. As Dr. Joe Dispenza puts it: "Gratitude is the ultimate state of receivership and invites good things back to you." The more gratitude you express in your relationships, the richer they get.

PART TWO

OVERCOME THE SHADOWS OF THE PAST

"You are not only defined by the things you love, but also by the things you hate."

Chapter 6

WHAT CASTS THE SHADE?

"It is in the darkest moments that our shadows shine the brightest."

A shadow of the past is any unreleased, persistent negative emotion you carry around, or, in other words, your emotional baggage.

What is a negative emotion? Any emotion that feels unpleasant and creates a state of suffering to any extent, ranging from a slight sense of sadness (like when you pass a dead squirrel on the road) to things that are difficult to process, such as rape, deaths of loved ones, or unfathomable incidents like the genocide of the Hutu and Tutsi in Rwanda, where neighbors slaughtered neighbors.

The former may be quickly processed and released, with many memories even deleted, while others remain persistent. The latter may be not processable at all in the moment, haunting the person who experience it for years or even forever. It has also been found that what is traumatizing for one person and haunts them for a long time may be quickly processed and released by another.

This, of course, doesn't mean one is a different quality of human than the other; it is just a matter of different life experience, values, beliefs, and perceptions of the situation.

What is the difference between "released" and "unreleased" emotions?

Inside the experience, an emotion is created. Numerous scientific studies indicate the close correlation of feelings and hormones.

Many emotions are clearly connected to certain hormones inside our body. For example, the feeling of being tired is connected to the hormone melatonin, the feeling of being awake is connected to the absence of melatonin and the presence of serotonin. It has also been discovered that the more serotonin is present, the happier one is. The feeling of stress and its qualities of sadness, anger, hurt, guilt, and fear are connected to the presence of stress hormones like cortisol and adrenaline. The feeling of love is attributed to oxytocin in women and mainly vasopressin in males. Endorphins suppress pain and can even lead to feelings of euphoria, as experienced by endurance athletes during the "runner's high." It seems like emotions often consist of a certain mixture of hormones. The fifty hormones in the human body and the possible quantity of each one illustrate the rich emotional life humans experience. As life continues and other experiences follow, the emotion fades, the hormones that were released in the moment get metabolized, and a new mix of hormones becomes prominent.

When you now revisit the memory, one of two things happens:

1. You remember how you felt in the moment, a conscious process.
2. The emotions that were created in the moment come up again, and you actually feel the way you felt when the event took place, your body releasing the exact mix of hormones once again.

For example, when I remember the moment my mother called and shared with me that my grandfather died, I was devastated and beyond sad. Today, I remember how I then sat in an empty office on a business trip and cried. I remember how I felt. The feelings that actually come up today are feelings of love and gratitude, while memories come to mind that I share with my grandfather, things he taught me like whistling on two fingers and how he made me laugh, like when I showed him how I can juggle three balls and asked him if he could juggle too, and he said, "I can only juggle four balls, you don't have four, do you?" The emotions I had at the time of my grandfather's death are processed and released.

As I was thinking about an example of a mild negative emotion and thought of roadkill, I remembered driving to a pickup soccer game when a blackbird darted out of the bushes to the right of the road, dove under my bumper, and just didn't make it. I pulled over, walked over to the bird, and saw that the poor thing was heavily injured but still alive. I had to make a choice of how to ease the bird's pain. I didn't see how the bird could be saved, so I made the hard choice of ending its life as quickly as possible. The emotions I felt in the moment came up immediately. This incident was about 20 years ago, but the emotions were still alive and well. I had not processed and released them for two decades.

Just like that, when I tapped into those moments of mediating my parents' arguments in the living room during conflicts with a partner, those emotions of sadness and fear came up again.

That brings us to the effect of emotional baggage. How does it work?

You have appropriate negative emotions in the moment, for example, during a conflict with your loved one. But that situation can bring up memories from past events that have unreleased emotions attached to them. The result is that those past, unreleased emotions then come up in the present, already stressful moment and get stacked on top of the appropriate emotions, which blows the total emotional response out of proportion. This, in turn, likely blows your physical response out of proportion. If your crocodile brain wasn't activated already, it jumps into action now. You then either say things that don't help the situation and wonder afterward, "Why did I say that?" but the damage is done. At the same time, you don't say the things that could alleviate the situation, i.e., express your love for your partner, listen and understand their view on the situation, show kindness and appreciation and instead of staying on target you go off on tangents.

There are three kinds of emotional baggage:

1. Negative emotions connected to people. These require forgiveness. We will talk about that and especially about the case of the transgressor not deserving forgiveness.
2. Negative emotions connected to events, like being attacked by a dog or having had a car accident. There is no one to blame; something happened to you. When you now see that dog breed or get into a traffic situation that reminds you of the incident, your body releases the stress hormones it released at the time of the event to prepare you for the worst.
3. A mix of both. In the case of rape, one needs to forgive the person and release the emotions that were created in the moment.

— Chapter 7 —

NEGATIVE EMOTIONS CONNECTED TO PEOPLE

"Forgiving means forgetting without deleting the memory."

Is it appropriate or possible to forgive a rapist? Does a rapist deserve forgiveness? No, they don't.

There are people who don't deserve forgiveness, such as those who want to see you suffer or impair your well-being. But what is the result of not forgiving them?

You harbor that emotion inside of you, and whenever something reminds you of that person, the negative emotions come up involuntarily, and you release stress hormones every time, impairing your well-being and entering a state of suffering. As long as you haven't forgiven, you cater to that person's cause. If that person wants to see you suffer, they'll rejoice to find that they got you to suffer so much more than just in the moment of their transgression.

In addition to that, decisions under stress are rarely as good as decisions that you make when you are relaxed and creative. Crocodiles don't think creatively. Crocodiles want to eat or prevent getting eaten.

Not forgiving a transgressor only serves one person, if anyone at all: the transgressor.

But doesn't not forgiving keep you safe from repeating your mistake of giving the transgressor the opportunity to harm you? It sounds logical, but the truth is that negative emotions cloud our judgment or can even drive us to make or repeat mistakes.

In 2003, the first dating websites emerged, and being single at the time, I explored that new technology. I met a girl online, we started chatting, had a few phone calls, and at some point, decided to meet. She invited me over to her place to watch movies. I wondered, what kind of girl invites a guy she has only chatted with online and talked to on the phone over to her apartment? At 23 years old at the time, I didn't care much but was excited for the prospect of what could happen.

I asked her what she would like me to bring, and she suggested vodka and Schweppes bitter lemon. I remarked that I would not be able to drive home after enjoying a few long drinks with her, and she was absolutely cool with that. We watched our movies, enjoyed our drinks, I stayed over, and nothing even happened. We had a good time, but I felt something was off. We stayed in contact for a while after that until at some point she told me a story about something that happened to her a few weeks before we met that left me in shock.

She had met a guy online, met him for drinks, he lured her into his apartment, got her drunk with vodka lemon, and raped her. I could not make any sense of what I heard, of how she set up our date. It made me sick to my stomach how I got involved in such a weird and sick twisted game. Then I learned.

Daniel Goleman writes in his book *Emotional Intelligence* about a game called "Purdy." It was discovered that after a school shooting where a mass shooter by the name of Purdy killed a number of students, in the wake of the event, groups of students started playing school shooting, alternating the role of the shooter and playing different outcomes with different numbers of students killed, "Purdy" getting killed, or no students getting killed at all.

Tapping into a memory, reliving it, pretending different outcomes, or even turning it into a game is a natural response and coping mechanism to release trauma. That's exactly what my date had done, and in retrospect, I hope that our experience was able to provide her with a sense of healing. It's what children do when they experience sexual abuse by an adult and then, in their attempt to heal from it, spread that trauma to other children as a child or later as an adult.

Bringing it home to forgiveness, one would have thought that the traumatic experience and the persistent negative emotions derived from it would keep my date from exposing herself to even remotely similar situations. Instead, it drove her to reenacting it and putting herself in a situation that could have led to repeating the traumatic experience or even worse.

That's what strong negative emotions can lead to if not released. Children of cheaters may cheat or get into relationships with cheaters, children of abusers may abuse or get into relationships with abusers, people who get cheated on may suddenly attract cheaters or start cheating themselves. Children of addicts may become addicts, alcoholics lose partners and child custody over their addiction and still carry on with it, gamblers lose everything and hope to win it back at the casino.

Forgiving someone doesn't mean that you will start liking that person again or trust them again or repeat mistakes.

It means "getting flat" with the person so that you take the emotional charge off them and can make the decisions that are right for you. It protects you from consciously or unconsciously finding yourself in a version of the Purdy game.

It means making the negative emotions "conscious," so instead of the feelings coming up unconsciously, often even without triggering the memory, you remember *how* you felt when the memory comes to mind but don't feel them anymore. At the same time, you preserve the learnings, which makes it as likely as possible that a situation like the traumatic one will never occur again.

There are three main reasons to forgive:

1. Someone wronged you.
2. Someone did something that is okay in the grand scheme of things, but you have a hard time dealing with it personally.
3. Someone left you, and you haven't been able to say goodbye properly or let go yet.

We already looked at an extreme case of someone being wronged, but what about the other two cases?

Sometimes people don't do anything wrong, but it deeply hurts. My daughter, for example, now 18 months old, will at some point go on her first date. As a dad, that will not be okay with me. In the grand scheme of things, it will be okay, though, so I will have to forgive her then and find my peace with it. Similarly, in relationships, partners have different sets of values and a different hierarchy of values that may even change depending on the environment or specific situation. Let's say a couple, Justin and Felicia, both value harmony and honesty. For Justin, harmony is more important; for Felicia, honesty is more important.

Now Justin receives news of which he knows it will upset Felicia. He comes home, Felicia is in a good mood, dinner is ready, and he is looking forward to a relaxed evening. He may choose to share his news the next morning. As he tells her what happened, Felicia gets upset. "You knew this yesterday already and DID NOT TELL ME???"

If their values were the other way around, he may have come home, she prepared dinner, picked a movie that she knows he likes, and he comes through the door and bursts out the news. She is sad, silently eats her meal, they do watch the movie, but she stays awake for hours and processes the news, wishing he had only said it the next day instead of ruining the evening.

Although you probably have a clear preference for how to go

about the situation, it is a matter of philosophies and not of right or wrong. If your partner happens to follow a different philosophy than you, your path to healing this relationship situation is finding forgiveness for your partner's way. Your partner may be able to contribute to that healing by acknowledging your values and view on the situation and apologizing, but even then, it is still yours to accept that apology and find the forgiveness.

If this is a burning topic in your relationship, skip to the chapter on apologizing. We will also explore this situation in more detail in the chapter "Changing Your Ways."

To summarize what forgiving means:

"<u>Forgiving means forgetting without deleting the memory.</u>"

Chances are that someone who says, "I forgive but I don't forget," has a hard time finding true forgiveness and may forgive consciously, but still negative emotions come up when thinking of the transgressor.

Once you have truly forgiven, you have forgotten the incident in the sense of the memory of it, and the past emotions don't come up involuntarily anymore when thinking of the person. But when someone asks you about the situation, you can still recall the memory. Even then you remember *how* you felt but don't feel it anymore.

How do you find that forgiveness?

The most powerful forgiveness process that I know of to find that healing on an unconscious level is the Ho'oponopono forgiveness process by the native Hawaiians. Visit www.imagine-evolution. com/forgiveness to find a guided forgiveness meditation based on the Ho'oponopono forgiveness process, in which I guide you through the process.

Sometimes a person's actions are not directed towards you but rather away from you. Someone leaves your life, ends a relationship, ghosts you in what you thought was a promising dating situation, or even dies. Each can be a confusing, hurtful situation that leaves you thinking if you could have done anything to prevent it.

Things happened the way they happened and could not have happened any other way. Why? Because they did. There is even a theory about time travel that if you were able to travel back in time to undo something, the time-space continuum would heal itself by making the thing happen again in a different way. I don't know if that is true, but as any thought about how the past could have transpired differently doesn't lead to any change anyway, I find it a very comforting idea. The bottom line is, all of these people need to be forgiven. In the case of a death, that may sound weird, but forgiveness and grief are closely related. Both are processes of letting go of something that doesn't serve you anymore and can't be undone.

Chapter 8

NEGATIVE EMOTIONS CONNECTED TO EVENTS

"You survived the abuse. You're going to survive the recovery."
- Mariska Hargitay

Sometimes things can be traumatic, and the culprit is not an individual: an accident, an encounter with a dangerous animal, a natural disaster, or the result of someone's actions, but you can't identify the transgressor.

In those cases, mental and emotional release needs to be found in other ways than forgiveness. A book has been written about this topic called *Mental and Emotional Release* by Dr. Matt James, and this is the most powerful process I have ever experienced to overcome negative emotions and release trauma.

Remember Lionel's encounter with the German Shepherd. For 60 years, the automatically released negative emotions got the best of him. After I took him through the mental and emotional release process, I asked him, "How do you feel?" He said, "All right." I was excited for him to experience the change. He told me that a weekend later he was going to meet a good friend of his, a guy who has three German Shepherds. Beautiful, sweet dogs that growl at nobody... except him.

As I checked in with him a week later, he said, "They were just nice dogs."

I followed up with him a few weeks later and asked him how things were going with German Shepherd dogs. He said, "I don't know, they're gone." Just like perception filters open when we learn about new things that serve us, perception filters that were opened by traumatic events can close once the baggage is released and the trigger serves no purpose anymore.

On my drives, I barely recognize dogs. Maybe Rhodesian Ridgebacks, as our dog Obi is one, and so I have an emotional connection to them. Just like those German Shepherds used to (negatively) stand out for Lionel because of the emotional charge and don't stand out anymore.

As I wrote the story of the blackbird above, I noticed the emotions of the situation coming up, and that I never released them. These were not emotions that were haunting me in any way, shape, or form, but when I tapped into the memory, they came up, and they were not pleasant. Being familiar with the Mental and Emotional Release Process, I was able to take a pause from writing this book, sit back, and release the negative emotions in minutes, releasing negative emotions I harbored for 20 years.

But that's not all. I used to have panic attacks for about 25 years of my life. And for most of that time, I was not even aware that I did. I just used to faint when giving blood. That was my "normal," that was just "me," and I knew how to mitigate it. I'd just lie down for the blood draw or, if I was allowed to consume food before, I'd have a large can of an energy drink... and still lie down for good measure.

Now giving blood is not a big deal that happens to an extent that it impairs one's life, but there were a few occasions where it reared its ugly head and became very unpleasant.

At some point, I would not only faint when I had my blood drawn but even while watching certain movies or when people would have conversations about drawing blood in any way, shape, or form.

I remember watching "Count Dracula" in an English class in high school just before summer break and... well... vampires draw blood. And as the count went about his business, I fainted, tipped over backward, and landed in the lap of a classmate. You can imagine the embarrassment. It also happened in movie theaters, for example, when I watched the movie "Blade." Those nasty vampires...

When watching videos at home, I could mitigate the situation, and my friends would know what's up when I moved from the chair to the floor and placed my feet on a chair instead. Think Pulp Fiction, where Vincent Vega enjoys a shot of heroin...

When I joined the military service, all members of my platoon of new recruits had to take a medical exam of which bloodwork was a part. I told the doctor that I would need to lie down, and he told me I should not be such a wimp and pull myself together. I would not faint.

I was the only one of 70 young men who fainted. Interestingly, there was often some latency between the blood draw and my reaction, in this case about five to ten minutes. We were all lined up when I stepped out and said, "I have to lie down for a minute..." and there I lay, 70 pairs of eyes on me, the platoon leader looking down at me saying, "Koch, you're the first human I've ever seen with a literally green face!"

What led me to decide to overcome my panic attacks were two incidents and one insight. Incident one was me almost fainting while driving on a German Autobahn and having to pull over. Incident two was me fainting in a movie cinema, and my date telling me that she'd only continue dating me if I saw a neurologist and have determined that I was okay. I complied, and the neurologist attested that I was having panic attacks and that that was not even that unusual. It was enough for me to decide that I wanted to overcome it.

Upon reflecting on the cause of my reaction to blood, digging up memories, I remembered a situation at the pediatrician with my mom and my brother. My brother, probably around eight years old at the time, got blood drawn, and being autistic and not understanding the situation, he was very adamant about not getting his blood drawn. As the pediatrician, as well as my mom, were even more adamant about the need for the blood draw, she and two nurse practitioners tried to hold my brother while the doctor tried to draw his blood, with blood squirting out left and right past the needle, and me standing there in shock, helpless, exposed to the situation without any means to have an impact.

Knowing what caused it did not change a thing. What released the persistent negative emotions from the incident at the pediatrician was the Mental and Emotional Release process, and it did so in minutes.

Since then, it has been years over which I had blood drawn multiple times, watched multiple movies at home and at movie theaters with previously triggering scenes, and had previously triggering situations that left me now unfazed. The most triggering incidents were probably the births of my two children. My mom used to joke that I'd for sure faint in the delivery room and would probably have to wait outside. I did not.

You can also find yourself in situations in which emotional baggage connected to another person and emotional baggage connected to experiences come together.

I once took a client through the Mental and Emotional Release process, and while releasing persistent sadness, she grew sadder and sadder. I stopped the process and asked her where she was stuck, and she shared a memory of a transgression by her father. I realized that before releasing the emotions from the event, she needs to find forgiveness. I took her through the Ho'oponopono meditation in which she found forgiveness for her dad before resuming the Mental & Emotional Release process in which she

released the shadows of the past that were keeping her stuck.

— Chapter 9 —

EMOTIONAL TREASURES

"Emotional Treasures are the sweets in your baggage."

Trauma and emotional baggage are significant topics in therapy and coaching for a good reason. However, what I've realized is that the opposite of emotional baggage and trauma doesn't receive much attention, despite being one of the most powerful tools to influence your state of being. In fact, I couldn't even find an expression for it, so I coined one: *emotional treasures*.

An emotional treasure refers to a wonderful memory with powerful positive emotions attached, capable of instantly evoking feelings like love, joy, gratitude, or bliss. These moments could include the birth of a child, a wedding, vacations, celebrations, your happy place(s), or even random memories such as hugging a child or loved one, or experiencing a happy, goofy, playful moment with a pet. Essentially, any moment when you strongly felt an emotion that served you or may serve you in the future, such as feeling powerful, confident, faithful, loving, compassionate, or courageous.

It's essential to be conscious of these moments and have them readily available to tap into when needed. In the chapter on mastering your emotional state, you will learn how to effectively utilize these emotional treasures.

Part Three

MASTER THE INSIDE GAME

"You are in charge of your mind and therefore your results."

Chapter 10

FOUR STATES

"You don't rise to the level of your hopes, but you fall to the level of your training" - Archilochus.

It was a warm spring day in May in Woodland Hills, California. I was sitting in my office on a video call when I heard my wife call me from downstairs. Her call pierced every bone in my body, and I jumped out of my seat. I knew something was terribly wrong. I dashed downstairs, my wife coming towards me with my naked, crying son in her arms, saying the words I will never forget in my life:

"Oh my god, oh my god, his skin is falling off!"

Only then did I see the patches of skin that were peeling off his tiny, one-and-a-half-year-old body. "What happened?" Felix had pulled a cup of hot soup off the counter, and the contents spilled over his torso. When my wife took his onesie off, parts of his skin stuck to it.

I took him in my arms, trying to comfort him as best I could, and looked in horror at his injuries, thinking about what to do. My horror, disbelief, pity for him, empathy for his agony, fear of what the treatment of his wounds might look like, and how he would look after it, maybe for the rest of his life, would not help him a bit. It would be reasonable and justifiable to focus on such thoughts, but they would paralyze me and make him suffer even more.

I started to breathe deeply and focused on the love I felt for him. I noticed that his wounds, despite covering a far too large portion of his little body, seemed to be only second-degree burns. I focused on the likelihood that he would heal quickly, that we would be happily playing in the pool again in two weeks, and that the scars would fade over time. All of this went through my mind in split seconds as we headed to the hospital, just five minutes away.

We dashed into the emergency room and were let in immediately – at least my son and me. It was Covid times, and the hospital's protocol didn't care about emotional distress, exceptions around burnt babies, or their families. We decided that I would be the one who stayed with him. A doctor quickly came and gave my son a morphine injection. His tears dried up, and I saw a first smile that had seemed days away.

Things were moving quickly – or so I thought. A few doctors dropped by, discussed, and after two hours or so, the decision was made to admit him to the burn unit. This was a brief happy moment: West Hills Hospital has one of the specialized burn centers in the Los Angeles area, and it just happened to be the closest hospital to our house.

Before being admitted to a room in the burn unit, my son had to pass a Covid test. I didn't think much of it at that moment, but it led to additional wait time. After a total of four hours, my patience had expired. And I felt I had been VERY patient.

I also realized that expressing my frustration in the way I felt it would probably not be appropriate toward the staff, whom I trusted were not lazy or delaying things on purpose. Feelings of resentment toward the nurses and doctors would not be effective nor have a positive impact on Felix or the situation. So, I headed to the reception, holding my still naked son in my arm, who looked like a lizard shedding his skin, and said, "Hey guys, I know you have a lot going on, and I want to be respectful to you and the other patients, but I would hope that a one-and-a-half-year-old with major burn injuries would be a priority. When can he expect to be admitted to his room?"

They checked on the status of the COVID test and told me it would take a maximum of 30 minutes. Thirty minutes later, I returned to the reception and said, "Guys, I really do want to be respectful to you and the other patients, but I hope you can appreciate that I am getting a bit impatient here. How would you feel waiting for over four hours with your child in this condition?"

A few minutes later, after almost five hours in total, we were following a nurse to the room where Felix and I would spend the next few days.

Immediately after our arrival, a doctor and a nurse came to dress Felix's wounds. I was not allowed to join them. In this case, what may seem cold-hearted made perfect sense to me. The idea was to prevent the sensation of pain and helplessness from being connected to the parent. Still, hearing my boy cry for me as he was taken away was heart-wrenching.

A nurse approached me with a few questions, and I asked her to give me a few minutes and headed to the bathroom.

Upon closing the door, all the pain, hurt, and anger I had bottled up over the past hours came to the surface, and I let it out. The past hours were the saddest and emotionally most painful of my life. A time where I had to stay on top of things and show up for my son. Now was the time to allow myself to feel and release the emotions and experience them fully. I cried. The anger about the hospital staff not making this little, helpless child a priority or not being able to. The arbitrariness of insisting on the Covid test. What would they have done if he had tested positive? Send him home??!! At the same time, not testing me, although I would be with him! And the anger toward my wife. Why was that cup on the edge of the counter? The anger was real and appropriate – what would have not been appropriate would have been directing it towards her.

I could have left a cup of hot coffee out the very next day. Felix could have grabbed a kitchen knife that I left on the counter a day before and required an ER visit because of that. I, my wife, and probably any parent are just as guilty of forgetting dangerous items within a child's reach at times. Scolding her for it would have just added to the pain and guilt she was already feeling, while it would not have had the slightest positive effect. It would have further impaired her well-being; it would have made me feel ashamed of myself afterward, and it would have damaged our relationship. She needed my support just as much as Felix did.

But the anger still existed; it was real. So, I let out the anger as well in that bathroom and said all the things in fantasy that I would never say to her.

After I let it out and let go of what I needed to release, I stepped out of the bathroom and went to the nurse. "What were your questions?"

Times like these are when all the personal development work you've ever done counts. You read your books, speak with your therapist, work with your coach, work through your events, seminars, and workshops, but what do your days look like afterward? You wake up, work out, have breakfast, go to work, have lunch, return to work, come home, do your chores, maybe have an hour for your hobbies and some time for your family, have dinner, watch TV, brush your teeth, and go to bed. What's the big deal? Little adjustments here and there, but sometimes... sometimes you find yourself in a situation where life calls. And like in a poker game, you now have to show your cards. Show what you have.

In that moment, you don't rise to the level of your hopes and dreams. In that moment, you fall to the level of your training. You run the programs that you wrote into your unconscious mind.

Only afterward, reflecting on it, did I notice how I had mastered my state of being that day.

My physical state – breathing deeply and standing straight and confident to stay composed myself and demonstrate confidence and faith to my son, my wife, and everyone we depended on for support.

My emotional state – tapping into love and gratitude rather than pain and despair; rising above my pain when I had to, but releasing the negative emotions when the time was right.

My mental state – focusing on positive outcomes, thinking about solutions instead of the negative implications and "what ifs" that were also possible.

My spiritual state – staying in a positive vibration and exuding it, while choosing to believe in a positive outcome.

After a few days of hoping, the doctors confirmed that Felix had only second-degree burns, and no surgeries were necessary.

Exactly two weeks after Felix pulled a cup of hot soup off the counter, we were back in the pool, playing as we had every day before the incident.

What determines the outcome of a situation like this is how we communicate with ourselves, which then has ripple effects on our communication with others.

Is your partner their own biggest critic and very harsh and un-forgiving with themselves? No wonder that's the way they speak with you as well, which offends you so much and makes you feel belittled and berated.

Are you your own biggest critic, and very harsh and unforgiving with yourself? No wonder your partner feels criticized, unloved, or disrespected a lot.

Are you reliable when it comes to being on time, and do you see it as the foundation of trust and respect? No wonder your partner feels under constant pressure, unloved, or disrespected when they see your frustration about them being a few minutes late.

Are you cool and relaxed and don't always follow through with the things you want to do? No wonder you agree to things your partner asks you to do, and when those things don't happen, you can't understand how it's such a big deal for them.

How do you communicate with yourself, and how does that resonate with your partner?

Here's the deal: You won't change them. But you can elevate your communication with yourself in a way that how they talk with you doesn't stress you out anymore. As you are less stressed, you will express less stress to them, and they will, in return, stress you out less. And you will find ways to inspire change rather than trying to impose it on your partner.

What is this "self-communication" all about? When you think of communication, you probably think about words. But many aspects of communication, especially most communication with self, have nothing to do with words. As you adjust your physical state, you just do it, no words. As you adjust your emotional state, you remember moments that created certain feelings, no words. As you adjust your mental state, that is where words come into play. As you adjust your energy, through listening to music, for example, again, no words. Words can have an influence, but much of communication is beyond words. So rather than communication = speaking with yourself, you "master your state of being."

In any given situation, we are in a certain state of being. We can be in a beautiful state of mind and experience love, gratitude, wholeness, bliss, happiness, joy, and many more. Or we can be in a state of suffering and experience anger, sadness, fear, hurt, guilt, shame, and so on.

A state of being is comprised of four sub-states: the physical, the emotional, the mental, and the spiritual state, see *Figure 5*. Is this true? I don't know. But I know with certainty that understanding your state of being like this is a powerful model that helps to master it, respond to adverse circumstances in an empowered way, and regain control quickly when you feel out of control. The four sub-states can be influenced individually, and when you change one sub-state, you change them all. How do the four sub-states interact?

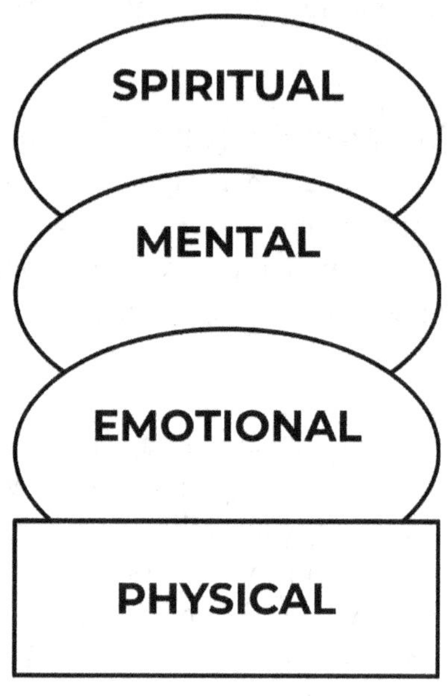

Figure 5

Janine just received a text message from her husband Frank: "Hey babe, I'm heading to the bar with Jeff after work tonight, will be home around 8. Love you."

Janine is on her way home and has the trunk full of groceries. She had planned to cook a nice dinner for the two of them, and her expectations of the evening just popped like a soap bubble. She now unconsciously alters her sub-states and initiates a cascade of events:

She starts feeling sad (emotional state) and releases the hormones of stress.
Her shoulders move forward as the feeling makes her slouch, she starts breathing a little shallower, and her chin drops. A camera

would now capture a sad human (physical state).

Now a little crocodile in her mind starts talking to her (thoughts) as she focuses on the impact of the news and tries to read Frank's mind.

"I have planned this nice evening, and now he tells me that he's spending it with someone else. That makes me really sad.

Actually, I have told him that I don't like him doing things like that. I have told him soooo many times to please ask me if there are any other plans and not just confront me with a decision...

I haven't only told him that, but he has acknowledged it as well. AND there have been times where he did call me to ask if it was okay. So, he DOES KNOW it!

That he knows it and doesn't do it today must mean that he is doing it on purpose. Why is he doing this on purpose? Did I do something wrong? Or does he just not care enough? Or are other people from work going to the bar as well? His secretary, too, who always looks at him in a way that makes me feel really uncomfortable?" (mental state)

Janine's focus and her thoughts feed back into her emotional state. Her sadness increases, and feelings of anger and fear come up as well. This influences her spiritual state – her energy and her beliefs. Energy-wise, it lowers her vibration and her energy level. Her beliefs around the rest of the evening and the following days take shape...

Local beliefs... "Now the whole evening is ruined, and I have to show him over the course of the next days that what he just did was not okay! It ruins the whole week, and Saturday we wanted to go to Kathy's baby shower..."

Global beliefs... "He hurts me over and over again. It's so un-loving. He clearly doesn't care about me and my feelings because when he has the opportunity to do something fun without me, he just does it. Maybe this marriage is not meant to be..."

As Janine goes through the (e)motions, the interactions of her sub-states happen unconsciously, releasing stress hormones and moving her into fight or flight or freeze mode. What will she do?

Fight? Tell Frank to get the f*** home, and if he does, confront him with his disrespectful, hurtful behavior, and interrogate him about who else was supposed to join them at the bar? Demand to check his phone to find evidence that his secretary was part of the party?
Or will she wait, elaborate on the thought cascade, and surprise Frank unpleasantly when he comes home from meeting his friend?

Flight? "If Frank can go out, what am I doing here? I'm going to head over to my parents', and whenever he is ready, he can ask me where I am and come and get me. I hope the night alone will make him consider how he made me feel."

Freeze? "I am going to get me a quick burger on the way home, a big milkshake, and watch TV all night until I fall asleep on the couch. When Frank comes home, I'll just say nothing. He'll figure out what he did wrong eventually when I give him the silent treatment."

A few streets away, another couple is in a similar situation.

Justin just received a text message from his wife Felicia: "Hey babe, I'm going to have a drink with Angie after work, will be home around 8. Love you."

Justin is on his way home and has a bunch of flowers, a bath bomb, and sushi takeout in the car. He had planned to have a nice candlelight dinner for the two of them, a relaxing bath, and then... But his expectations of the evening just popped like a soap bubble. He now unconsciously alters his sub-states and initiates a cascade of state changes:

Justin starts feeling sad (emotional state) as his body releases the hormones of stress. His shoulders move forward as the feeling makes him slouch, he starts breathing a little shallower, and his chin drops. A video camera would now clearly capture a sad human (physical state). Now a little crocodile in his mind starts talking to him (thoughts) as he focuses on the impact of the news and tries to read Felicia's mind.

"I planned this nice evening, and now she just tells me that she's spending it with someone else. That makes me really sad. Actually, I have told her that I don't like that. I have told her so many times to please ask me if there are any other plans and not just confront me with a decision... I haven't only told her that, but she has acknowledged it as well. AND there have been times where she did call me. So, she DOES KNOW it! That she knows it and doesn't do it today must mean that she is doing it on purpose. Why is she doing this on purpose? Did I do something wrong? Or does she just not care enough? Or are other people joining her as well? Probably her creepy co-worker John, who is always undressing her with his weird gaze?" (mental state) His focus and his thoughts feed back into his emotional state. Justin's sadness increases, feelings of anger and fear come up. This influences his spiritual state—his energy and his beliefs. Energy-wise, it lowers his vibration and dampens his energy level. It changes his...

Local beliefs... "Now the whole evening is ruined, and I must show her over the course of the next days that what she just did is not okay! It ruins the whole week, and we wanted to go on a road trip..."

Global beliefs... "She disregards me over and over again. She clearly doesn't care about me and disrespects me whenever she has the opportunity to do something fun without me. Maybe this marriage is not meant to be..."

As Justin goes through the (e)motions, the interaction of his sub-states happens unconsciously, released stress hormones, and move him into fight or flight or freeze mode. What will he do?

Fight? Stop at the next trash can and dump the flowers and the bath bomb. Tell Felicia to get the f*** home, and if she does, confront her with her disrespect, her hurtful behavior, and find out who else was supposed to join them at the bar? Demand to check her phone to find evidence if this John guy was part of the party? Or will he wait for her to come home from meeting her friend, elaborate on the thought cascade, and accuse Felicia of cheating?

Flight? "If Felicia can go out, what am I doing here? I'm going to head over to Phil's, and whenever she is ready, she can ask me where I am at and beg me to come home. If she doesn't, I'll just stay at Phil's. He recently divorced and will enjoy my company."

Freeze? "When I get home, I'll eat both sushi meals and play video games until I fall asleep on the couch. When Felicia comes home, I'll just say nothing. She'll figure out what's up."

Each couple has a conflict. Conflicts may be stressful situations, but some people handle them exceptionally well and prevail in a way that helps them create a future that others only dream of. Should couples have conflicts? Would you even have conflicts if you were in a relationship with Mr. or Mrs. Right?

John Gottman is very clear in saying that based on his over 40 years of scientific research, conflict in marriage is not only inevitable but perfectly normal.

But is there really a similar amount of conflict in healthy and unhealthy relationships? Think about it this way:

You can't even stop having conflicts with yourself. Do you know what they are called?

- Decisions that you have to make.
- Your mistakes that you discover.
- Essentially every situation where you wished reality around you was different.

Every time you have to make a decision, you are in a conflict with yourself. "Shall I apply for a job at this company or that company?" "Shall I order takeout or cook?" "Shall I go to the gym or sleep a little longer?" "Shall I date Pete or Kevin?" "Shall I study law or engineering?" "Is this just a temporary misunderstanding, or should I end this relationship?" "Shall I start my diet today or tomorrow?" "Chicken or steak?" "Shall I ask Julia if she wants to marry me?" "Shall I ask her in private or in a football stadium?" "Should I rent or buy?" "Is this the right market to buy a house?"

Every time you discover a mistake you made, you are in a conflict with yourself. "I scored an F on the test." "I made a dent in my car." "I forgot to brush my teeth." "I gave a scammer my password." "I accidentally threw away something I cherish." "I accidentally threw away something my partner cherishes." "I just moved in with someone who turns out to be an addict; I didn't know." "I paid for this subscription that I haven't used in 8 months."

You are in a conflict with yourself in every situation where you wished the reality around you was different. "My partner broke up with me." "My dog died." "The gas bill is way higher than I thought this month." "It rained every day during my vacation." "Someone made a dent in my car and left the scene." "My dog bit a neighbor's dog." "My partner cheated." "My partner bought themselves a toy for $2000 without telling me." "Why is he wearing THAT shirt?"

All of these conflicts start out as conflicts within yourself or within your partner that can then become conflicts between you and them.

As you can't stop having those conflicts with yourself, you can't stop having conflicts with your partner. And in addition to that, your partner has those conflicts within themselves as well.

How you go about your conflicts with yourself is likely how you will go about conflicts with other people, and the same holds true for them. Are you harsh and unforgiving to yourself? Does your partner criticize you for being harsh and unforgiving to them? What about the other way around?

Mastering your state of being helps you go about the conflicts within yourself in an empowered, forgiving, yet effective way that gets you the results you want to see to become an empowered lover.

In the next four chapters, we will deep dive into each of the four sub-states and explore the tools you can use to elevate each one. Not every tool will be the right one in every situation, but as you practice them, you will have powerful interventions available wherever you go. These interventions not only serve you in your relationship but in any difficult situation you encounter, like pre-sentations, meetings with your boss or a challenging employee, job interviews, or life situations like the one I experienced with my son that you will hopefully never encounter.

Chapter 11

THE PHYSICAL STATE

"Your actions speak louder than words."

Your physical state is the part of your being that can be recorded on a video camera. What do you see when you experience a person in fear? The person will likely be out of balance, having most of their weight only on one foot, physically and mentally unstable, and easily influenced (tipped over) by outside forces. Their hands may be hidden in their pockets or behind their back, or they may be fidgeting. Their shoulders can be hunched, and they breathe shallow, letting less oxygen inside their body. They appear pale and sweaty. Their body is in survival mode, ready to fight, flee, or hide. When you find yourself in such a state, what can you do?

When my parents observed me as a teenager with hunched shoulders, they sometimes gave me a nudge in the back and told me to stand straight or stand tall. I can't recall ever reacting positively to their approach. After all, I was a free human and could arrange my body in space however I pleased! But what if you made that choice on your own and held a positive inner representation of yourself in your mind's eye at the same time?

TOOL: STAND PROUD
A real change takes place when you stand proud. In this moment, you connect a positive emotion with the desirable inner representation of its outward expression: both feet get rooted on the ground, your body weight evenly distributed, you take a deep breath and pull your shoulders back, your hands relax or return to a more expressive position. You reconnect with the essence of who you are and who you want to be.
Get up out of your seat right now and change your position to standing proud. Pay attention to how your body is arranged in space and how it feels. How does it affect your mental state and your energy level? Try to hunch and experience how it now feels awkward.

Standing proud can become a tool in your self-mastery toolbox to adjust your state of being at any given time when you find yourself under some kind of pressure, when you feel afraid of something, or when you find yourself in a crucial conversation with a boss, spouse, child, or co-worker.

Now, *knowing* all of this is only the first step. Remember, all learning is not the addition of knowledge to the brain but the change of behavior. If you leave it at this, you will either forget it or emerge from a critical situation, remembering that standing proud may have made a difference if you had only remembered it during or before the conversation. Thus, to make it effective and really learn it, you must integrate it into your life and practice: stand proud under the shower every morning, stand proud when you unlock and lock your front door, stand proud in the queue at the supermarket, stand proud during casual conversations with family members, co-workers, and friends, stand proud when you brush your teeth, sit proud as you drive to work, sit proud as you read this book. It will become second nature, and especially when you find yourself in an uncomfortable situation, you will automatically remember to stand proud. As a side effect, it will improve your posture.

Before you enter a challenging situation, a crucial conversation, or even on a challenging phone call, a positive expression on your face can make all the difference. Have you ever noticed that you sense people's smiles over the phone?

TOOL: GRIN LIKE THE CHESHIRE CAT

You probably know Alice in Wonderland, or at least you know of her, and in this story, there is a cat with an insanely wide grin.

Pull off a grin as if you wanted the corners of your mouth to touch at the back of your head and hang your teeth out to dry. When you do so, you activate trigger points in your cheeks that activate the production of positive hormones. The positive hormones will make you feel happier; the happier feelings will make you think more positive thoughts; the positive thoughts create happier feelings. You will feel silly and goofy, and a slight smile will remain on your face. A happy person is a confident and creative person.

When I receive a phone call that may turn out to be challenging, I always smile like the Cheshire cat before picking up the phone, and I often do it before I record a video. Smiling like the Cheshire cat targets only the physical state but has an immediate effect on the emotional state, which then leads to a change in your mental state and your spiritual state. Standing proud primarily targets the physical state but adds an emotional component for an even more powerful result. Remember, all states go hand in hand. As soon as you change one state, you change them all.

How do you think it could alter Janine's and Justin's state if they continue driving but sit up proud and put that smile on their faces?

Many of the things that apply to humans also apply to animals. If you will, you can take many behaviors of animals as a model for human behavior. I had such an experience with my dog. Obi is a Rhodesian Ridgeback and used to inhale his food like a vacuum cleaner. I wanted him to eat his food more slowly, so I let him change his physical state from excited to relaxed before he would be allowed to touch his food. Every time I prepared his food, he danced around, getting up on his hind legs, ears up, tail wagging. I am sure you have a picture. So, I let him lie down and only gave him the "okay" command when his tail stopped moving and his ears went down. After a few repetitions, he became a very well-mannered, slow, even picky eater.

Now you may say, "Interesting, I can see that working with a Rhodesian Ridgeback, but good luck trying that with a Labrador!"

Before I had my Ridgeback, I had a Chocolate Labrador. He did eat like all Labradors eat – by inhaling his food. I googled how to get a dog to eat slower and found (and tried) various tricks: Adding ice cubes to the food slowed him down by 25%. Adding water to the food slowed him down by 50%. Better, but it did not actually slow him down; I had just increased the quantity by adding water. The real change came when I altered his state, when I only let him eat after his physical state had changed from excited to relaxed, and repeated it until it became a habit. Even the ravenous Labrador became a slow eater. Just like that, changes in your physical state trickle through your emotional state, over your mental state, right into your spiritual state. It is very powerful.

You may have heard of the former German Chancellor Angela Merkel. If you google her, you will come across many pictures where her hands are together, and her thumbs and index fingers touch. This gesture is called the steeple. A variation of the gesture is one where every finger touches the respective finger on the other hand.

TOOL: STEEPLE

Have every finger touch the respective finger of the other hand to form a steeple. This gesture sends a strong signal to your unconscious mind: "I am confident. I know what I am doing. I know my stuff. I am an authority." It also sends the same message to the unconscious mind of the person you speak with. And that's probably why Germany's ex-chancellor, Angela Merkel, this kind and timid-looking lady, does it around other statesmen.

"Will people notice when I steeple?" Probably not. It is something humans do anyway when they feel confident, and it doesn't matter if you feel confident and then steeple, or if you steeple and raise your level of confidence by doing so.

But isn't that faking it? Is consciously changing one sub-state faking it? When you feel out of control and consciously do something that gets you back into control, isn't that the same as before unconsciously doing something that made you feel out of control? I don't think so.

The Navy SEALs, for example, use a technique called box breathing to find (or regain) calm in overwhelmingly stressful situations. How stressful? Bullets-flying-around stressful.

TOOL: BOX BREATHING is a breathing technique that activates your parasympathetic nervous system to move your body and mind into a state of calm. This is how you do it:

1. Breathe in over the course of 6 seconds.
2. Hold your breath for 6 seconds.
3. Breathe out over the course of 6 seconds.
4. Hold your breath out for 6 seconds.

You do this until you're calm or for as long as the challenging situation lasts. If you are in a conversation, box breathe while the other person speaks. I promise, nobody will notice. If six seconds are too long for you, start with four seconds.

You read earlier about my panic attacks. After going through the mental and emotional release process, the underlying negative emotions that held my triggers in check like iron shackles were gone, but the response was still programmed into my nervous system. So, whenever I got into a situation in which I knew I, in the past, would have dropped into a panic attack, I box breathed.

For the birth of my children, as I waited outside the delivery room for my wife to get dressed, I box breathed and continued to do so during the delivery. Afterwards, my wife told me that when I came in, at first, she thought I was one of the doctors. That was the level of confidence I exuded.

If you have ever experienced a panic attack, then you know that the trigger is one thing, but if it wasn't awful enough, then comes the fear of not being able to stop the attack, which exaggerates the feeling of helplessness and being out of control. After you interrupt or prevent the panic cycle a few times with box breathing, you become confident that you are not at the mercy of your unconscious mind anymore, and the trigger fades.

Other activities that you can do to alter your physical and, therefore, your overall state:

- Take a cold shower.
- Exercise, like doing a few squats or push-ups.
- Take a walk.
- Dance in your living room.
- Meditate.

Chapter 12

THE EMOTIONAL STATE

"You're all in your feelings."

The emotional state is the realm of your feelings and emotions, the language of your unconscious mind. Considering the close correlation of emotions with certain hormones in the body, you can say that your emotional state represents the chemical state of your body. Every emotion that you feel coincides with a special mixture and quantity of hormones. Every feeling you have, every emotion you have is the precursor to a motion. Emotion is energy in motion, and that energy is looking for an outlet.

When Justin and Janine receive the news that their spouse plans to spend a few hours with other people, potentially people who would like to be in a relationship with them, fear kicks in, just like in a deer in the forest.

He stands there, grazing, enjoying himself and the fresh green grass, until a pack of wolves shows up. Instantly, the body of the deer is thrust into survival mode. The hormones of stress kick in – cortisol, adrenaline – blood is drawn away from parts of the body that can be taken care of again in the case of survival: creative thinking, digestion, reproductive system, immune system. Blood vessels that support those systems contract under the influence of the stress hormones. It makes no sense to fight a virus if you are not alive to enjoy the virus-free life. Blood pressure increases, arteries that pump blood to the muscles widen, and send as much blood as possible to the muscles that are needed to fight or run, and to the part of the brain that is tasked with quick reflexes and identifying dangers, like a member of the wolf pack suddenly darting out of the bushes to the left.

Our deer jolts off and runs as fast as he can, closely followed by the pack. He is fast, he knows the terrain, and makes it to safety. In the next approximately 30 minutes, the stress hormones get metabolized, and the deer relaxes, starts grazing again, and continues enjoying his life.

The same process happens in humans when we are confronted with a threat. We don't encounter too many real wolves these days, except if you live in certain areas of the US and may occasionally encounter a coyote on the hiking trails. Then again, we all have our own wolves to fight: bosses, co-workers, call center agents, police officers, spouses, kids, bad drivers, dogs, clowns, and even non-living things like deadlines, horror movies, the news, or elevators. As you read through the list, you might have come across something that, for you personally, has a positive connotation, for example, the word "dog," while for others, just reading the word "dog" brings up memories of a traumatizing experience that immediately releases stress hormones.

Just like that, the thought of being on stage and in the limelight in a couple of minutes can scare some people and excite others. Did you know that anxiety and excitement happen in the same part of the brain? The difference is how you process it. For slight anxiety, nervousness, it can even be sufficient to intervene on the physical level. You can say, "The difference between nervousness and excitement is a deep breath."

Looking at the list above, you can see that a fear response, despite being triggered by your unconscious mind, may not be the most beneficial reaction to the situation. No relationship expert has ever given the advice: "When your spouse makes you angry, fight as hard as you can!" Or for someone suffering from road rage: "When you encounter a bad driver, fight him until you win and teach him a lesson!" There are situations when a fight cannot be avoided, like when you are being attacked by a criminal or an aggressive dog or black bear, but otherwise, keeping your cool, staying centered, and being in a state of mind that allows you to come up with a creative solution is the golden way.

As Justin and Janine read the text messages, all they want to read is a love note from their beloved, who is excited to get home, but upon reading the news, their "babe" morphs into a ravenous hyena plotting the demise of the marriage. Their unconscious mind is triggered and goes off on autopilot.

What they don't know is that we have permanent access to all our emotions at all times. They are stored in our memory. The process of seeing and interpreting images does not happen with our eyes but with our mind. That means our brain cannot distinguish between something that is happening right now in front of us and a memory from the past that we are recalling. Thus, other than the deer that only feels fear as it sees the wolves, we can sit on our patio or lie in bed and remember a situation, like that co-worker who acted so disrespectfully this morning. Involuntarily, we recall the images from this morning and see again what we saw, hear their snarky words again, and feel the feelings of anger, frustration, and disgust again. Feeling those feelings means the hormonal glands in our body start releasing the same cocktail of hormones that they produced in that live moment.

As frustrating as this experience is, it harbors a gift, a secret power that you can use to your advantage. An almost magic trick that can be the difference that makes the difference between failure and success, health and disease, winning and losing, growing or sabotaging a relationship:

Just as you were once controlled by random thoughts that led to negative emotions in the past, you can now consciously recall positive memories and enjoy the process of creating desired, empowering emotions whenever you want them and take charge of your emotional state, independent from the environment you're in.

TOOL: Tap into **EMOTIONAL TREASURES**. Remember a time when you felt an emotion that you want to feel right now – confidence, for example. Recall a specific moment when you were confident and close your eyes.

Visualize what you saw in that moment. Where were you? Were you inside or outside? Who was with you? What were they wearing, and what were you wearing? Recall the details as specifically as you can.

Now, focus on what you heard in that moment. Were people saying something? Were you saying something? Were there sounds around you? Try to remember the auditory details as specifically as possible.

How did you feel in that moment? Indulge in the feeling and place your attention on the emotions flowing through your body once again.

To intensify the feeling, instead of one instance, recall two or three situations in a row.

Example:

Increase your happiness:

Close your eyes and go back to a time when you felt grateful. Recall the specific moment and visualize what you saw in your mind's eye. Hear the sounds you heard and feel the feelings you felt when you were filled with gratitude.

Now, go back to a second time when you felt grateful. Recall the specific moment and once again visualize what you saw, hear what you heard, and feel the emotions you experienced during that grateful moment.

Examples of such moments include the birth of a baby, a special birthday celebration, a wedding, graduation, promotion, winning a competition, receiving a special present, hearing kind words from a special person, an engagement, or any situation where you helped someone, and the help was well received. You can also think of moments when you witnessed someone else helping another person.

Again, for your unconscious mind, it's the same whether your sensory faculties are experiencing live sensory input or if your virtual sensory faculties are tapping into your imagination and memory, see *Figure 6*.

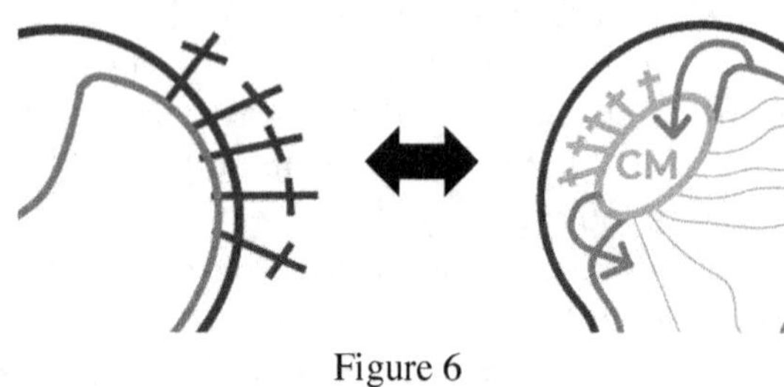

Figure 6

Both are equally real to your unconscious mind, and it is your choice which ones you use to create your emotions. You have the ability to feel any way you want at any given time if you choose to do so.

Most of us were raised thinking that the experience we have creates an emotion, but some people even believe the emotion *is* the experience. How can two people sit side by side, exposed to the same reality, and have a 180° different experience? Like the couple driving in a car and the child suddenly raises a question from the back seat: "Hey dad, where are all the assholes that are around when mommy is driving?" Or the other couple that is driving down the highway, and dad in the passenger seat points out a crazy driver that mom on the driver's seat had not even recognized.

Two fans of opposing soccer teams watch a match. A player gets fouled, and the referee blows his whistle. After seeing the incident in slow motion from five different angles, both spectators still walk away with a different perception.

A few minutes after reading their text messages, Janine and Justin become aware of their emotions. Instead of believing their anxiety is "just them" and swimming with it or projecting it onto their partner, they know that it is a trick their unconscious mind is playing on them, and they have the tools they need to overcome themselves.

They remind themselves of situations where they were deeply in love and how important their partner is to them.

Justin remembers the day he sat on the beach at sunset with Felicia and felt this deep love and thought to himself, "I want to marry this woman."

Janine remembers last Valentine's Day when Frank brought her breakfast to her bed and had prepared a day full of surprises.

As his feelings have shifted to love, Justin changes his perspective and understands how important it is for Felicia to socialize, and that it's his memory of his ex-girlfriend cheating and constantly flirting with other men that made those initial emotions come up. He sits up proud, to match the positive emotions he just tapped into, and texts back:

"Hey, my love, thank you for letting me know. The thing is, I have a bunch of flowers for you, a bath bomb, and your favorite sushi in the car, and I had hoped to have a relaxed evening for the two of us. If you have something important to discuss with Angie, I'll just leave the sushi in the fridge, and we can enjoy it tomorrow. I'd love to see you earlier tonight, though, if it's possible to meet Angie another day this week."

As Janine remembers how much she loves Frank and how responsive he mostly is to her needs, she softens as well. She understands that it is important for him to socialize, and that it's her general anxiety that made those initial emotions come up for her. She sits up proud, to match the positive emotions she just tapped into, and texts back:

"Hey Babe, thank you for letting me know. If you have something important to discuss with John, I understand. What I haven't shared with you yet is that I bought groceries to cook your favorite curry tonight and had hoped to watch the latest episode of the Mandalorian together. Let me know if you can reschedule with John or if I shall cook tomorrow instead?"

Relationships and spouses can get a little rough around the edges. In fact, very rough. And if it's not the spouse... wait to share a household with a toddler. If you've been through that already or are going through it right now, you may still be smiling or nodding...

My son has told me, "I don't need you," "I don't like you," "Leave me alone," and it was gut-wrenching. It was also obviously not his assessment or essential view of his relationship with me. I also, and way more often, hear "I love you, Papa" or "I want to cuddle with you" during play or when we get ready for bed.

The dark moments are dark. Humans experience frustration, and when they do, they express it, and that can hurt. That can feel un-loving. That can seem disrespectful. It usually feels like a precisely targeted sniper shot in your direction that hits you where it hurts the most.

Here is the good news: It may feel like it but it's most likely not a sniper shot. Instead you're really just too close to an explosion and happen to get hit by shrapnel. That doesn't make it a happy moment by any means, but finding the strength to experience an expression of frustration without responding forcefully by reacting with harsh words that start the blame carousel is a conquest of human spirit and consciousness. <u>The ability to absorb expressions of frustration in an empowered way without becoming frustrated yourself can make the difference between making and breaking a relationship.</u>

Have you ever been on the blame carousel? This is how it works:
Person one jumps on and sets it in motion by blaming, criticizing, being defensive, making a sarcastic remark, being contemptuous, or making a joke that's not taken well.
Person two deflects the accusation and makes an accusation in return, accelerating the carousel. Now accusations, criticism, and such fly back and forth, turning the carousel faster and faster until both supposed lovers fly off, dizzy and hurt.
Again, expressions of frustration are natural and can't be avoided 100 percent of the time. How can you respond to an expression

of frustration from your partner in an empowered way and avoid jumping on the blame carousel?

I call my favorite metaphor for processing your partner's frustration the Star Trek strategy. I don't know if you're a fan of the franchise, but chances are you have at least heard of a show called Star Trek and know that in this show, a spaceship to be found called Enterprise. This spaceship Enterprise sometimes comes under attack by alien spacecraft. The Enterprise has a force field around it, an energy shield that absorbs enemy fire and the occasional asteroid. If the Enterprise didn't have this energy shield, enemy fire would damage the hull of the ship, kill crew members, the Enterprise would need to be repaired, which would take a long time, cost, and effort, and it may even leave a scar.

Kind of what happens when you feel insulted or even in the case of name-calling, like being called a bitch or asshole. It goes right into your heart, it hurts, you need to forgive it, and it may leave an emotional scar.

As the Enterprise has its energy shield, this energy shield absorbs the enemy fire and protects it from damage. But it comes at a cost. It still requires energy to keep the energy shield up, and if fired upon too often, it can deplete, and real damage happens.

Here's the good news: You have an energy field as well. It's not as neatly defined as the Enterprise's, and it doesn't exude an eerie glow when hit, but it exists, and it protects your emotional state in moments of stress. This is how you can harness its power:

TOOL: The STAR TREK strategy
When your partner insults you in a moment of their frustration:

1. Acknowledge how it makes you feel. Become aware and name your emotions (to yourself).
2. Understand that what you're experiencing is not an attack that shows you how you are not loved, disliked nor disrespected, but you are just witnessing an <u>expression of frustration</u> of your partner.
3. Say (or think) "This just makes you a husband who calls his wife a bitch, I love you." or "This just makes you a wife who calls her husband an asshole, I love you." This reaffirms to yourself (and possibly your partner) that their words have not harmed or touched you in any way. It eliminates the need for an apology from your partner. They told the world who they are and how they felt, and did not define who you are.
4. Notice that cortisol and adrenaline levels in your spouse (and maybe in you as well) may be too high to improve the situation with words at this point.
5. Respond with kindness. Your kindness does not condone their behavior, but rather demonstrates your love for them. Offer to do something for them. If you already know of something, take action, such as bringing them a glass of their favorite beverage.

If the situation doesn't deescalate, it may be time to create some space between you and your partner for a bit. Here's how:

> **TOOL: CREATE SPACE** by saying, "I am really stressed right now and need to take a breather. I'll spend the next 30 minutes at [location]." Then return a bit earlier, like after 28 minutes or so, to resume the conversation.
>
> By doing this, you make it about you. ("I'm going to step out so you can calm down" will probably not help much.)
>
> By doing this, you build trust in a moment of frustration—a time where many couples sow distrust by leaving to an undisclosed place for an undetermined amount of time, leaving their partner guessing and in some degree of fear. It's a time where partners may just engage in shouting matches or punish with the silent treatment.

Good locations to spend that time can be the garden, a walk, a park, a room in the home, the car, or using the time to do chores or even do something for your partner to demonstrate that you don't appreciate what they said, but you appreciate them.

Creating space is not running away, stonewalling, or giving the silent treatment. It is an effort to create an environment for you and your partner where stress hormones can be metabolized and to prevent further escalation. You build trust by saying what you do and doing what you say, and when you return earlier, you even overdeliver.

When a phone call gets too heated, some people just hang up the phone. That's a good thing. If you do that, you already know. If you are a person who doesn't do that and feels hurt or disrespected by your partner hanging up the phone, notice that they do that not to hurt you but because they recognize their own emotional state and know that if they stayed on the phone, they may say things that are even more hurtful than hanging up. I know it can be hard, but try to understand it as an expression of appreciation for you and the relationship. Take a moment to relax. They'll either call you back, or you can give it another try 30 minutes later.

Alison Armstrong in her audiobook *Celebrating Partnership* talks about the rage monster that lives in every woman, and when it comes out, it spits fire and says what it takes to inflict hurt and disrespect to make the partner feel the pain they feel. Alison, in her talk, apologizes to every man who has been exposed to the rage monster.

I don't feel privileged to apologize on behalf of women, but I believe that understanding the rage monster as an expression of frustration can alleviate the pain it causes and help to let it bounce off the male energy field while finding the empathy and compassion to help heal the source of frustration of your beloved.

The male counterpart of the rage monster is probably the robot that comes out and tries to logically mansplain the impossibilities and possibilities of certain situations. Something like:

She: "I saw you staring at my friend Katie. Do you want to have sex with her?"

He: "You think I would cheat on you with Katie? She doesn't even look that good and also, she is married."

I apologize for every mansplanation you have ever received from your man. Forgive him, as he doesn't know what he's doing... The female response of "Oh, so if she looked better and wasn't married, you'd consider cheating on me with her?" just leaves him startled in disbelief, and he has no idea how to get out of this. "No, no, I meant... sigh."

Ladies, what he means is: "Babe, I love you and the kids so much, I would never do something horrible like that!"

Gentlemen: Say that!

You see, elevating your emotional state can go hand in hand with elevating your partner's emotional state.

Back to your emotional state. Here are a few other ways to elevate it:

- Listen to your favorite music.
- Watch a comedy show.
- Call a friend.
- Meditate.
- Mental and Emotional Release.
- Go for a walk.

Chapter 13

THE MENTAL STATE

"I've had a lot of worries in my life, most of which never happened."
– Mark Twain

Your mental state represents the **thoughts** you have, or in other words, the things you say to yourself inside your head (or even out loud) and what you **focus** on. Your thoughts and your focus are the language of your conscious and unconscious mind.

Upon receiving their text messages, Justin's and Janine's focus was primarily on themselves: "This makes ME feel sad, disrespected, hurt." "I am going to teach him/her a lesson, so s/he finally gets it and never does it again!" "Look what I have done for him/her, and now s/he makes me look really stupid!" Their thoughts are circling around what their partner's behavior means now and for the future:

"S/he doesn't love me."
"S/he doesn't respect me."
"S/he doesn't care about my feelings."
"S/he did it on purpose and will do it again and again."
"Maybe s/he is not the right partner for me!"
"Maybe s/he is about to cheat or leave me!"

These thoughts express a certain degree of anxiety around the future but also express how much their partner means to them.

What is the difference between fear and anxiety? I remember a hike I took into the Sespe Condor Sanctuary with a friend to enjoy the natural hot springs in the middle of nowhere. We were out of cell phone reception almost immediately, and we pitched the tent about 14 miles/22 km away from civilization. As I woke up the next morning and stepped out of my tent, I was surrounded by pristine scenery: I stood in a valley, surrounded by rolling hills next to a crisp mountain stream, the sun was just rising, birds singing under a beautiful blue sky. I went for a swim in the stream, then prepared breakfast. While breakfast was heating up, I started thinking about the things that could potentially go wrong: A bear could show up, a cougar could show up, I could get bitten by a rattlesnake, I could break my ankle on my way back, just to name a few.

My reality looked very different, though: I was in a beautiful spot, I was safe, no danger was present. All the things that could create negative feelings (stress hormones) were only inside my head. The anticipation of things that were unlikely to happen.

How many people base the majority of their decisions on potential dangers that rarely come true? Of course, the potential dangers I may or may not have gotten into were real possibilities, but how would investing energy in pondering them help master them if they did become a reality? I thought of the possibility of an encounter with a wild animal before I headed out. I bought bear spray, and I carried it so that I could pull it out swiftly, and I had practiced doing so.

I also educated myself about rattlesnake bites and how to respond to them. I learned a few interesting things:

- Most rattlesnake bites are to the hand and not to the leg or ankle.
- When you get bitten by a rattlesnake, hike out. It takes a few days to kill you, so the advice is to hike out and get to a hospital. As we were pretty far out, one of us would have hiked out with only the essentials and get a helicopter.

I felt prepared and comfortable and didn't spend much time pondering the risk of rattlesnakes.

Revisiting the situation and going back to the potential threats over and over again would have had the opposite effect. In my mind, I would have faced a bear and a rattlesnake again and again and again and released the stress hormones, as the brain can't distinguish between a bear or snake in front of me and a bear or snake that I am imagining. Those stress hormones would have narrowed my focus and impaired my creative thinking, impaired my relaxation, and my overall well-being. I would have started my journey home more stressed, more nervous, more preoccupied with what is happening inside my head (wrestling a virtual bear) than enjoying my environment, and through that distraction and not being fully present in the moment, I would have increased the risk of injury or getting into a dangerous situation.

As we were hiking out, my dog Obi and I walked past a bush, and when my friend was next to the bush, the bush started to rattle. Never have I seen someone jump that far. My friend was startled and shaken. We peeked under the bush, and there was the snake. A huge pitch-black rattler, and we had walked past it by just a few inches. It had chosen not to bite us.

I realized rattlesnakes are not ferocious beasts waiting for a chance to make a dude's life miserable but are mainly concerned with preserving their own life and their poison, a rare commodity that they need to be resourceful with as they need it to catch meals.

The snake didn't mind one or two passersby, but upon the third, it decided to spread the news of its existence so that it wouldn't fall victim to the apparent stampede that was going on.

A few miles later, Obi and I passed by another bush, and this one rattled while Obi was next to it. Now Obi and I were on one side of the bush, my friend was on the other side, and he wasn't happy. Still shaken from the last snake encounter, he started to poke at the bush with his hiking stick.

"So that's why most rattlesnake bites are to the hand," I thought.

"What are you doing?" I said.

"I want to see it!" was the reply.

I said, "I'd love to see it, too, but what I'd love even more would be for us to get home safe, so please just make a huge circle around the bush, and let's move on."

And so, we made it home safe and sound but with a few profound learnings. One was a deeper understanding of Mark Twain's quote. You may fear that your partner cheats, but controlling their environment, looking into their phone on a regular basis, or questioning their whereabouts is like poking the bush. Not because there is something dangerous lurking in the phone but because your partner will only be able to endure the distrust and disrespect for so long.
Being prepared for what could happen isn't manifesting it. It is the opposite. You're now free to put your attention on enjoying the beautiful things, knowing that when tragedy strikes, you have a plan to pull out of your pocket.

Master your focus:
The time to focus on the danger is for a dedicated amount of time where you plan your response in the unlikely case that misfortune finds you. Then focus on whatever pleasant thing you set out for. Focus back on the danger when it appears, and cross that bridge when you reach it.

Confucius put it like this: <u>A bird sitting on a tree is never afraid of the branch breaking because its trust is not on the branch but on its wings</u>. If you hike the backcountry unprepared, hoping for bears and rattlesnakes to stay away, you may feel uncomfortable and on high alert all the time. I don't know if bears can sense stress hormones like dogs, but if they do, you're now making it even more likely to fall prey.

If you walk into an exam unprepared and hope for easy questions... have you ever noticed that professors seem to have a sixth sense for the unprepared? My fellow students and I used to rant about how the professors would often probe the unprepared students so deeply while asking the prepared students so few questions that they asked themselves why they spent so much time studying so hard.

Even as an empowered lover, your relationship is not guaranteed to last. No relationship ever is. But as an empowered lover, you know that you are doing everything in your power to make it as likely as possible that the marriage will last, and if it fails, you know how to cope with it, preserve your learnings, and ascend to an even more compatible partner.

Our mind is always active, and as long as we are not consciously focusing on something specific, it runs the scripts that we programmed into the unconscious mind in the past through repetition and through experiences that were combined with strong emotions. Information + Emotion = Memory.

Justin and Janine had programmed their unconscious minds to quickly determine threats of being cheated on. Janine's dad had cheated on her mom multiple times. She remembers him coming home with the stereotypical lipstick mark on his shirt, the fight that ensued shortly after, and the eventual divorce after years of her mom letting him get away with it.

Justin was cheated on by two girlfriends before he met Felicia. Janine and Justin both know "consciously" that they are loved and safe, but the previous experiences thoroughly programmed their unconscious minds.

It does not matter what the conscious mind today thinks of the situation of the past. At that time, an imprint was made in the unconscious, and that imprint is still as deep today as it was when it was made. Even after releasing it, the mind may habitually employ the thoughts it defaulted to in the past. The difference is, without the baggage, you can now influence them.

How can you alter those thoughts?

You may have noticed that stopping a thought is impossible. You can't stop a thought because you need to think something. When you stop thinking, it leaves a void, and that void will be filled with something else or with the same thought again. The mind always thinks, and it thinks about what your focus is directed at. So,_to change your thoughts, you need to change your focus, and the thoughts will follow. It is as simple as it is effective.

In 1970, Walter Mischel, a psychology professor at Stanford University, conducted a famous study that would become known as the Marshmallow Test. The purpose of the study was to understand when children develop the ability to delay gratification. He sat children down at a table, a marshmallow on a plate in front of them, and instructed them that they could eat it, but if they waited 15 minutes, they would get a second one. The results varied between kids eating the marshmallow immediately, managing to wait, and kids nibbling at the marshmallow. You can find a video of marshmallow tests on YouTube for your amusement or self-study.

I am mentioning the experiment here not with a focus on delayed gratification but with a focus on how the kids who were able to endure the 15 minutes did it. They shifted their focus. They turned around on their chair or covered their eyes and moved their attention away from the object of desire. They invented games with their fingers that drew all their attention. Again, you can't change your thoughts; you can only change your focus, and your thoughts will follow.

Whenever you look at a situation, you look at it from a certain angle or through a certain frame. That frame gives meaning to what you experience and keeps your thoughts within it. In Janine and Justin's case:

"My partner informs me that s/he won't spend time with me but with someone else, which means s/he likes someone else better.

Chances are, the person presented to me is just a smokescreen for a person of the opposite sex they may betray me with."

Reframing the situation can shift your focus and offer you new and empowering ways to see a circumstance and create new outcomes for a situation that at first glance seems not okay for you. Just like the smart kids moved their attention away from the marshmallow for fifteen minutes to get two marshmallows, you can shift your attention away from judging the negativity of your partner's behavior.

Instead, you can shift your attention to alternative meanings, to not get two marshmallows but create a relationship situation that makes you and your partner feel loved and respected. <u>The meaning any situation has is the meaning you give it.</u>

TOOL: MEANING REFRAME
When you catch yourself in a state of suffering...

1. Become aware of your feelings and name them.
2. Place your attention on what you are focused on-the meaning you are giving the situation right now. Likely, you are focused on how you are at the effect of your partner, on how your spouse can impair or is impairing your well-being.
3. Find a different meaning that the situation can have, which gives you the ability to act differently, thus changing the reality for you and for the person or people in front of you so they may respond with different behavior as well.

Example:
Your spouse yells at you. You feel disrespected, wronged, hurt, and find his/her behavior inappropriate. That is the meaning you unconsciously give the behavior. Have you ever yelled at someone whom you respected? Most of us have (my hand is raised, too). Even if you haven't, you will find an example of someone who yelled at somebody they deeply respected. So, if one can yell at someone they respect, then yelling doesn't necessarily mean disrespect. What else could it mean? How about that the person does not feel heard? Even a respectful person may yell if they don't feel heard. Looking at the behavior through that frame gives you the opportunity to find a response that comes from love and understanding rather than confrontation. Perhaps you can make him/her feel heard.

Justin habitually focuses on how he is the plaything of his wife, at her mercy, at the effect of the reality she imposes on him. He acknowledges feeling the feelings of sadness and being disrespected. He wonders what other meaning the things she does could have. "It's important for her to socialize," "Her friend may have a problem, and Felicia is a great person to seek advice from," "Maybe she had a bad day at work and wants to blow off steam to avoid coming home frustrated"...

Instead of focusing on himself and his own preferences, Justin decides to shift his focus to Felicia's needs. "How can I support her best? How can I make her feel valued, loved, and at ease? How can I communicate with her so that she knows I had plans as well, in case she was expecting a boring evening? I mean, normally, I'd have no problem with her meeting a friend after work."

TOOL: CONTEXT REFRAME

When you find yourself in a situation where people or circumstances make you feel angry, frustrated, or sad, it can help to reflect on the context of the situation. Can you imagine a context in which the behavior of your partner can be appreciated?

Example 1: Your spouse is lying on the couch. You habitually label their behavior as lazy and feel left alone and disrespected as you're doing chores. You have the impulse to judge them or give them a task. You place your attention on how such conversations went in the past and chuckle as you become conscious of the pattern. You ask yourself, "In what context can I appreciate this behavior?" If the house were on fire, you would appreciate that your spouse doesn't sprint head over heels outside in panic but stays calm and collected, calls the fire department, saves important valuables, saves the dog and the cat, and guides the family swiftly but controlled away from the danger.

Example 2: Your spouse gets intense when defending their position, not backing down but fighting to get their point across. You wonder why they are arguing in such a disrespectful, even hostile manner and why you can't just have a relaxed discussion about the topic. You wonder if there could be a context in which you can appreciate that behavior... If your spouse or your children were in danger, you would want your spouse to protect your family (or family's assets) in that exact way. You might say, "It's just more fun to work with tigers, although you get a swipe once in a while." You're proud that you have a partner who can show up for themselves, and you don't need to be concerned about them when you're not around.

Justin wonders if there are situations where he can appreciate what Felicia is doing right now. He loves how closely she listens when he comes to her with a problem. That she is so outgoing and fun is one thing he really loves about her, and outgoing, fun people like to go out and have fun.

Your situation today is the result of your thoughts, feelings, and actions in the past. How you deal with any circumstance you find yourself in depends on the meaning you give it and the context in which you place it, see *Figure 7*.

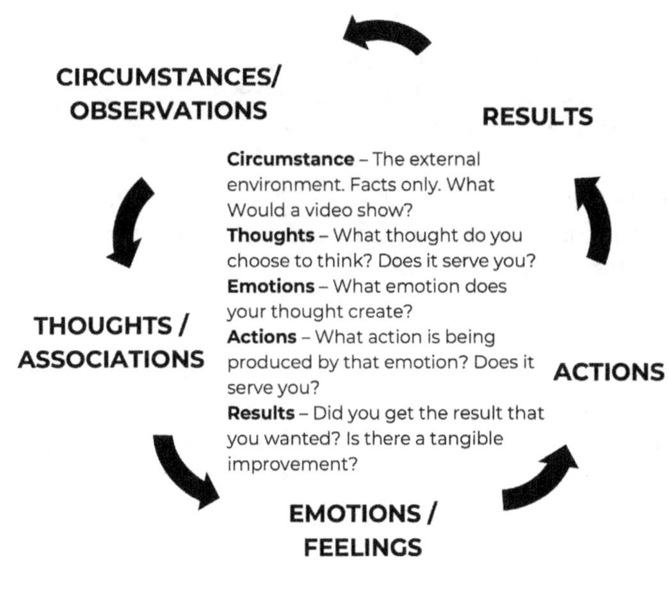

Figure 7

As your thoughts swirl around in your head, have you noticed that it can feel like someone is speaking every thought to you? At least, that is the experience of many people. This voice in your head doesn't mean you're going crazy; it's normal. Most people even have many different voices in their head – their own voice, their parents' voices, their grandparents' voices, their siblings' voices, their partner's voice, their friends' voices, and even the voices of ex-partners. I even have voices of deceased people in my head.

Some of those thoughts or voices are empowering, while others are negative and disempowering. For example, your mother's snarky remark when you do something that you know she wouldn't appreciate, or an angry "you" chastises you and tells you how stupid you are or were. When you think about it, you notice that what that voice says may not even be true, but it talks to you anyway...

TOOL: THE VOICE OF TRUTH

When you say to yourself, "There will be another day tomorrow," what voice is saying that? Or when you say, "I have two legs," repeat those phrases a few times in your mind and notice the voice. Pay attention to its volume, pitch, and tonality. This is your voice of truth.

Now, let's test a negative thought that you sometimes have, that you know is not true, and listen to the voice that tells you that. This is one of the voices that lie to you and bring you down.

Next, correct yourself and tell yourself the truth, using the voice of truth. For example, if you think, "I am not lovable," correct it by saying, "I loved myself enough to XY" (where XY represents something you have actually done, such as "have worked out this morning/yesterday, have meditated, ate healthy..."). By acknowledging something you have truly done for yourself, you provide undeniable evidence that you love yourself. Remember the voice of truth when an unpleasant voice in your head speaks to you, and correct it.

A variant of the voice of truth is chanting a mantra. A mantra is a repetitive phrase or sound used in meditation or spiritual practices to focus the mind and evoke a specific intention or state of being. If you want to adopt a belief that you would find useful but catch yourself telling yourself the disempowering opposite or if your life reflects the fact that you don't believe it yet, you can chant a mantra that instills the belief in you that you would like to adopt.

The book *The Big Leap* by Gay Hendricks introduces what the author calls the "Ultimate Success Mantra." I personally use it and have made a slight modification. This Mantra is your go-to mantra for any situation you would like to see improve, regardless of the quality of the situation you're in. It doesn't matter if it's a happy or sad time in your relationship, if you're homeless or a millionaire, if you're in the best shape of your life or have cancer. It is especially useful for breaking through any "glass ceiling" you may encounter.

TOOL: THE ULTIMATE SUCCESS MANTRA

"I expand in success, abundance, health and love, as I inspire those around me to do the same."

Wait a moment for your unconscious mind to talk back at you in whatever negative way it may.

Then repeat the mantra.

Say the Ultimate Success Mantra to yourself, pause, and let the voice that lies to you respond and belittle it. Then just repeat it again to show that voice that what it says is meaningless.

You can use the Ultimate Success Mantra to talk yourself to sleep, say it as the first thing when you wake up in the morning, and any time in between, such as during a drive.

Chapter 14

THE SPIRITUAL STATE

*Spirituality is not adopting more beliefs and assumptions but
uncovering the best in you." – Amit Ray*

Your spiritual state consists of your **energy** and your **beliefs** in any given situation. This includes religious beliefs as well as local beliefs such as "Here we go again, now we will argue and fight for the next hours..." or even global beliefs like "Maybe this relationship is not meant to be."

In Part One of this book we discussed the human energy field and what it could look like. This chapter is about how you experience your energy field and how you can influence it. You can understand your energy as a field with both qualitative and quantitative aspects.

The qualitative aspect is the vibration you are in, which can be a positive or high vibration when you experience positive emotions and you are in a beautiful state or it can be in a negative or low vibration when you experience negative emotions and are in a state of suffering.

The quantitative aspect refers to the intensity of the vibration. These four combinations provide a useful model for different states and offer options for effectively influencing your state.

1. You can be in a low vibration with a high intensity, such as rage, anger, or paralyzing fear.
2. You can be in a low vibration with a low intensity, like sadness, blame, guilt, hurt, or frustration.
3. You can be in a high vibration with a low intensity, experiencing peace, happiness, joy, or comfort.
4. You can be in a high vibration with a high intensity, feeling love, gratitude, ecstasy, or bliss, *see Figure 8.*

Figure 8

Low vibration, high intensity; in this state your body is flooded with stress hormones, curse words are used, shouting matches happen, objects may start flying, and verbal, emotional, or even physical abuse can occur. I haven't come across a relationship situation that would benefit from this state, except if you need the adrenaline to muster some extra strength to protect your partner from a wild wolf. In that case, you don't need to do much to access this state; your unconscious mind will take care of that.

Most people who find themselves in a low vibration, high intensity state desire to change that state as it is a highly uncomfortable experience. (Reframe: If you find your partner in this state, notice how much pain they are in.) This state is dominated by the presence of a high amount of stress hormones, and remaining inside an argument in this state is unlikely to lead to a productive solution. A solution that arises within an argument like that will be rather forced by the other person giving in or pretending to give in out of fear that this energy may be acted out further and will come at the detriment to oneself, the other person, and the relationship.

When you find yourself or your partner in such a state, the first step is to move to a place where you can metabolize the stress hormones without being triggered further by using the CREATE SPACE tool mentioned in the chapter on the emotional state.

Once you are alone, the following activities can help you relax and regain your composure:

- Listen to relaxing music.
- Name and acknowledge the emotions you feel.
- Exercise.
- Go for a walk.
- Box-breathe.
- Practice Wim Hoff breathing.
- Meditate.
- Spend time with your pet.
- Call a trusted friend or family member who you know will not fan the flame but empathize and help you reframe and find productive solutions without judgment.
- Do an act of kindness for your partner.

If this state is driven by fear, it is especially dangerous as predators pick up on it. The gazelle with this energy signature is the one the lion prefers to pick. Does that make it the gazelle's fault that it was eaten? Of course not. If you find yourself in recurring situations where you feel this level of fear, prepare yourself so that it stops. The person who doesn't prepare for a bear attack isn't responsible for it, but the one who is prepared will either not get into a situation like that (no food in the tent) or has the tools and practice to make it more likely to fend it off when push comes to shove (has bear spray ready).

What you need to avoid is spiritual bypassing. Spiritual bypassing means using spiritual practices or reframing a situation to feel better instead of dealing with the problem at hand. For example, going for a hike in bear or rattlesnake country with no preparation and just focusing on positive things. Or getting sued and just sitting back, meditating, and being confident that if you're just positive enough, the law of attraction will handle it for you. Or saying that studying for a difficult exam is just obsessing over something negative and watching a comedy show will put you in a good vibration to create a positive outcome. Or getting into a relationship despite red flags because you think you can change them. Or having a history of being abused or worse and not seeking therapeutic help or acquiring self-defense skills that you will then probably never need, but they change your vibration and deter abusers.

Low vibration with low intensity can be an appropriate state. When you receive news about the death of someone who is close to you, when you get hurt or disrespected by your partner, or when you receive bad news at work or at home.

The grieving and forgiveness processes happen in this state, as well as working through sadness or overcoming guilt, hurt, embarrassment, or shame. It may be appropriate to remain in this state for a while or move out of it slowly.

This state also serves you when you build rapport with and support someone who has suffered a loss or personal hardship.

When appropriate, you may choose to try one or more of the following activities to raise your vibration:

- Talk about your pain with people who can help you overcome it.
- Talk to other affected people or maybe just sit together with them in silence.
- Experience someone else's presence to feel safe and comforted.
- Tap into your emotional treasures.
- Listen to uplifting music.
- Meditate.
- Practice the Ho'oponopono forgiveness meditation.
- Write down your feelings and experiences.
- Focus on the learnings from the event.
- Watch motivational videos.
- Engage in productive/creative activities like making music, preparing food, cleaning/tidying up, organizing, gardening...
- Call a trusted friend or family member who you know will not fan the flame but empathize and help you reframe and find productive solutions without judgment.
- Take a cold shower.

- Express appreciation and gratitude towards people you feel close to.

A **high vibration with low intensity** is the state most people spend most of their time in and is the most desirable state, most of the time. It encompasses emotions like peace, happiness, joy, contentment, comfort, being in flow, feeling close to someone, and many more.

There can be situations where you may want to move to a lower vibration as you empathize with and comfort a person who is close to you and is going through a painful situation or has suffered a loss.

You may want to move to a higher intensity as you prepare for a public speech or presentation, join a celebration, or get ready for participating in a sports event.

To move to a lower vibration to empathize with another person, tap into the feeling of the other person by creating an inner representation of their situation or remember a time when you experienced something similar. Give them 100% of your attention, touch them slightly if appropriate, listen carefully, or even just sit in silence with them.

To increase the intensity of your high vibration, one or some of the following activities can help:

- Listen to energetic music and raise the volume.
- Exercise, but not to exhaustion.
- Watch motivational videos.
- Spend quality time with your loved one.
- Express your love and gratitude for your partner, speaking their love language.
- Meditate.

A **high vibration with high intensity**, although feeling great, can be inappropriate in many settings. An obvious one being when you want to fall asleep. The following activities can lower your vibration to a point where you still feel positive but with a lower intensity:

- Meditate.
- Listen to relaxing music.
- Read.
- Practice yoga or exercise.
- Take a bath.
- Enjoy a massage.
- Go for a walk.
- Take a cold shower.

You may have noticed some activities that can be used to alter your spiritual state in different directions, such as meditation and music. Music is a vibration in and of itself, and we tend to adapt to the vibration of our environment, i.e., the music around you.

In meditation, you can hold the inner representation of the desired state in front of your mind's eye and experience your state changing towards it. Other activities have already been mentioned as means to alter other sub-states, and often one activity targets multiple sub-states simultaneously. Cold showers, for example, are a physical exercise, but it is almost impossible to exit a cold shower in the same spiritual state as you entered.

Besides your energy, the spiritual state is also comprised of your beliefs. Do you believe the higher power, your unconscious self, or a loved one have your back or are sabotaging you? Someone who catches themselves thinking, "Maybe this is not meant to be," essentially believes that a higher power cares for them, their family, every one of the eight billion people on Earth, every animal, plant, amoeba, bacteria, and virus, and has a conscious intention for the future of each. Maybe that is the case. Personally, I don't think so. But I believe the higher power is a force that we can tap into, and the more effectively we do so, the more it influences the outcome.

You tap into this higher power through prayer, meditation, or by simply elevating your emotional state and then taking action. In fact, you're always connected to it and just influence how. As the saying goes: "God helps those who help themselves." From my understanding, God pays just as much attention to lip service and good intentions as anyone else. Decisions are made not thought.

This is the philosophy behind the law of attraction, and it has its place in relationships because we do attract and detract people, states, and circumstances that serve us, as well as those that don't serve us.

As there are people who believe in the almost magical power of manifestation and those who don't believe in it, I want to start with a scientific explanation to satisfy the skeptics.

It has been proven over and over that a person's expectation has an influence on the outcome of a situation. We don't need to look further than the placebo effect. Big pharma acknowledges it, and they wish they didn't have to. A patient expecting a medication to work raises the likelihood that it will. It's not only a "thought." The placebo effect means that biological and chemical processes are being set in motion that create the healing. But only in the person who really believes. Really believing means believing on an unconscious level. Big pharma knows how to use the placebo effect to their advantage:

- Blue pills work better than red pills.
- The more difficult the name of the medication, the better it works.
- The more expensive a medication is, the better the results.
- If it's administered by a person with authority, like a person who wears a white robe and a "Dr." in front of her name, the better it works.
- All these aspects target the unconscious mind.
- The placebo effect does not only work in us, but we make it work on other's as well. Placebos work in animals, too.

Our expectations not only change the perception of an inert sugar pellet in a way that makes our unconscious mind alter the biology of the body, but it can also affect the quality of our vision, or rather, how the visual information that reaches our retina is interpreted by the brain.

A person who expects a parking spot right in front of the store is more likely to recognize a shopper who just enters their car to leave or the open parking spot next to the handicapped parking spot. A person who believes they never get a spot in front may overlook the shopper who enters their car or perceive the parking spot next to the handicapped spot as one of the handicapped spots. Of course, the person who believes in manifestation will celebrate how she "attracted" the spot.

Either way, manifestation is a humble experience, and someone claiming causality by thinking something into reality will get in trouble at some point. For example, when a spouse buys a lottery ticket, and their partner claims they manifested the win. Or a supporting partner claims causality in any financial success that the spouse worked very hard for. It is true that the support for the spouse, emotionally through encouragement, physically by sharing household chores, and mentally by helping to rehearse meetings, interviews, and presentations played a role. It is also understandable how claiming too much share in the other person's win will likely not improve the relationship, as does dismissing the supporting partner's help as meaningless.

It becomes even clearer when we look at the manifestation of negative outcomes. Every one of the 2,224 people on the Titanic manifested the iceberg, but only a few would had a reasonable chance to prevent the collision. You have manifested everything you experience, although your role in the causality may have been relatively insignificant.

Most events, especially events in relationships, are co-creations. Whether Felicia's text message leads to a divorce or not is not only in her hands but in Justin's hands as well. Justin can respond with understanding and compassion, or he can send an angry, snarky, sarcastic text back, and Felicia can then double down on that. Or she can absorb it gracefully, with empathy, reassure Justin, and they can either spend the whole evening together or enjoy the night from 8 pm on until their bedtime.

I do want to quickly touch on the possibility that the law of attraction and the act of manifestation may have some merit. If you don't care for this, you can move on to the chapter on meditation.

Dr. Joe Dispenza offers the explanation that our intentions, thoughts, our visions, and inner representations are signals that we send out to the quantum field that connects all things. When you then experience resonating emotions, these then provide the "magnetism" that draws the thing you thought of back to you. If you think something positive and feel positive emotions, the positive thing may become more likely to happen. If you have a negative thought and feel negative emotions, the negative things may become more likely to happen. This gives a good explanation of why not every thought about cancer leads to a tumor and why few lottery tickets result in a win: A signal without a matching emotion likely dissipates with no effect. We looked earlier into the electromagnetic waves that the brain sends out. Equivalent to our brain, our heart also emits an electromagnetic field. Researchers at the HeartMath Institute, a nonprofit research and education organization, found that they were able to detect the electromagnetic field of the heart at a distance of up to ten feet outside of the body. That doesn't mean that it stops there; this is just as far as the sensitivity of their measurement devices went. Again, as of now, the law of attraction seems to be just a hypothesis based on ideas and anecdotal evidence.

Speaking of anecdotal evidence, here are two experiences I had that believers in the law of attraction may celebrate, while skeptics may still understand them as lucky coincidences. Very lucky coincidences.

Story 1: A friend of mine visited me from Germany and told me that he was doing this thing with a friend of his: Each was transmitting the other person an object in their meditations that the other person did not know about. She had done it before; for him, it was the first time, and he was excited to see what would happen. He told me what object he was sending her and how he came to choose it while he was excited about receiving her object in one of his future meditations. A couple of days later, we went to a breathwork session together, held by a shaman in Los Angeles. We enjoyed the session, conversed with the shaman afterward, and he invited us to go to dinner with him and a few friends. We agreed, had a great time, and as we left and walked back to our cars, the shaman pulled a stone out of his pocket, a turquoise, and told my friend that he had been carrying this stone in his pocket for three years now, and he felt it was time to pass it on to him. My friend was grateful and excited. The next morning, he had a FaceTime call with his meditation friend. After their conversation, he walked up to me, pale and shaken. "You won't believe what happened!" he said. "When I showed her the stone, she turned pale and said, 'That is the object I am sending you in my meditations! Do you remember the necklace I have with the turquoise stone? I am sending you that stone!'"

Story 2: My son had these "Dr. Brown's" baby bottles that have a special ventilation system so that the baby can drink continuously without having to let air back in. The ventilation system consists of a straw and plug that goes on top of the straw. As we were cleaning the bottles in the dishwasher, two of the straws came loose, dropped on the heating coil of the dishwasher, and melted. I looked online for spare parts and found a pack of two, just what I needed. As they arrived, we now had the right amount of straws again but too many plugs, so I threw away the excess plugs. A couple of days later, I was looking for plugs and I realized that I had thrown away one plug too many, but the trash had already been picked up. I felt a bit stupid and wished that plug was still there. About a week later, I came home from a drive, and as I walked from my car to the entrance of our house, I saw a little white object in the corner of my eye. Looking closer, I saw one of the plugs lying on the ground next to where I put the trash cans on pick-up day. The only objects that fell out of the full trash can were a plastic fork and this plug.

Experiences like these point towards the possibility that our thoughts may even interact with a quantum field to draw certain experiences and realities towards us. One can say that reality is how we perceive with our senses all that we've created.

But I can appreciate it if you continue to call it luck.

Meditation

You may have noticed that meditation impacts your physical, emotional, mental, and spiritual state. I mention it in this chapter because I like to see it as a spiritual practice. As such, I despised it for most of my life. In fact, my conviction was that meditation is something hippies in tie-dye indulge in while burning incense and sitting on funny pillows. Until I read again and again that CEOs meditate, and I became curious.

How does meditation work and provide its benefits?

The feeling of stress and the hormones of stress are designed to move your body into a peak state – for defending yourself against a physical threat, fight or flee. It diverts the blood flow from parts like the digestive system, reproductive systems, or immune system to the arms and legs. It also diverts the blood flow from the creative part of the brain to the ancient 'crocodile' part of the brain.

That used to happen and made sense for humans that can run into a wolf or bear any time. Today it happens when we get triggered by bosses, employees, coworkers, family members, deadlines, horror movies, the news, and many others. Situations that rather require creative thinking than strong limbs.

Nature designed the hormones of stress to be experienced once in a while in exceptional situations, but our modern lifestyle can lead to stress being an ever-present feeling which the body is not de-signed for. It can lead to daily suppression of the digestive system, reproductive system, or immune system, and one may experience lower sex drive, weight loss/weight gain, and with a constantly lowered immune system, frequent illnesses or chronic illnesses and compromised elimination of mutated cells…

As if we weren't exposed to enough outside stress factors already, we add inside stress factors by remembering real ones from the past and stressing out over those memories. You may have experienced being in a perfectly relaxed situation when suddenly a stressful thought conquers your mind out of nowhere…

Your body behind your eyes can't distinguish between the wolf in front of you and the wolf you remember. A thought comes in, you stress over it, cortisol is produced… and the thought has fulfilled its purpose and fades away without you having made a decision nor taken action.

But why do our unconscious minds send us those memories in the first place if they don't help?

Because one of its tasks is to keep the body in a "normal" chemical state. The unconscious mind doesn't distinguish between good and bad, only between "normal" and "abnormal." Which is good in many cases. If water levels in our cells drop and we get dehydrated, the unconscious mind catches that and brings it to our conscience, which gives us the chance to choose to drink.

But it can also happen with negative things. Like the smoker who taught his body that a certain level of nicotine is normal. When the nicotine level drops below a certain threshold, his unconscious mind notices it and brings it to his attention. Then the conscious mind assesses if smoking right now would be appropriate and if so, the smoker goes and has a cigarette. This again is an unconscious process: The smoker does not need to pay attention to setting one foot before the other, opening the door, pulling out the pack of cigarettes, and lighting one. That all happens unconsciously while he thinks about the next meeting, what he's going to watch on TV that night, or thinking about past memories. After smoking the cigarette, his nicotine level is back in balance.

What happens between the nicotine level being in balance and out of balance?

Not much: Time goes by and the cycle repeats, see *Figure 9*.

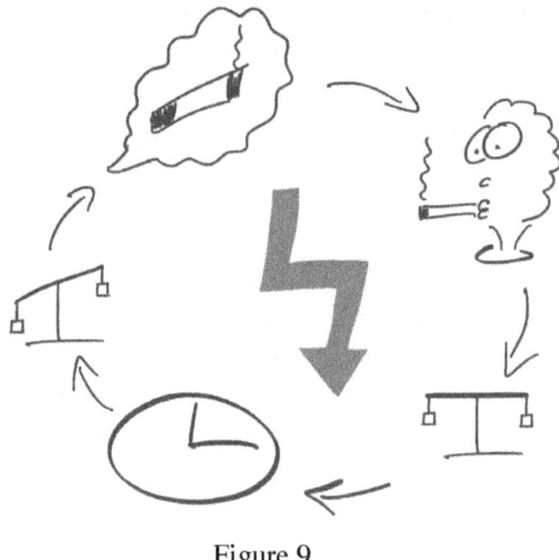

Figure 9

Just like that, we have taught our bodies to be used to a certain level of cortisol. And when it gets out of balance, our conscious mind sends us a thought of a figurative wolf. We ponder it and don't even need to go outside... just by remembering it, we stress out again, raise our cortisol level, and the thought fades. Time goes by, and the cycle repeats.

So, if thoughts can make us release stress hormones, and stress hormones suppress our immune system, then thoughts can make us sick. If thoughts can make us sick, can thoughts make us well, too? See *Figure 10*.

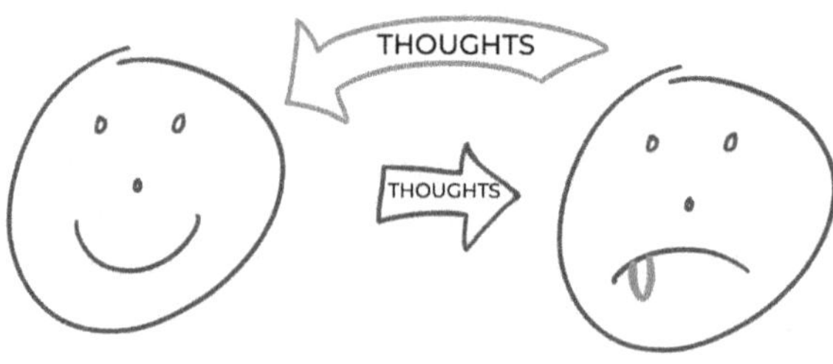

Figure 10

What are we thinking about day in, day out anyway?
In their recent 2020 study titled *Brain meta-state transitions*

demarcate thoughts across task contexts exposing the mental noise of trait neuroticism, Julie Tseng and Jordan Poppenk estimate that we have over 6,000 thoughts per day. Many of those are repetitive, circling around…

- The past – pulling up memories.
  or
- The predictable future.

The only thing those thoughts do is create feelings and keep the body in our chemical "normal," so that we feel the same every day. This is generally good because it makes us emotionally stable and reliable.

Our brain uses 20% to 25% of our total energy consumption, and a good portion of that energy is wasted on things we can't change. So, when can we actually change? There is only one moment: NOW.

Instead of allowing the past and the predictable future to siphon off our energy, when we stay in the present moment, we can use it to make real changes. Now is the moment when you can have a thought you never had before. Now is when you can be creative and create things that you never had before, like painting a picture, building a business, writing a book, having ideas that you stereo-typically have in the shower or in bed at night, or making a change in your relationship, see *Figure 11*.

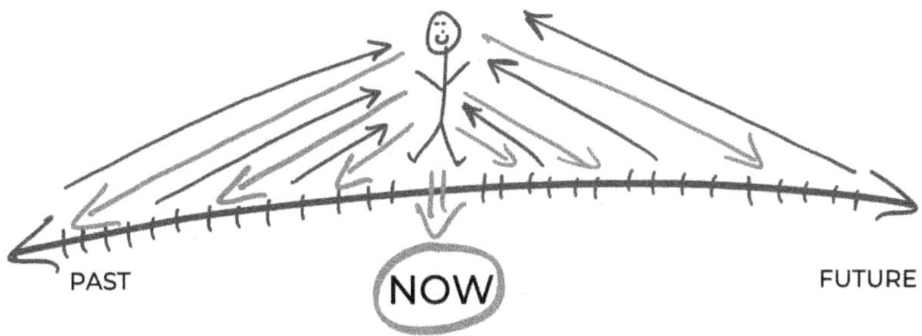

Figure 11

How can you get in the now and harness that brain power?

In meditation, you practice observing and controlling your thoughts by controlling your focus and taking your power back. By focusing on your breath, your heart, or the words of a meditation guide, you bring your attention to something that is happening in the present moment. Consequently, your thoughts are then in the present moment and directed at something that does not trigger a stress response. Essentially, you don't control your thoughts, but you control your focus – and your thoughts follow.

Here is the challenge: As you turn your attention away from stressors and towards beautiful things, your unconscious mind will notice a drop in stress hormones and send you stressful thoughts to get that cortisol level back in "balance," and you might get VERY uncomfortable. However, since you are in control of your focus, you can acknowledge the intrusive thought and place your attention back on the now. By staying in a low-stress state, you teach your body a new cortisol normal. As a result, it sends you fewer stressful thoughts in the future.

As you think fewer stressful thoughts, you produce less cortisol, and your body maintains its blood flow with the immune system, digestive system, and reproductive systems. This promotes your health, weight, sex drive, and normal sleep quality. You enter an energizing cycle.

Supporting your physical, emotional, mental, and spiritual state...

By placing your attention on things that serve you in your meditation, you practice being in control of your focus and keeping your attention on the things that serve you outside of meditation as well. As you control your focus and, thus, your mental state, the other sub-states follow, and this ability becomes available to you in moments of adversity, such as a conflict with your partner. You can say that <u>how you do something is how you do everything</u>.

Meditation and Manifestation

By focusing on what you truly want (sending out a clear intention) and tapping into beautiful emotions (drawing the things you love to you), you may manifest a relationship and other things you love, see *Figure 12*. As you train your body to appreciate a state of low stress, stressful thoughts will naturally be replaced by beautiful ones, and you'll live your life in a higher vibration, with positive things naturally finding you. Alternatively, if you prefer, the positive emotions and expectations will enable you to more readily interpret neutral things as positive and have more patience when your preferences are not met.

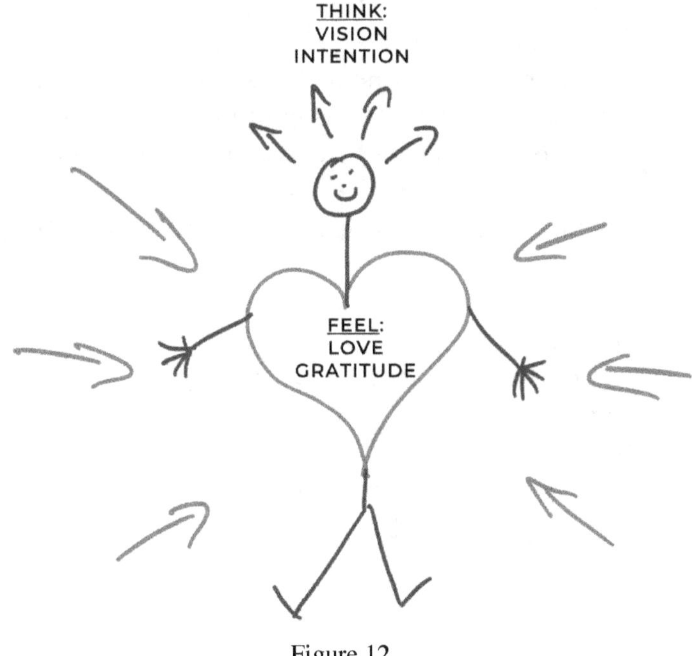

Figure 12

TOOL: MEDITATE

Start a meditation practice in a way that fits your lifestyle, for example:

- The simplest form of meditation:
  - Find a place where you are undisturbed (your office, your car, the restroom).
  - Set an alarm for 5 minutes (or how long you want to meditate for).
  - Close your eyes and place your attention on your breath.
  - When you notice that your thoughts wander, acknowledge them, and refocus on your breath.
- Other ways to mediate:
  - 5 - 15 minutes of mindfulness exercise (breathing consciously and remembering moments of love and gratitude or your happy place) or guided meditation in the morning.
  - Breathwork (For example try the Wim Hoff Breathing technique).
  - Take a walk a day and listen to a guided meditation on your walk.
  - 5 - 15 minutes of guided meditation or gratitude journaling in the evening.
  - Chant your mantra loud or in your mind for the time you want to meditate or in bed until you fall asleep.
  - Fall asleep listening to a guided meditation.

Mistakes to avoid:

- If you miss a meditation or notice that you forgot to meditate for a day or week or month, relax. Getting frustrated about meditation is the opposite of what you want. Now you've created a weird construct in which meditation adds stress to your life. Just close your eyes and focus on your breath…

- There is no "bad meditation". Even as an advanced meditator you will have meditations where it is difficult for you to maintain your focus and your thoughts run wild and are hard to control. That's fine. Those are probably the most important ones.
- Isn't five minutes too short? A five-minute meditation is better than no meditation. The most important thing is building a meditation habit. If you want to meditate longer, go ahead.
- What's the next step? Find guided meditations on YouTube, check out my guided meditation on www.imagine-evolution.com/meditation or look into Dr. Joe Dispenza's guided meditations, which I like a lot.

Part Four

LOVE-BASED LANGUAGE

"It's not about having loving intentions. It's about making your partner feel them."

Chapter 15

WHAT IS LOVE?

"Baby don't hurt me." - Haddaway

Shouldn't all relationships be Love-Based Relationships? Yes, they should. But there are also power-based relationships with a clear hierarchy between the partners. Things done for a person in power can appear to be done out of love, making it very tempting to use your power to "make" your partner do something. However, this impairs the relationship. Countless people have found their spouses cheating or filing for divorce and exclaimed, "WHAT???!!! After everything I've done for you??!! I pulled you out of the gutters, gave you a life you never dreamed of, and now YOU leave ME??!!"

What they gave their partner may have seemed like a dream come true on paper, but they never gave them respect and appreciation for who they are. They tried to mold their partner to their liking, attempting to change their ways, act more confident, more driven, and more self-sufficient, while disregarding their artistic inclinations, values, beliefs, and so on.

If you find yourself in either side of a power-based relationship, don't fret! Elevating your relationship is within your reach.

There are also arranged marriages. An arranged marriage can still be a Love-Based Relationship, but if it's not, this book provides the tools to transform it.

There are fear-based relationships. A relationship that is about to end often becomes a fear-based relationship, where one or both partners already have one foot out the door. They start fantasizing about a new partner or even looking at new apartments, making secret preparations in case of a separation. However, they stay in the relationship out of fear of the unknown or because of a secondary gain.

All these relationships can be transformed into Love-Based Relationships. But what is a Love-Based Relationship? What is love?

You can look at love from a romantic point of view, and you can look at love from a scientific, logical point of view. It is natural to despise the latter at least a little bit – if not with a vengeance. The nature of love fills tons of literature, so it will only be briefly touched upon here. I am going to share my personal take, and you may adopt it or dismiss it. You have a true choice.

From a romantic point of view, love kind of... just is. It is this beautiful, fulfilling, fuzzy, amazing feeling inside of us when we feel deeply connected on an intimate level with another person – a person we love. We experience butterflies in our stomach, and we would risk or even give our lives to save them. We want to spend as much time together as possible for the rest of our lives.

Scientifically, the matter appears more straightforward. Certain chemicals get released, with oxytocin being the most popular one. Through the simple act of repeatedly having sex, our bodies and minds become wired together. We become attached, and severing those ties proves to be painful.

You can also see love as "unconditional appreciation." A person you love can do a lot of horrible things to you, and you may still stay by their side.

I like to use dogs as a metaphor. A dog loves you. You can kick your dog, and it will come back. But if you kick it every day, at some point, it will either run away or bite. And if it bites, it's because it wants you to stop what you're doing so that the relationship can heal and continue. In that context, a shouting match makes sense as two hurt people trying to restore love in a disempowering way.

In human relationships, people stay with alcoholics, gamblers, cheaters, physical and emotional abusers. If you find yourself in a situation like that, you will find the tools in this book to influence the situation in a way that allows you to make the choices that are right for you. That can mean leaving, or it can also mean forgiving, acknowledging change, stopping people-pleasing or enabling, and setting and enforcing boundaries so that the behavior that hurts you no longer affects you. The relationship will either heal or end. Either way, you will be able to experience the outcome with confidence and love for yourself and the other person.

Most people treat love as a noun and forget that love is also a verb. When you feel love, you express it. When you express love, you feel it, not only your partner. Both go hand in hand, and expressing more love is the easiest way to strengthen it and your relationship.

Chapter 16

THE SECRET TO APOLOGIZING

"An apology is a gift that helps the other person find forgiveness."

I remember my wife coming to me and telling me that what I did made her feel hurt. I can't even remember what it was about, but I have a very clear recollection of my response to her: "No, I did not. I do not have that power to make you feel any kind of way!" I mansplained. "It is your perception that makes you feel the way you do. Don't blame it on me!"

I did this for the first four years of our relationship as I was listening to the wrong gurus. Now, they are not completely off, because that your perception makes you feel a certain way and reframing it can help you make the need to forgive another person obsolete and can be very empowering advice. When you were wronged.

If you try to impose this explanation on your partner, then it becomes mere manipulation. Here's how to fix it.

We talked about forgiveness already, and apologies are closely connected to forgiveness. Apologizing is what you do when you acknowledge the part you played in a situation that caused pain to another person, and you want to help them find forgiveness and healing.

An apology can be an admission of guilt and fault and just one of several things you can do to make up for it, but most apologies in relationships are not and admission of guilt or fault. Most apologies are an empathetic acknowledgment of the part you played in a situation and the expression that you wished that you could have influenced the situation in another way and prevented your partner's negative perception or feelings.

This must not be misconstrued with the ever-apologizing person who goes about their business doing whatever they please while disregarding their partner, thinking that apologizing will fix it every time. If you feel your partner is like that, it may be time to set and enforce effective boundaries.

On the other hand, I believe people who never apologize just don't know the power they are giving away to elevate their relationship. I must confess, I was amongst those people for the longest time.

It was a distinct moment when I realized that an apology can be separate from guilt.

In early 2021, I came inside from feeding our chickens, and my wife was visibly frustrated.

"Where were you!?"
"I was outside feeding the chickens," I replied.
"DID YOU NOT HEAR ME!?"
"No, I did not. What's going on?"

And here came the story: My wife was pregnant with our daughter; it was the first trimester, and that can be hard on the stomach. And as she hurried to the bathroom, she wanted me to take our son so he wouldn't have to bear witness. I didn't hear her, so she was on her own.

She told me later that it was kind of cute as he patted her back, but I would have loved to help and spare both of them the experience.

Was there anything I could have done differently? Was I guilty of anything? No, but I wished I had been there to support her, and so I said, "I am so sorry that I wasn't there!"

Would it have been justified to feel attacked? Would it have been justified to feel disrespected? Would it have been understandable to defend myself, mansplaining how I had not been able to help and how it was inappropriate to speak to me with an angry and loud voice? Sure. And it would have led… nowhere. It may have even created the impression that I had, in fact, heard her and was trying to obscure it or just not taking any responsibility for it. It may have created the impression that I did not take her situation seriously and tried to downplay it. It may have been understood as disregarding her feelings and trying to downplay them. Although justifiable, reasonable, and exercised by millions of spouses every day around the world, responding with frustration on my end would have been to the detriment of our relationship, if only for the next hour or that day.

That begs the question, do we make each other feel things? There are plenty of gurus in the personal development world who claim that one person can't make another person feel anything. That your feelings are the result of your perception and not of the other's actions. Or even that you choose your feelings. I believe that is utter bullshit.

When Justin and Janine read the text messages from their partners, they felt something. Instantly and unconsciously. Upon their reply, Frank and Felicia will feel something, instantly and unconsciously. If they don't receive a reply within the timeframe they expected to receive it, they will also feel something the second they become aware of it.

Imagine your partner cooked dinner, and you said, "Hey honey, thank you so much for the delicious food, go ahead and relax, I'll clean the kitchen and join you after."

The next morning, honey walks into the kitchen, and it's sparkling clean. Honey will feel something. Instantly and unconsciously.

If honey walks into a hot mess, though, that still looks just the way it looked after dinner, then honey will feel something very different. Instantly and unconsciously.

Honey won't tip her chin with her index finger and say to herself, "How should I feel about this… what should I feel about this… I got it: I am very sad and disappointed that pumpkin didn't do what pumpkin said pumpkin would do!"

We don't choose our feelings. At least not the initial ones. We can feel those initial feelings, acknowledge them, reframe them, and do all the good things from Part Three of this book, but our partner still played a part in this. Rarely, very rarely the partner does not play any part at all. Maybe when you thought they misplaced an item, and it was really you.

You make your partner feel, and they make you feel. Your happiness and your partner's happiness are deeply intertwined. By virtue of being in a relationship together, you gave your partner an emotional remote control that they hopefully use with care and responsibly.

Especially many men – And I was a vigorous member of this group – proclaim that when their partner feels hurt by them, that they did not *make* them feel hurt. They would never stab a knife into their partner's feelings and twist it. No, they love them deeply! It's natural to explain how hurting them wasn't the intention. Assigning the sole responsibility for their wife's or girlfriend's feelings to their wife's or girlfriend's perception and mansplaining it in all detail just makes sense… *to him.*

Until she is hurt or sad or frustrated because of something else. Then he not only acknowledges his influence on her feelings but may even get upset if she doesn't respond well. A work meeting, a stressful day with the kids, her best friend made a snarky remark, the scales showed too high of a number, whatever it may be. Now the man of the house pulls up his sleeves to *make* her happy again.

He does something nice, makes a compliment, says something funny, changes the light bulb that broke five weeks ago, yet she doesn't show any sign of happiness. He thinks, "Why does she not respond to my efforts? I didn't do anything wrong. Should I not be the special one who has the power to make her happy? Maybe I am not. If it's not me, who is it? Why does she disregard me? Why does she blow me off, me, the nice guy who worked his butt off all day and now meets Debbie Downer…"

Or when he gives his wife a birthday present, imagine she'd look at him and say, "What should I feel about that? Let me think… babe, I choose to feel happiness upon reception of your gift! Thank you!" Awkward, right?

NOW, it is not only accepted that he can make her happy but even taken personally if he can't.

Here's the deal. <u>You make your partner feel. You can make your partner happy. But only within a certain scope and when they are open to it</u>. When you show your partner appreciation and gratitude, they will feel happier afterward than they did before.

But when your partner is frustrated, sad, disappointed, then a kind word may not make that big of a difference. <u>As long as there hasn't been a magic syringe developed that can suck out that cortisol and adrenaline in an instant, you won't be able to "make" your partner happy in such a moment.</u>

Here's the good news: There is something you can do. When your partner is frustrated, you can show an act of kindness, like bringing them a glass of their favorite beverage or asking if there is anything you can do for them and then say, "Hey babe, I'm going to be in the living room for the next hour. Just come to me when you want to talk." Doing that shows them that you care for them and that you're holding space. Now you have created an environment that makes it as easy as possible to metabolize those stress hormones, calm down, and resume the conversation.

And how does an apology fit in? If you did play a part in your partner's negative feelings, be it through something you said, something you didn't say, or your purposeful or unintended absence, then your apology shows that you empathize with their situation and that you would love to have done things differently.

How to apologize to the feminine and the masculine

You may have heard the terms feminine and masculine energy, and I like to use them to illustrate differences between the genders. At the same time, all genders have masculine as well as feminine energy in them. In the context of apologies, you can say that the feminine gets her feelings hurt. She may feel hurt, sad, guilt, ashamed, unimportant, not good enough, and so on. And she can be "made to feel that way." The masculine, on the other hand, doesn't have feelings. I sometimes joke that men have feelings too: hunger and thirst. Of course, men have feelings, but the masculine doesn't. The masculine gets disrespected, attacked, disregarded, blown off. In short, a negative experience is forced on the masculine.

Apologizing to the feminine in the way she needs to hear it makes no sense to the masculine. She wants to hear "I am sorry that I hurt you" or "I am sorry that I *made you feel* sad." The masculine immediately revolts and says, "I did not make you feel that! I would never stick a knife into your feelings and twist it! How dare you accuse me of that!" And so, it makes sense to him to mansplain her experience and his true intentions. Ever happened to you? Forgive him as he doesn't know what he's doing. If he stood next to his queen in the kitchen with a long kitchen knife and she turned around suddenly, touching the blade and cutting herself, he would obviously apologize profusely. Sure, he didn't move the knife in her direction, but he did hold it, and if he hadn't, she would not have cut herself. He would never say, "Oh, as I did not cut you on purpose, your pain is not real." Just like that, he accidentally wielded the words or showed the behavior that led to the hurt feelings.

Apologizing to the masculine is just as counterintuitive to the feminine. He wants to hear "I am sorry *that* I disrespected you." The feminine immediately revolts and thinks, "Excuse me? I deeply respect him! I love him! I would never disrespect him!" Then she says, "I am sorry that I made you FEEL disrespected!" Ouch. That just pours salt in the wound and adds insult to injury. A consecutive disrespect of the experience. "I don't feel disrespected,

I was disrespected!" If she stood next to her king in the kitchen with a long kitchen knife and he turned around suddenly, touched the blade and cut himself, she would obviously not say, "Oh, you must feel like you have a cut, sorry for making you feel like that." Just like that, he needs her to acknowledge his perception of the experience. You can say the masculine is interested in the cause, the feminine is interested in the result.

Should you explain yourself after the apology and share your intentions? Only when it's asked for. In most cases, the apology will suffice, and explaining yourself will appear like you're taking it back and not taking responsibility for the part you played in the situation. You can safely assume that your loved one knows that s/he is loved and that you are a person of basic goodwill and that your transgression did not have the intention to cause harm.

TOOL: APOLOGIZE IN THEIR LANGUAGE

How to apologize to the feminine (Person says you hurt their feelings):

"I am sorry that I MADE you feel [feeling]"

How to apologize to the masculine (Person says they were disrespected, blown of, disregarded...):

"I am sorry that I [experience] you."

Are there situations where an apology is not enough?
Certain transgressions require more actions than an apology to achieve forgiveness and rebuild trust.

I don't recommend permanent gifts like jewelry or other expensive items as a means to apologize. Who wants to wear a cheater necklace or drive a cheater car? Major transgressions like cheating may require other measures. A token like flowers can be part of it, but a significant investment in changing one's own ways, such as investing in therapy or a coaching program, sends a strong signal from the cheater that they regret their actions and are willing to invest time and resources into ensuring it won't happen again. The same holds true for physical abuse, financial abuse, or the consequences of addiction. A partner who chooses to stay after such actions shows exceptional love and appreciation and needs to see tangible actions to rebuild trust. I believe that if the transgressor is not open to that or if their partner settles for lip service, then a necessary contribution to healing the relationship is missing.

An apology also needs to be a "forever apology," which means you repeat the apology for the rest of your life every time the topic comes up and reiterate that this is what the other person can expect. This is the kind of apology I gave my sister, and this is the apology I gave my wife when I finally came around. I am deeply sorry for every time I made my wife feel any sort of negative way and even more for every time I deflected the part I played in the hurt she felt and added insult to injury by telling her it was just her perception. I told her that I now understand how hurtful it was to hear that from me and that this is a forever apology that I will only repeat for the rest of our lives when it comes up. I did have to repeat it, and I may have to a few more times, but the occasions become less and less.

Here's the good news: You don't need to publish a book about it. However, it is appropriate for your partner to test that forever apology to build trust in it, while it is likely not even a real test but the hurt surfacing as long as it has not been released. Asking, "Hey, how many more times do I need to say I'm sorry? When are you going to get it?" renders any apology that has ever been made on this topic and any actions that were supposed to rebuild trust meaningless. You just moved the relationship back to square one after the transgression.

TOOL: FOREVER APOLOGY

"I want you to know that this is a forever apology. Whenever this topic comes up for the rest of our lives, I will only apologize because that's all I can do. I am sorry. Please forgive me."

TOOL: WORDS TO APOLOGIZE WITH

What words should you use to apologize?
The maybe three most important phrases to apologize:

1. I am sorry.
2. I apologize.
3. Please forgive me.

The power of words increases from one to three. "I am sorry" is something you may say after someone bumps into you in the supermarket.

"I apologize" carries more intent and purpose, but it can also be perceived as impersonal or pretentious, so you need to try it out and find how your partner needs you to express an apology. How they apologize is a good indicator, but if in doubt, ask.

"Please forgive me" is the most powerful expression, as it doesn't stop at the partner, but it begs a response. If that response is a "NO!", then that's a good thing because it helps your partner release their negative emotions. If your reply is "Okay, I understand. I really messed up, and I am very sorry," then chances are your partner may approach you later and say they forgive you, or you can ask them for forgiveness again at a later point in time. You can also combine expressions like "I am sorry, please forgive me."

Reversal

What if your partner does not apologize? What if your partner just explains their intention or tells you how your feelings are not valid but just the result of your perception?

1. Please allow me to apologize for your partner on their behalf. I am sorry that your partner makes you feel that way. Please forgive him/her.
2. Be vulnerable with confidence. When you tell your partner how what they did made you feel and they deflect it, that adds hurt and begs a response that teaches them how they are not responding appropriately. You mansplaining or womansplaining back is not that response. You have probably experienced how that just makes either of you go off on tangents, down rabbit holes that don't serve you, and just escalate the situation. Welcome to a free ride on the blame carousel. The appropriate response is just repeating how it made you feel: "I feel hurt that you brought yourself takeout and did not think of me." "What's the big deal? I thought you had eaten already. You could have asked me to bring you some!" "I know, I still feel hurt that you did not ask me or get me some, too." "You always play the victim." "I don't feel like a victim. I just feel hurt that you did not ask me or get me some, too." You see how being vulnerable with confidence means communicating powerfully instead of forcefully.
3. The insight that your feelings are the result of your perception is still empowering when it comes from the inside out. Remember that your partner loves you and respects you, and they explain their intention not because they are callous and not interested in your feelings, but because they really did not intend to hurt or disrespect you and hope they can reframe it for you. As it seems to them that you think it was their intention, that hurts or disrespects them. Little do they know how much easier it would be if they just apologized for the part they played and explained only

when asked. But mansplaining or womansplaining that to them will work just as well as them elaborating on their intentions...

I want to end with a story about my probably biggest transgression in my marriage that my wife will probably talk about until the end of our days. Two months before our son's delivery date, I went with my wife to a regular OBGYN checkup at which they had a few concerns and sent us to the hospital. My wife asked me to get her hospital bag, which she had carefully prepared months before already. I had the idea that we should not "manifest" an early birth that would lead to our son ending up in the NICU and removed items from that bag.

Believe me, I feel embarrassed as I am writing these lines, but I felt very confident at the time. I am very blessed that I am married to the kindest woman on the planet who not only endured it but also my mansplanations on top of it. It took me months to realize how doing so was hurtful, disrespectful, and caused unnecessary distress in an already overwhelming situation and apologize. Needless to say, at this point in the book, I gave her a forever apology that I do need to repeat once in a while. I am deeply sorry, my love. Please forgive me.

As you read earlier in this book, despite being born two months early, our son is well, and no one would ever guess that he was a preemie.

Chapter 17

BOUNDARIES IN RELATIONSHIPS

"Setting and enforcing a boundary is a two-step process."

Boundaries are a crucial aspect of living in a healthy, loving, respectful, trusting, long-term, Love-Based Relationship. Each person has their own unique set of things that are okay for them and those that are not okay for them.

- One person is punctual and needs others to be on time as well; another person is relaxed about being on time and others being on time with them.
- One person has strict boundaries around their privacy; another person wants to share their phone PIN and location with their partner and have access to theirs.
- One person may have nutritional boundaries based on religious beliefs, health conditions like gluten intolerance, permanent preferences like being vegan or vegetarian, or temporary preferences like diets. Another person can and wants to eat whatever they please.
- One person may need to lead an active lifestyle and exercise daily, while another person does not exercise.
- One person may be adamant about movie genres they don't watch, while others watch anything or even particularly enjoy these types of movies.
- One person may have certain privacy needs like needing to be alone in the bathroom, while another person may be open to sharing the bathroom no matter what.

Some of these examples may strike a chord with you, either because they are particularly important to you or your partner, or even because you and your partner butt heads on a regular basis on one or some of these issues.

What is a boundary? A boundary is something that you put around you to protect your autonomy, personal needs, well-being, and values. What is not a boundary? A rule, for example, is not a boundary but a behavior that you and your partner agree on and also have an idea of what happens if the rule is broken.

A one-sided rule is imposed on somebody and takes away from their autonomy by attempting to control their actions, decisions, or behaviors to serve a preference of yours.

We follow a lot of spoken and unspoken rules in our relationships that foster a loving, respectful, and trusting relationship. An attempt to implement one-sided rules creates disharmony at best or creates an imbalance of power and control and fosters distrust.

How can you distinguish a boundary from a rule? Many people call rules that they try to impose on their partner boundaries, so how do you know?

A boundary is not a boundary when your partner can avoid the consequence by doing the thing in secret or when the only way to enforce it is through punishment, see *Figure 13*.

When it comes to boundaries, you're always able to enforce them (although you may not dare to). You will read more about rules and how to establish them at the end of this chapter.

Figure 13

The first step to creating or respecting a working boundary is to know about its existence, in case it's your partner's boundary, or to make your boundary known to your partner. People with weak boundaries often get hung up on this first step and have a hard time setting a boundary, communicating it openly and transparently. On the contrary, they may struggle with accepting another person's boundary as well, possibly due to an unconscious understanding of "As I don't have any boundaries, my partner doesn't need boundaries." Or, if the relationship has already turned sour, "Why should I respect boundaries when mine are not being respected?"

From the perspective of a person with weak boundaries, a partner can easily appear as a narcissist who purposefully doesn't respect boundaries. But when a boundary is not effectively communicated or enforced, it's unlikely to be understood or even respected. It then becomes a matter of chance to be respected, at best.

One may say, "But isn't it natural and obvious that...?!" As you read through the list above, some of those points came naturally and obvious to you, and you wondered how anyone can see it differently. Well, people can and do. And will. And if that's your partner, then your relationship happiness will depend on your boundaries game.

TOOL: SET AND ENFORCE A BOUNDARY WITH LOVE

The boundaries game is a two-step process:

1. **Set**
   And
2. **ENFORCE**
   Your boundaries

- Set the intention to "set and enforce your boundary with love."
- Your boundary will not make your partner happy. Pick a moment when they are open to hearing about it. Meet a frustrated response with compassion.
- If possible be fun, playful, and charming.

Enforcing a boundary means taking action and altering the environment so that it cannot be violated except through abusive behavior.

Setting a boundary is a matter of communication and making that boundary known, while enforcing a boundary is a matter of action. Enforcing the boundary can be accompanied by words, but only the action matters. Both setting and enforcing are ideally done with love. That means in a positive, encouraging, playful, and maybe charming way to reduce the likelihood of the boundary being understood as an attack that your partner needs to defend themselves against.

Still, being confronted with a boundary is never a happy place. It is, by virtue of its existence, a conflict of preferences that are as opposite as they are natural to each partner. The person experiencing the boundary has a desire to overcome it and find a way to render it meaningless.

This is in and of itself not a narcissistic behavior. It is an inherent human trait to find and conquer boundaries. Think of children. A baby is confronted with the boundaries of its own existence like not being able to crawl, then walk, not being able to speak, and not being able to fulfill any task that requires fine motor skills. Then, later in life, the toddler is confronted with boundaries that are being artificially introduced by her parents, such as TV time, which food to eat, which items to play with, or which closets to open and which to keep shut. The purpose is not to annoy the child but to keep them safe and help them become a responsible, considerate, and productive member of society.

At some point in life, our ego gets added to the mix, and the existence of a boundary becomes a matter of debate and expression of liking or disliking a person. Daddy was loved a minute ago, but now that he insists that the fridge door needs to be shut, he may hear "I don't like you."

What does a clash of boundaries look like, and how can you overcome it?

Justin doesn't need privacy in the bathroom. Felicia does. Justin has no problem walking in and grabbing a tissue while Felicia does #2. "What's wrong with him?" That's exactly what Felicia is wondering. If Justin were in a relationship with Janine, it would be no problem at all. But he happens to be in a relationship with Felicia, and it's a constant source of conflict. After much hesitation, she brings it up in a conversation with her good friend Angie:

"Every time he comes in, I feel so violated in my privacy and feel so exposed. I yell at him, and he just mansplains how it's not a big deal and how I need to relax and that it doesn't even smell that bad. It's creepy and embarrassing!"
Angie wonders, "Can't you lock the door?"

"I shouldn't have to!" Felicia gets visibly agitated. "It's the most normal thing in the world. You knock on the door, you wait for an answer, and upon hearing that answer, you make the choice that your partner prefers! I do it with him all the time for three years, and for three years, every couple of weeks, he bursts into the bathroom, showing me that my feelings mean nothing to him!"

"I hear you. I know how frustrating that is because my husband used to do the exact same thing. I even slept at my parents' for a night because of it, to show him how angry it made me. Nothing. Finally, I talked with my parents about it, and my dad said:

"Setting a boundary means putting up a fence. Violating a boundary means the person who is supposed to be kept out by the fence climbing over it. Now you can do one of three things:

1. You can move the person to the other side of the fence and raise the fence to a height that it can't be climbed anymore.
2. You can move with the fence, so the person is outside, and then raise the fence to a height that it can't be climbed anymore.
3. You can decide that it's not worth it, tear the fence down, and focus on other battles.

But many people opt for option 4: Shouting at the person every time they trespass, thus validating their presence on their side of the fence. It may make their presence on the wrong side of the fence a little bit more uncomfortable, but if the alternative is being ignored, most people opt for receiving attention rather than being ignored outside of the fence. Throwing a fit at someone who crosses a boundary is not enforcing it; it's playing games and sabotaging your relationship with that person. Enforcing a boundary means making it impossible to penetrate.

So, stop playing games and sabotaging your relationship, lock the door. If you forget it, get up, leave him in the stinky room, go to the other bathroom, and clean up later. Will he be happy when he finds the door locked? Of course not! The purpose of a boundary is not to make the other person happy. The purpose of a boundary is to keep the relationship a safe place where both partners can show up authentically and make happiness possible.

So, he may try to walk in and find the door locked. He may feel disrespected or hurt and express frustration. It is important to anticipate that and respond kindly, caring, and understanding, and apologize for making him feel the way he does. If he asks or in a calm moment, you can ask him to knock and wait until you say if you're comfortable with him coming in or not. If he honored the boundary, he wouldn't even be able to tell that the door is locked.

A boundary is also not a tool *to* change another person's behavior. That may be the result but the intention is to keep you safe. You can lock the bathroom door behind you for the rest of your life. But there is a possibility that he may start to knock and not even try the door handle when you say "no". At some point, maybe after a few months, you may forget to lock the door or choose not to when you trust that he will knock and respect your boundary."

After my dad told me that, I decided to try it out, and of course, my husband was not happy, but he quickly accepted the new boundary, and at some point, he really started to knock, and eventually, I stopped locking the door."

Felicia left the conversation deep in thought...

Setting and enforcing your boundaries with love means conveying them so that it becomes as likely as possible that they will be received well or at least with minimal frustration on your partner's end.

If you've been in a marriage for many years, maybe decades, and you now set and enforce a boundary, then it is only normal for your spouse to think something like "Oh, why is this suddenly a problem? You've been okay with it for years. Do you not love me anymore?"

This is not a narcissistic manipulation attempt; this is a serious, natural concern!

Here is how I recommend approaching it:

"Hey babe, there is something that I need to speak with you about for a long time, but I feel a bit uncomfortable bringing it up, and I am a bit nervous because you could misunderstand it. But it is something that is very important to me. Is now a good time to talk about it?"

If your partner says "no," acknowledge that. Demonstrate that it is okay for you, and that it is important for you to catch him or her at a time where they are open to receiving the information. It's a *true choice*. If you force it on your partner, it becomes significantly less likely that they will receive it well or even follow it.

Other examples of setting and enforcing boundaries:

Boundaries around movie genres: Set: "I don't watch horror movies." If your partner starts a horror movie, find out if watching a different movie is an option; otherwise, leave the room.

Workout boundaries: Set: "I need to work out at least three times a week. What days would you prefer me to work out?"
If no agreement can be reached, take your partner's lifestyle into account, show flexibility around working out in the morning or evening, inform your partner about your workout times, and work out at those times. Remain open to renegotiate.

Nutritional boundaries: Set: "I don't eat meat."
If your partner prepares a meat dish, make or order something else for yourself.

Privacy boundaries:
"I need you to share your location with me and need to know your phone PIN."
Set: "I am not open to permanently share my location with you at this time and need to keep my phone PIN private for now. I may change that at some point in the future, but for now, it's important to me. I am happy to share my location on a case-by-case basis."
Enforce: Share your location only in specific situations and don't

disclose your phone PIN.

You then have the opportunity to build trust by handing your phone to your partner to take pictures, access the navigation app, or on other occasions. They can build trust by respecting your boundary. Eventually you may feel comfortable enough to volunteer your PIN.

Boundaries around timeliness:

Set: "I need to be at the appointment on time and have to leave at 3 o'clock at the latest."

Enforce: Help your partner be on time by reminding them two hours, one hour, 30 minutes, 15 minutes, five minutes, and one minute before departure. Leave at 3 o'clock alone if you have to, and apologize if necessary.

You see, setting as well as enforcing boundaries is a calm and peaceful process. It will likely cause some frustration on your partner's end, but compare that to years of feeling hurt and disrespected because you didn't dare to show up for yourself.

You also notice that respecting the boundary doesn't require action on the other person's end, while violating it would require an act of force, if not to say abusive behavior. If that happens the question becomes, how safe are you in your relationship and what do you have to do to get to a safe place?

In some instances, a partner may even have a boundary around your boundary and break up. But imagine if your partner broke up for any of the examples described above. Could giving up something so important (to you) still lead to a sustainable Love-Based Relationship?

It gets tricky when a boundary was violated for years, and you find yourself in a marriage with kids, fearing that if you set and enforce a boundary now, it may tear the family apart.

Firstly, if your partner loves and respects you and is a human of basic goodwill, that may be a fear but not a real possibility, and mustering the courage to set the boundary will be easier than expected.

If you try to set the boundary and your partner responds with the

D-word, then seeking help from a coach or therapist is advised. The problem is likely deeper.

You may enter a gray zone when something that protects your autonomy restricts your partner's autonomy or when something that ensures your well-being impacts your partner's well-being. If you can't set and enforce a boundary with love, you will have to create a rule together with your partner.

Rules

Again, one-sided rules are constructs that are not designed to protect someone's autonomy, personal needs, well-being, and values but an attempt to restrict a partner's autonomy for one's personal gain or preference. The problem with rules is that they can be avoided by doing the prohibited thing in secret.

Here are some examples of rules:

- Always wearing the wedding band.
- The partner can't talk with certain people about certain topics.
- Any rule around chores.
- Any rule around using the joint bank account.
- Not watching porn.
- Not doing drugs.
- Having no friends of the opposite sex.
- Not going to strip clubs.
- No sex with people outside of the marriage.

None of these rules are problematic in and of themselves when they are mutually agreed upon. They become a problem when they are one-sided.

You can declare any of these rules a boundary, but if push comes to shove, you can only enforce them effectively by demonstrating your frustration, up to ending the relationship. I want to share one example of a rule and then talk about how you can make rules work.

As a teenager, my dad implemented the rule that I need to wear a bicycle helmet. Arguably, a smart and understandable rule, born from a concern about the safety of his children, with lots of examples of how wearing a helmet can save lives, including a friend of mine who fractured his skull in a bicycle accident for not wearing a helmet.

Thankfully, the kid survived.

At the time, bicycle helmets were not widely adopted yet, and especially "cool kids" did not wear them, or at least that was my conviction.

As my dad faced pushback, he tried his best to convince me, including buying me a helmet of my choice, no matter the cost. Yet, I would not wear my helmet, so the only thing my father could think of was telling me that if I didn't wear my helmet, he would lock up my bike, and I would not be able to ride it.

Since my father hadn't figured out how to be omnipresent, I would indeed wear my bicycle helmet. Until the end of our cul-de-sac, at which point I habitually took it off, hung it over the handlebar, and rode my merry way.

When my parents weren't home, I wouldn't even bother to wear it at all. There was one other thing that I knew would make it difficult to enforce his rule. He was very adamant about his kids being athletic. My primary use for the bike was to get to other sports like tennis and soccer, so if he locked my bike up, it would have become very tedious and sometimes even unreasonable for me to get there, which would make him unhappy as well.

One day, I was headed to soccer practice, and at the end of the street, my dad drove around the corner, surprisingly early home from work. I believe it was a very eye-opening moment for both of us. He stopped, I stopped, he rolled down his window and said, "Don't you want to put on your helmet?" I looked him straight in the eyes, said "Of course," and put it on.

And so, we parted ways, my bike stayed unlocked, I kept up the charade so that my dad would save face, and I learned about what Stephen Covey later explained as the *circle of concern* in which my dad was operating in regard to that matter.

What could boundaries around me (not) wearing my bicycle helmet have looked like? "I will not go on a bike ride with you if you don't wear your helmet." In that case, my dad would have protected his well-being by preventing himself from seeing his son risk his life.

This morning, before I wrote this section of the book, I went for a walk with my son. As we were walking, he pulled his arms inside his vest. I stopped until he pulled them out again to prevent him from risking falling flat on his face. At the same time, I cannot prevent him from doing that when I am not around. Back at home, I had him do it again in front of the bed, gave him a little push, and he fell flat on his face on the soft mattress. Hopefully, I was able to create a learning experience in a safe and controlled environment, and he understood what would have happened on the street. Now I have to settle with being faithful when I am not around.

You see, for rules to work, it's not about how much sense they make. What makes a rule work is that it is *mutually* agreed upon or at least a *true choice*. <u>Without a choice, there is no commitment.</u> A rule can only be a boundary while you are present, enforced by removing yourself from the situation.

People love rules, but only when they have a part in making those rules. There are many ways to respond to rules, of which following them is only one. When you play a board game with one or more people, for example, you can follow the rules, try to convince the other person(s) to change the rules, cheat when you have the chance, or quit the game, with or without flipping the table.

More often than not, enforcing a rule that the partner does not agree to is hard because in every incident, you lose as well, at least your happiness, and in the worst case, the entire relationship.

It is stressful to keep an eye on your partner to make sure the rule is not broken, in case you feel your partner would like to break it, or if your life experience programmed your unconscious mind to be convinced that breaking that rule is a constant threat.

Even though your rule comes from a place of fear, your partner will likely understand your enforcement of the rule as controlling behavior.

Your partner will feel especially controlled and deprived of their autonomy when complying with the rule deprives them of fulfilling one of their own needs. What could that look like?

- A rule around who your partner may communicate with and what:
    - You choose people or groups of people they are not allowed to talk to, like a person they work with.
    - You choose topics they are not allowed to talk about with (certain) other people, like friends or family members.
- A rule that disregards or attempts to invalidate a partner's boundary and then calling that a boundary. Like "It's a boundary of mine that bathroom doors are unlocked all the time!"
- A rule about what your partner can eat, or food that cannot be in the house because you happen to be on a diet.

In these situations, you very likely foster distrust, resentment, and set your partner up for failure, thus setting the relationship up for failure.

Setting an effective rule depends on an open conversation, sharing your needs, and asking for help and agreement from your partner. Maybe they have an idea that can make it easier or offer an alternative that you haven't thought of. Offering a *true choice* makes it most likely that the rule will be followed.

In case your partner violates a rule that both of you agreed on, sharing your feelings and being *vulnerable with confidence* around the incident is the most powerful response you can show to keep your partner feeling safe, honest, and to encourage them to comply with the rule. If it becomes a constant source of conflict, it may be opportune to agree on establishing consequences for violating a rule. Breaking a rule means taking from your partner without permission. A consequence is not a punishment, but a token of appreciation to give a little bit back after you have taken something without permission.

If you show your frustration in an unloving or disrespectful way, your partner may even take the rule off the table that they followed out of kindness. I also don't advise breaking the rule yourself to "show your partner how it feels". The chances of that improving the situation are slim. Likely, it just validates their rule break and weakens your position to reinstate the rule.

But what if your need for the rule is so strong that it feels like a boundary and your well-being depends on it? Then ending the relationship may be inevitable, and it is important to ensure early on in dating that your next partner is on board with this rule. For some rules like "we don't have sex outside of our marriage," the response may be clear. However, the response may become unclear if the rule is actually broken, leaving you confused and open to forgiveness under certain circumstances. I recommend checking in with your support system, friends, family, or even a therapist or coach.

In some instances, you may find that a rule you want to implement may be important for you, but your partner is not open for it. Then seek help to empathize with your partner, find how other couples solve the situation and develop a compassionate response.
Even if your friends and confidants support you in fighting for your rule, the first step will be to put yourself in your partner's shoes, process your own pain, and ask yourself what makes your partner need to express this behavior that you detest. Find genuine empathy and compassion and approach them with genuine curiosity and the intention to truly understand.

In the case of cheating, for example, the cheater has committed a transgression that no reason can justify or defend. However, by virtue of being in a relationship with that person, it is important to ask the question, "What part did I play in this?" People whose needs go unmet for a long time and don't see a chance to have them fulfilled inside the relationship may choose one of four responses: make a change, settle with the status quo, end the relationship, or get their needs met somewhere else. And of course, there are habitual cheaters who just cheat, no matter what. If the latter can be ruled out, the empowered thing to do is to introspect, even if you decide to end the relationship, to avoid a similar situation with a future partner. I want to be very clear: If you've been cheated on, there is no blame, shame, guilt, or fault to assign to yourself. You have done the best you could with the resources you had available at the time. Now it is time to build new resources.

Reversal

There is no reversal. If your partner does not respect your boundaries, then they need to be enforced. If your partner responds with abusive behavior, then you need to take the necessary action to stay safe, maybe with the support of friends, a coach or a therapist. If you discover that you're talking about a rule, not a boundary, then it will only work by getting their buy-in, and you may need to have many conversations until you become able to drop the rule or they become able to follow it.

Chapter 18

MASTERING FRUSTRATION

And God said, "There will be frustration".

When we bought our house, before I started the renovation, I stood in front of it and said out loud, "Mistakes will be made."

Mistakes were made. Some were little oopsies, some cost thousands of dollars.

You will make mistakes; your partner will make mistakes. Both of you have made mistakes. Sometimes you turn around, knock a pencil off the table, say "oopsie," and pick it up. Sometimes you drop a plate. Sometimes you crash a car. "Oopsie."

Every one of your "oopsies" causes frustration in you to some degree, and your partner will be exposed to that frustration. Every oopsie of your partner causes frustration in them that you may get exposed to. And, of course, there are mistakes that are only mistakes from the viewpoint of the partner.

One of the biggest pitfalls I see people fall into in relationships is:

1. Not being able to stay composed in the presence of their frustrated partner.
2. Expressing frustration in a way that projects it onto their partner, demanding some kind of fix from them.

If you have a hard time keeping your composure when your partner expresses frustration, it is likely a result of fear. Anxiety creeps in as you see your partner in a bad mood, and thoughts circle around:

- How long will he/she stay in that mood?
- Is he/she going to do something that affects me negatively?
- I want to have a nice evening; that may not happen.

- I need to be very careful now, so that the situation doesn't escalate.
- Is it my fault?

The ideal way to handle the frustration of a partner is:

1. Acknowledge how it makes you feel and label your emotions.
2. Frame it as, "My partner is frustrated, that's okay. Everybody gets frustrated sometimes."
3. Show an act of kindness and express that you are available to talk.
4. If they want to talk, listen. When you have an idea of how they can solve their problem, ASK if they are open to hearing it. If they are not open, say "okay" in a genuinely appreciative tone. I can't count the number of times I did that, my wife said "no," and then asked me a few minutes later to share. My intention was never to manipulate her into doing that. If she doesn't, it's cool with me, and that happens, too. Every time you ask your partner if they are open to hearing an idea, you offer a *true choice*.

When you get frustrated, you have an opportunity to build trust. Imposing your frustration on your partner doesn't. Here is a guideline that can help you master your frustration to create an outcome that serves you best.

1. Acknowledge how you feel and label your emotions.
2. Release your frustration through the tools in Part Three of this book, for example, deep breathing, calm music, a walk outside. If necessary, move to a space where you are unlikely to get triggered and can metabolize those stress hormones without projecting your frustration onto your partner. (This is not an excuse to lock yourself in for a few days or to take a trip to the bar or your parents' for a few days and stop showing up for your responsibilities).
3. Default to kindness. Do something kind or beneficial for your partner and/or yourself, like:

    a) Clean.
    b) Tidy up.
    c) Organize something, like your closet.
    d) Do chores (Take the trash out, empty the dishwasher, do laundry).
    e) Meditate.
    f) Massage your partner.
    g) Bring your partner food.
    h) Hug your partner.
    i) Buy them a gift. (Don't shop for yourself to manage your emotions).

4. If your partner was the reason for your frustration, tell them what you observed as a camera would have recorded it. "You acted like an idiot" is not an observation. "I came home, and the trash was still full" is an observation.

5. Share with your partner how it made you feel. "When I came home, and the trash was still full, it made me feel like you're a liar" is not a feeling. "When I came home, and the trash was still full, I felt sad and disappointed" is a feeling.

6. Ask them about what you would like them to do now to improve the situation. "Could you not be an asshole" is nothing one can actually do. "Would it be okay for you to bring the trash out as agreed?" is something one can do to instantly fix the situation.

7. If you encounter pushback, accept it, be empathetic without starting the blame carousel.

Preventing frustration

Master your expectations. Offer your partner *true choices*. A true choice is a choice where they are free to pick either option. Offering a true choice doesn't mean becoming inauthentic, giving up your preferences, or pretending your preferences don't exist.

It does not mean giving up your preferences because, of course, you have a preference; otherwise, you would not have asked your partner to do what you asked them to do.

It also doesn't mean pretending you don't have a preference.

Authenticity is a relationship pillar without which the relationship is hard to sustain.

Offering a true choice means finding genuine appreciation for your partner picking the option that is not your preference.

Sounds great in theory, but what does that look like in practice? How can you appreciate what you don't, in fact, appreciate?

First, you choose to want to. With what intention? You want your partner to fulfill as many of their needs and wishes and as many of your needs and wishes as possible. Humans are much more likely to give from a place of choice and free will than from a place of force. When your partner anticipates an adverse reaction connected to one of the options you gave, it creates pressure and adds negative emotions to the option you'd wish for them to pick, which may lead to one of two consequences.

1. Your favorable option becomes unlikelier to be chosen, by virtue of negative emotions detracting us from the thing they are connected to.
2. If it is picked, there is less or even no commitment to it. Worst case scenario, they lie to you to keep the peace in that moment.

<u>Without a choice, there is no commitment</u>.

You may enter a cycle of your partner telling you what you want to hear to prevent a negative consequence and then not following through as they hope...

- You'll forget.
- There'll be an opportunity to renegotiate.
- To at least delay the negative reaction.

In situations like that, I often see the following pattern:

Felicia asks something.

Justin says yes.

Justin doesn't act on the agreement.

Felicia gets angry.

Justin says he didn't say "no" because he feared her anger.

Felicia says she just got angry because Justin lied; it would have been okay had he just said "no".

Felicia's response is justifiable and makes sense. Her behavior is understandable, but it sabotages the relationship. As Felicia gets angry, Justin hears her explanation, but it contradicts his experience, and her voice and tonality contradict her words. The fact that Felicia *is* angry *now* validates his experience and confirms to him that he was right to prevent experiencing that anger in the moment when Felicia asked the question.

Felicia needs to understand that making a moment where she asks a question a safe place and offering true choices is the first step to getting more of what she wants and needs. She needs to stop delivering punishments when Justin makes a "wrong" decision.

What are punishments? Withholding affection or even tangible things like items, withdrawing previous agreements ("As I don't seem important enough for you to do this, I don't want to go to the party anymore"), but in essence, even an expression of frustration like a scoff, rolling your eyes, or a sad face.

How can you prevent that?

After choosing that you want to find appreciation for it, set your expectations before you ask the question and prepare yourself for the possibility that your request will be rejected. Tell yourself and understand that it is not only normal, but it is good to allow your partner to show up authentically. Stay aware that offering them a true choice strengthens the relationship and improves the likelihood that they will give you what you want next time from a place of love and care.

Then ask the question. There are ways to ask for a favor that increase the likelihood of a positive result:

- Would you be so kind to...? (Most people believe they are a kind person or at least strive to be; most people appreciate demonstrating their kindness and feel good about doing so)
- Babe, could you do me a favor? Upon a positive response (and only then), ask your question.
- Hey Hun, I'd love for you to...?
- Hey Babe, would it be possible for you, by any means, to...
- Honey, it would mean so much to me if you could...?
- Do you want to...?
- Can I trust you to...?

Find the expression that sounds most authentic to you and maybe even practice it in front of a mirror.

If you get a negative response, give your partner the benefit of the doubt that they would have really loved to fulfill your wish, but the reason for not doing it in this moment is very important to them and not a declaration of your unimportance. Say "Okay, I understand" and go about your business. One of four things will happen:

- They'll say, "Actually, I think I can squeeze it in."
- They come to you a few minutes later to do it.
- They don't do it, and when you approach them the next time a few hours or days later, they remember that nothing negative came from saying no and feel safer in the relationship.
- They really can't or don't want to do it.

What if your request is very important for you *in this moment*? First, ask yourself if that is true. If so, think about when the last really important request happened. If you come to notice that every one of your requests is important, you've made three or so already today, then it may be time to reconsider your time management and what you can do to make your requests less important.

If you use your requests to your partner as a means to feel loved, supported, acknowledged, and tend to display frustration when you don't get a positive result, chances are your partner does not do those things from a place of love but from a place of fear. Unconsciously you know that already, but until now, you didn't know how to break the cycle. Now you do.

If your request is very important, and the last important one was a few days ago, try to cut a deal:

"Hey babe, it would mean a lot to me if you could do it right now. Is there anything I can do for you that would make it easier for you to do it right now?"

Maybe there is, and they will gladly accept your offer. Maybe it just illustrates that you are willing to give something in return and motivates your partner to do it immediately.

I remember a night when I went to bed, and my wife still had her nightlight on, and I asked her if she could turn it off. She said "no." I said, "Okay" and turned around. A few minutes later, she turned it off.

As you try it out and pay attention to your partner's response, you may notice how in the past, you would have started an argument about it ("Look, I want to sleep, and I can't sleep with a light on. It's so disrespectful of you to keep the light on while I want to sleep...").
Offering a true choice can not only lead to a faster result but often to a result at all, while keeping the amount of frustration to a minimum.

What if she hadn't switched off the light? Either I may have fallen asleep anyway, or I may have asked again half an hour later. Maybe I would have asked if I can do something that would make it easier for her to switch it off. I could have asked how she feels about leaving the light on, knowing that it makes it difficult for me to sleep, and hope she'd find empathy or share a reason that I can empathize with. If she denied my request again, I'd say "Okay" as there would be no way an argument could elevate the situation. It was genuinely a true choice of hers.

What constitutes a negative reaction to a request being denied?

- Withholding appreciation.
- Withholding touch.
- Taking back previous agreements.
- Raising your voice or even name calling.
- Trying to make the spouse feel guilty about not doing it.
- Threatening consequences like "you wait until you ask me anything next time!"
- Responding cynically or sarcastically.
- Judging them as egotistic, narcissistic, selfish...
- Even just scoffing, rolling your eyes, or displaying any kind of disapproval.

"But how does my partner know it is important to me?"

By virtue of you having asked. You wouldn't ask your partner anything just to keep them busy, have them jump through hoops, or out of envy that they can relax now, and you still have stuff to do. You genuinely want the best for your partner, and they know it. So the fact that you ask them means it is important to you. And the fact that you stay cool in the face of rejection shows them that it was really about you getting help and not about "getting them to do something."

TOOL: OFFER TRUE CHOICES

Before you ask your partner to do something for you, set your expectations and find appreciation if they have to say no. Ask your spouse the question in a way that inspires agreement:

- Would you be so kind to...? (Most people believe they are a kind person or at least strive to be; most people appreciate demonstrating their kindness and feel good about doing so)
- Babe, could you do me a favor? Upon a positive response (and only then), ask your question.
- Hey honey, I'd love for you to...?
- Hey Babe, would it be possible for you, by any means, to...
- Honey, it would mean so much to me if you could...?
- Do you want to...?
- Can I trust you to...?

These expressions increase the likelihood of a positive result and create a sense of choice for your partner.

What if your partner agreed to do something, but you later discover they didn't follow through, and they may have even pretended they would do it to avoid your anger at the time?

Instead of getting angry, give them an experience of how you handle disappointment. Be vulnerable yet confident and say, "It makes me very sad that you said you would do that and didn't follow through. Trust is important to me, and I love you. I hope you can be honest with me next time. Is there anything you need right now?"

This approach is powerful in maintaining open communication and fostering trust.

Reversal

What if your partner asks you for something that you are unable to do in that moment? Consider using one of these phrases or create your own authentic response:

- I'd love to do that for you right now, but I can't.
- I'd love to do that for you right now, but I can't. Would it be okay if I did it at time X?
- I am currently in the process of doing X, and I'll probably be done at time Y. Please remind me if I haven't completed it by time Z.
- I am currently occupied with X. Would you like me to interrupt that for you, or would it be okay if I finish it first?
- Maybe there is something they can do to help you while you help them. If so, ask them, "I am wondering how I could help you right now. Could you lend me a hand real quick, and I'll be able to help you even sooner?"

What if your partner responds with frustration when you can't fulfill their immediate need?

- Ask them how it makes them feel, then apologize for causing those feelings/ their experience and express your regret that you can't fulfill their request immediately.
- It's okay for both you and your partner to feel frustrated at times. Remember, you are not solely responsible for your partner's happiness. Act with compassion by doing what is right for you with compassion, rather than doing something wrong out of compassion. This means showing compassion for both your partner and yourself.

What if your partner presents you with a choice where they have a clear preference and you know they will get angry if you don't cater to it?

- Make the choice that is right for you. Your partner can be right but wrong in the way they express it (yell, curse,....). If they are right, don't let their demeanor negatively affect your decision. Responding to frustration with kindness is a super power.

- If you find yourself in a situation where you feel the need to lie, but you have experienced that your partner's reaction later would be, "I'm mad because you lied, not because you said no!", consider sharing your fear about it. Remember, *fear* of your partner's negative reaction *is not a valid reason to avoid telling the truth but a valid reason to show courage* and be honest.

What if your partner asked you to do something, you agreed, then forgot and now they are frustrated to an extent that you feel hurt or disrespected?

Do it anyway. If you promised to take out the trash and didn't, you can empathize with your partner's frustration and fulfill your commitment. Your partner's expression of frustration does not justify taking back your commitment.

After taking out the trash you can say, "I am sorry that I forgot to do it, but it still hurt me how you yelled at me for it."

Even if you get pushback on that in the moment, if they love you and are a person basic goodwill and empathy, they will ponder that.

Chapter 19

BUILDING RAPPORT

"The greatest gift you can give another person is the quality of your presence." - Brian Tracy

Rapport is the genuine unconscious mental and emotional connection between two people or one person with a group of people. In rapport, you are "dialed in" to the other person and "get them," and they get you. In rapport with another person, you give them your attention and receive theirs, understanding or even sharing their needs, feelings, and problems, while they understand yours, creating the possibility of creating new solutions with two brains instead of one.

Is rapport an artificial technique or persuasion trick?

No, humans build rapport naturally when they communicate with each other. In almost every friendly, loving conversation you have, you build rapport with the other person. As naturally and unconsciously as we do it in positive conversations, we can commonly forget to do it in moments of conflicts or even "break" rapport.

Like speaking with a toddler in easy phrases during happy moments, but when she is irritated or frustrated and has an even harder time comprehending language, many parents become elaborate and use long, difficult sentences to explain why something is not okay.

Thus, it's often not about learning something new but about becoming conscious of things you do well in positive situations, so you can consciously do them in moments of conflict to support moving the dialogue back into solution creation mode.

How does building rapport work?

Communication is not only the spoken word. In fact, only 7% of communication lies in the content of what we say, but 38% lies in the voice/tonality/tempo, and 55% lies in our body language. Building rapport means tapping into the full spectrum of communication. Psychology professor Albert Mehrabian at the University of California, Los Angeles, laid out the concept of this 7-38-55 rule in his 1971 book *Silent Messages*.

TOOL: BUILD RAPPORT

The basic principle to establish rapport is to *match and mirror* the other person:

- Posture (how they arrange their body and arms/legs in space)
- Proximity (their comfortable speaking distance)
- Gestures (e.g., as they take a sip of water, you take a sip)
- Voice/Tonality/Tempo (especially important in phone conversations)
- Content/Terminology (e.g., when they talk about the weather, you respond with something weather-related before changing the subject. If they have typical phrases they use, use them too)
- Breath (use your peripheral vision)

Matching and mirroring means adapting your way of conducting yourself to the other person in a natural way, with a little delay (if you did it in a hectic, immediate way, that would be called mocking and mimicking and breaks rapport). Establishing rapport can also lead to the other person liking you more. Why? Because people like people who are like themselves, people they share traits and preferences with.

Let's talk about the elephant in the room: Is building rapport manipulation?

You can build rapport with the intention of changing someone's view on something or with the intention of influencing someone's behavior.

That's often the reason to initiate communication in the first place. Manipulation means trying to force one's agenda on someone and disrespecting that person's autonomy, which breaks rapport. If you ask someone to hand you a glass of water and they do it, you influenced them but you did not manipulate them. If you told them to hand you a glass of water and promised a punishment if they didn't or presupposed what negative meaning it would have if they didn't, then you would have manipulated them.

Building rapport is taught as a strategy in sales because it makes you appear more likable and trustworthy. By virtue of being in a relationship with your partner, you have a degree of liking each other and trust established already. What people who teach building rapport as a sales strategy often forget to share is that as you build rapport, you not only make it easier for the other person to hear, understand, and agree with you, but you also open up yourself and make it more likely to genuinely hear, understand, and agree with the other person. In fact, if you have a hard time "getting" your partner, building rapport can make the difference.

I have almost magical moments with my children on a regular basis when they try to tell me something and I don't understand the word. First, I ask them to repeat the word, and if I still don't understand it, I say the word in the exact same way they say it and repeat it a few times. In most cases, this leads to me magically grasping the meaning of the word.

I remember a hike with my son, and suddenly he said, "uoc." I said, "What?" He repeated "uoc." I repeated the word a few times, looked around, and said, "Oh, a rock!" as we were walking past a massive boulder.

As a salesperson, building rapport helps you understand the needs of the customer better and get what they really need instead of just advertising features and benefits of a product.

As you build rapport and match your physical state with your partner's physical state, you start seeing the world through their eyes and understand and empathize better with them.

But when you try to be like them, doesn't that mean pretending you are different and becoming inauthentic?
No, it just means tapping into the full spectrum of communication and communicating effectively in a way that makes it as likely as possible that they will understand you and you will understand them. Kind of like me writing this book in English is what I need to do to make it as easy as possible for you to understand what I am writing. Had I wrote this book in my mother tongue, German, you could still decipher it with the help of a translation app, but it would make it very difficult. You would have likely not made it to this chapter.

I believe our characters consist of things like our values, beliefs, sense of humor, likes and dislikes and more but not the language, body language, or voice and tonality we use to express them.

Consciously not building rapport would be like me writing this book in German, as this is "me," and expecting everyone to brush up on their German skills before having a conversation with me. I'd have a lonely time in the US and lots of conflicts.

How do you know when rapport is established?
You can feel it. It is a warm and fuzzy feeling of being connected, and the hormone oxytocin may be at work.
You may also notice how 100% of your attention is with the other person, and 100% of their attention is with you. You and they create a "rapport bubble" that shields your attention from outside influences. You blend out the other conversations in the restaurant around you, the noise of the music, or the TV. It will take effort for someone to interrupt; they may have to say your or your conversation partner's name once or even a few times. You can understand

a rapport bubble as merged energy fields.

There is also an objective way to check if you are in rapport with someone by *pacing and leading* them. After matching and mirroring for five to ten minutes, change your posture and see if the other person follows. Yesterday, I was sitting at the dinner table with my laptop open, and my 18-month-old daughter sat next to me watching a video. At some point, I put my head in my hands, and a few seconds later, she did the same. Not only was it very cute, but it also showed that we were in rapport.

You may wonder, "Will your partner notice it?"

Again, building rapport is something humans do with each other anyway all the time, so no, they won't notice it. Probably not even if they know the concept. They may become conscious of being in rapport with you, but there is no way of knowing if it was established consciously or unconsciously, nor by whom. People who learn about rapport sometimes notice it when other people are in rapport. I remember having had a conversation with a colleague at work, and we were both leaning back, our hands behind our heads. A coworker came in and said, "Oh, you're in rapport!" We hadn't even noticed. If your partner knows about rapport and notices you establishing it, it will rather be conducive to the conversation as it directs their attention to something you two have in common, and that you're putting effort into understanding them.

Reversal

What can you do when you can't establish rapport with someone?

Sometimes a person consciously or (more likely) unconsciously doesn't want to be in rapport with you and will break it as soon as it has been established. They may even get irritated if you reestablish it. I have seen that happen twice in my life, but it can happen. There is not much you can do about it, and chances are the conversation is not happening under the premise of basic goodwill. It may be better to pause the conversation. You can also say, "I feel really disconnected from you right now and would like to change that. How are you feeling right now?"

Another way to build rapport in a situation like that could be going for a walk together. As you walk side by side, it's easy to synchronize your steps with the other person. You don't necessarily have to step with the same foot, but you can step with your right foot when your partner uses their left foot.

It can also mean that your conversation partner sends non-verbal signals that they are not open to finding consensus. If you sit opposite at a table, they may place items as barriers between you and them or point their feet away from you or even towards an exit when they want to leave the conversation.

Use your sensory acuity to influence the situation in a positive way. If they want to leave and you initiate the end of the conversation, you reestablish the connection and leave the conversation on a positive note. They experience relief, feel understood, and you set the stage for a positive next conversation.

Building rapport can also be understood as the friendly merger of energy fields, as the earlier mentioned "rapport bubble" insinuates. If there is a friendly merger of energy fields, is there also an unfriendly one?

The book *Pitch Anything* by Oren Klaff describes a thing called frame psychology. It means that whenever two people meet, each one brings their frame to the situation, and only one frame will prevail while the other frame will be absorbed. He identified frames like:

- The power frame, where the person with more power will absorb the other person's frame.
- The moral authority frame, where one person asserts moral superiority of their cause or motives over the other person's.

- The analyst frame, where one person overwhelms the other person with detailed questions that put them on the defensive.
- The time frame, where the frame holder imposes urgency on the other person to make them cater to their needs.
- The prize frame, where the frame holder creates scarcity around a prize that the other person would like to attain and makes them qualify for it.

You may find yourself or your partner holding any of those frames in conflict situations. If you find yourself doing so, notice how imposing a frame on the other person contradicts the true choice principle. Take a break, restart the conversation, and build rapport instead.

If you find your partner holding any of those frames, chances are they are not purposefully trying to manipulate you but just running communication patterns that they have been running for decades and that have their origin in their childhood. Here's how to counter each of those frames:

- **Power Frame**: You counter with a "power-busting frame." That means you show a humorous or playful small act of defiance or denial. For example, if your partner wants you to leave something alone, you look at them and touch it with your finger.
- **Moral Authority Frame**: "Maybe you're right, let me think about this." That gives you time to regroup and assess a response without the pressure of the moment.
- **The Analyst Frame**:
  - If you make a suggestion and your partner demands a lot of details that you haven't thought of yet with the intention to dismiss it: "I'd love to talk about the details with you at some point, but what's important for me right now is if you generally like the idea if it turned out doable?"
  - Your partner may throw the analyst frame at you in the form of "What have you done for me?" and then dismiss

every example you give. In that case, it can be best to counter with a moral authority frame and say, "I am surprised how you cannot remember anything I have done for you, and I don't feel comfortable like this. Please tell me a few things that I did for you?" If they can't come up with anything, it makes no sense to continue the conversation at that moment. Conversely, your question will ring in their mind and help them remember things while you take a break from the conversation.

- **The Time Frame**:
  - Empathize: "I understand how important it is for you, but I can't make a decision right in this moment."
  - Sometimes things do need to happen immediately to prevent negative consequences.
    - That begs the question: What is the difference between a threat and a consequence?
    - A threat is a man-made punishment. "If you do X, then I 'have' to do Y."
    - A consequence is a force that the partner can't influence. "I hear the trash truck outside, and I am in a zoom meeting. If you don't bring the trash out now, we'll sit on full trash cans for a week."
  - The time frame can show up in relationships as ultimatums. Ultimatums don't work. They can't because the response to an ultimatum is never a true choice, and without a choice, there is no commitment. If you receive an agreement, you're completely in the dark if it will be followed up upon or if it is just a means to buy time. If it is followed up on, it's because of a deeper understanding that could have been reached more effectively, while the way it was achieved leaves a bitter taste that damages the relationship. If you tend to give ultimatums, find empowering alternatives, and I hope you find leverage to do so in this book.
  - If you're faced with an ultimatum on your partner's end, there are different options:
    - Assertive: "Then you may have to do [consequence]

right now. I am not able to continue the conversation like this. Let me know when we can talk about a solution in a loving and respectful way."

- Just leave the conversation and pretend the ultimatum was never expressed to save your partner from the embarrassment of having to take it back or escalating the situation.
- Use the **CREATE SPACE** tool, and when the conversation can be resumed, empathize. "Hey, I understand how important this is for you, and I want to find a solution with you that both of us can live with."

- The prize frame can look like an ultimatum without a time constraint. It may be used in a playful manner, for example, around intimacy. "I will give you this, if you do that." While it's often not a negative thing, the relationship will suffer if love, respect, trust, or intimacy become a prize that needs to be earned. If you are inclined to use the prize frame in such a way, you may be able to find more empowering solutions in this book or by working with a coach or therapist. If you are faced with a prize frame, the most empowering thing for you to do may be to understand it as an expression of frustration and of needs not having been met for an extended amount of time. Instead of insisting on it being removed, take your time to empathize, listen, and fulfill your partner's needs. Your partner may be right, but wrong in the way they express it.

Sometimes in relationships one partner want's something that the other partner is reluctant to give. Using the prize frame means using force to get it. The soft and loving approach is to offer a deal.

Building rapport increases the chance for all other tools in this book to work and can be done in any situation, be it a conversation in person, via video call, or phone call. It can even work via email and text, for example, if you use the "seems like/looks like/sounds like" tool in the next chapter.

Chapter 20

EMPATHY AND COMPASSION

"If you don't feel heard, listen better."

Most people agree that empathy and compassion are pillars of a healthy relationship. However, empathizing with a partner is not always easy, especially when both you and your partner are frustrated.

The spectrum of empathetic people ranges from "empaths," who naturally and intensely feel the emotions and experiences of others, to individuals who struggle to tune in to other people's feelings. Both ends of the spectrum can be frustrating experiences. Always feeling the emotions of everyone around you can be exhausting, while not understanding how your partner feels can lead to frustration and a sense of disconnection. Many marriages have ended in divorce due to this issue. By avoiding the pitfalls outlined in this chapter, you may prevent such an outcome.

Pitfall #1:
Telling your partner how they feel.

When you accurately describe your partner's emotions and they appreciate it, you have successfully empathized, and everything is golden. But. If you're slightly off in your assessment, you're wrong and the connection breaks.

Even if what you say is true, but your partner doesn't like how they feel, the connection breaks. For example, saying, "Why are you so angry?" may elicit the response, "I'M NOT ANGRY!"

As an empath, this can be particularly frustrating because you already know how they feel – you can feel it yourself. It's as frustrating as when you have no idea and mansplain to them how they *should* feel.

I learned an effective method of empathizing with others from the book *Never Split the Difference* by Chris Voss. The book explores negotiation tactics, such as how to achieve your objectives in a negotiation with a terrorist while being unable to fulfill any of their demands.

I'm not suggesting that you should view your partner as a terrorist, but if a particular communication approach even works with a terrorist, it should also work with friends, strangers on the street, coworkers, bosses, family members, children, and spouses.

I started using this method and witnessed immediate results, not only at home but also with clients and in text messages. I recall a distraught soon-to-be father sharing his struggles in a dads' group on Facebook, and upon applying this technique, his response was, "Can I talk to you on the phone?"

TOOL: SEEMS LIKE/ LOOKS LIKE/ SOUNDS LIKE

Here is my golden rule to empathize with your partner (or anyone else).

You start your sentence with one of three (almost) magic words:

- It seems like
- It looks like
- It sounds like

So, instead of saying, "Why are you angry?" or "Why are you so frustrated with me?" you say, "It seems like you're very frustrated about something right now" or "It looks like it really upset you that I forgot to bring out the trash."

Now, a few things happen:

- By using "it seems like/it looks like/it sounds like," you demonstrate that you have put thought into the well-being of your partner and invested time and effort to understand them. You thought about it, you thought about it, and after careful consideration, it now seems to you...

- Instead of mansplaining or womansplaining their feelings to them, you show that you may be wrong. Even as an empath, you may understand how they feel, but they would use a different word for it. As an emotionally illiterate person, on the other hand, you just need to memorize the words for certain feelings, and if in doubt, just use "frustrated." They'll probably respond by giving you the exact feeling, and then you can use that word.

- You also shift the focal point of the problem away from them (you are the problem because you have feeling X) or from you (I am the problem because I made you feel X). Instead, you direct it to a behavior of yours or an experience of theirs, something that exists outside of both of your personalities. Now you can both look at the issue together from the same perspective and solve it as two lovers.

- It is also an open-ended question that invites the other person to open up to a genuinely interested, caring, loving person who is listening.

What's so spectacular about this? People use "it seems like/it looks like/it sounds like" all the time. How is this revolutionary?

I found the answer to that question in another book that also has nothing to do with relationships: *The Happiest Toddler on the Block* by Harvey Karp.

We use effective communication all the time when we are relaxed and share our thoughts with other people in pleasant situations or if someone comes to us with a problem that we are not emotionally involved in. Things can turn sour, though, when we're invested in the topic of the conversation and things don't meet our expectations or if we get triggered along the way.

This resembles a pattern that most parents fall into when speaking with their toddlers. In happy moments, when the kid does something good, they say things like "Yay, good job, good catch!" or "Do you want more banana?" Easy sentences, few words, straight to the point.

When the kid throws a tantrum, suddenly parents use long, elaborate sentences, difficult words, words the child doesn't hear very often and is not used to. In a moment where the crocodile brain is the active region, the toddler's limited comprehension is further reduced, and the simple language would already be a challenge. But the parent addresses the intellect instead of the crocodile brain. It is understandable, justifiable, reasonable – and leads nowhere.

Over time, you have become unconsciously competent in certain language patterns, but remember that all learning is state-dependent. Just because you have learned something in a positive state doesn't mean it is available to you when you are in a frustrated or stressed state.

As you notice that you've used "it seems like/it looks like/it sounds like" all along, you realize that you are unconsciously competent in using those words when you are in a positive state. Now, you start to consciously use those words in moments of conflict, which may feel awkward at first. As you use those words and get a positive response, you start feeling more comfortable using them and become consciously competent in using them in difficult times. As you practice it more and more, at some point, you start using them unconsciously in difficult moments. A great part of the coaching process is making clients aware of what they are unconsciously competent in and transferring it to other life situations.

Pitfall #2
You tell your partner what they should do.

How often do you do with delight what other people tell you to do? You probably have the highest success ratio with a toddler when you tell her to do something, but even with a toddler, you'll butt heads on a regular basis.

We tend to think that being in a superior position, like having more knowledge on a subject or having some kind of influence on how happy their life is, should be leverage enough to be listened to and considered... but is it?

If you're the parent of a toddler, like I am at this time, you know that is not the case. If you are a child or partner of a person with an addiction like alcohol or cigarettes, you will have learned that all the scientific evidence in the world won't change their mind. Telling people what to do is a justifiable, reasonable, understandable endeavor to influence a person's beliefs, values, and actions. And it is moot.

So, what *can* you do?

1. Wait to be asked. It can take a very long time, but when your spouse asks you for your opinion, feedback, or advice on a topic, seize the golden moment. It will pass quickly, and it may not come again for a long time.

    Now it counts.

    Sometimes people respond, "Oh, *now* you want to know! *Now* you're asking. *Suddenly* you're interested! You know what? Go ask someone else!" Blowing them off in the moment the partner is open, just to return to the pattern of telling them and berating them later on. Then maybe even saying things like, "A week ago, you even asked me, and now you don't want to hear about it anymore?"

    That's right – and they missed the opportunity to create a real change and instead used it to feed their ego with a slight.

    The frustration you feel when you get asked as if you had never had a conversation about the topic is understandable, justifiable, and reasonable – and you need to overcome it in this unique chance to break the cycle and instead find instant appreciation for their openness.
2. Ask for permission and offer a *"true choice"* to do so. When

you ask for permission, you create an opportunity to get into position (1.). The likelihood that you will be granted permission is minimal, but every time you respond with genuine appreciation, you build trust and work up to a yes.

Here is another tool to help your partner open up more.

TOOL: MIRROR YOUR PARTNER

Mirroring means repeating the most important part of their last sentence or the most important three to five words of their last sentence as if you were saying them to yourself in deep thought. This needs to be genuine – you need to genuinely think about that sentence. It entices your partner to elaborate further to help you think about it better. And as they do, they think about it more themselves and reflect on their own words. They feel more understood and closely connected.

Have you ever had a problem and approached your partner, boss, friend, or someone else, only to have the answer come to you as you asked them the question? You're not alone. It is one of the mysteries of the human brain, and you can use it to help your partner, family member, co-worker, employee, or boss find new solutions to old problems.

"But will they not notice it and call me out?" No, because it is a normal and genuine behavior that humans use in conversations anyway. You may initially feel discomfort consciously using this technique for the first few times, but with practice, it will become second nature.

Instead of telling your partner what to do, provide them with the opportunity to figure it out themselves. If the best and logical option aligns with what you would like them to do, there is a good chance they will come up with it on their own. And if they don't, telling them directly can often sour the conversation instead of making a positive difference.

What if *I* need empathy?

Hopefully, as you approach your partner, they can show you empathy as well. However, if they are unable to do so, it could indicate that they are preoccupied with their own emotions and unable to assist others in managing theirs. Asking for permission to share your feelings can increase the likelihood of their receptiveness.

What if my partner is *never* open?
If your partner consistently displays an unwillingness to be open, it may indicate a deeper issue. They may truly never be open, or their behavior may give you that impression, but it is possible to address this issue from your end. Speaking with a coach or therapist can be the next step if the tools in this book do not lead to a change in the dynamics of your relationship. Asking them how they feel can be a simple and helpful starting point.

TOOL: FEELING INVENTORY

Ask: "How are you feeling right now?"
It is such an easy question, but it is just as easily overlooked.

If your partner consistently shows disinterest in your feelings, it is likely that they are also disinterested in their own emotions. They may use expressions of feelings as a means to achieve specific goals, such as using stress as an excuse to exit a situation or saying "I love you" to gain intimacy.

By asking them about their feelings, you direct their attention to their own emotions and the concept of feelings in general. This brings feelings to the forefront of their mind. Eventually, they may ask about your feelings in return. It's important to create a positive atmosphere around these discussions. After a few days or weeks, when you ask again and they have finished sharing, you can playfully say, "Are you going to ask me back?"

Ideally, you should ask them to ask you about your feelings when you are in a positive mood, or at least able to share your feelings in a positive context. Your response should encourage them to ask about your feelings more often. This is not the time to bring up years of perceived neglect.

"But that's what I'm feeling!" It's important to recognize that you have other feelings that you can choose to focus on, such as feelings connected to success at work or the achievements of your children. Over time, you can transition to discussing deeper emotions.

The other side of empathy is making it easy for your partner to empathize with you. <u>Be vulnerable with confidence</u>. Many conflicts escalate because one partner feels hurt or disrespected and expresses it to the other. The other partner may deflect, shift the blame onto the first partner, respond with cynicism or sarcasm, or engage in other unhelpful behaviors. Partner one feels blames, blames back and the blame carousel spins.

Felicia: "It was really hurtful when you called me a bitch!"
Justin: "oH, WaS iT?" *rolls his eyes*
Felicia: *explodes*

In that moment you can make a *forceful* or a *powerful* decision. It is justified and reasonable to respond with frustration and make your partner feel your anger. However, the result of such a response is often jumping on the blame carousel.

Here's what the conversation looks like when Felicia stays vulnerable with confidence.

Felicia: "It was really hurtful when you called me a bitch!"
Justin: *rolls his eyes* "oH, WaS iT?"
Felicia: "Yes, it was very hurtful."
If Justin continues to insult or escalate, Felicia can recognize that he is overwhelmed with stress hormones and say, "I need to take a

break from this conversation. I'll go for a walk and be back in 30 minutes." This is a powerful response.

Who should empathize in a conflict?

In conflicts, as a general rule, the person who is more upset should speak first. How do you know that's not you? By virtue of you thinking of this rule you know you're not the most upset one. Relax, take deep breaths, or practice box breathing and allow the other person to express their emotions. Then, ask for permission to respond.

In summary, if you feel that your partner doesn't ask about your feelings enough, try asking them more about their feelings.

Hurt people hurt people

It's important to note that the concept of "hurt people hurt people" should not be used as an excuse to unload your emotional baggage on your partner and then dismiss their negative response with the justification: "Sorry, hurt people hurt people. I can't help myself."

If you realize that you have hurt someone, it is appropriate to own it and apologize for your actions. If your partner wants to know what led to your behavior, you can share it while emphasizing that it doesn't justify what you did and repeating the apology.

The real value in understanding "hurt people hurt people" is to develop empathy for the person who hurts you. This doesn't mean you should tolerate boundary violations or allow yourself to be mistreated, but rather to approach the situation with compassion and *do the right thing with compassion instead of the wrong thing out of compassion.*

If the hurt inflicted by your partner is a verbal expression of frustration, the tools in this book can help you create a shift in your relationship and hit the brakes on the blame carousel.

If the hurt your partner is inflicting is physical abuse, financial abuse, cheating, or drug abuse, then seeking outside help from a therapist, coach, or possibly even a lawyer or the police may be advised.

Asking your partner about their feelings is a great way to find out what is going on with them and to show them that you care. However, asking questions can become a delicate balancing act when the stress hormones in a frustrated partner make them hyper-vigilant for any kind of threat, such as assuming that you're trying to set them up, assuming you have already made up your mind, assuming you have ulterior motives, or assuming your question is a disguised attack. You can avoid that to a great extent by first acknowledging and expressing understanding for every answer you receive before asking the next question.

The most important word to avoid when asking your partner about a potentially irritating topic is "why." "Why" is a trigger word for many people, possibly because it is a typical teacher's question, or a question parents ask when their child has done something obviously wrong, or a question that bosses, partners, and many others ask after a decision has already been made.

You can avoid triggering the negative effect of the word "why" by starting your sentence with the words "how," "what," or "do" instead.

TOOL: REPLACE THE WORD WHY

~~Why are you angry?~~
What made you upset (about...)?
How are you feeling?
Do you want to talk about it?

~~Why did you do that?~~
What made you do that?

~~Why are you doing that?~~
What makes you do that?
How much longer do you need?
Do you want to continue doing that or is there something else you can do?

Reversal

I taught replacing the word "why" for quite a while as a coach when something unexpected happened. My son, who was then two years old, asked me, "Why do you do that?" and I got triggered. By a two-year-old.

I thought to myself, "How dare you why-question me!" and didn't know what to say. The first question I asked myself was, "Why does he ask that?" I found the answer pretty quickly: That evening, he threw a toy and my wife said, "Why do you do that?!" There it was. I felt so silly being triggered by a two-year-old and thought he probably just genuinely wants to know why I do what I am doing. So, I consciously took the charge off the trigger and henceforth just answered his questions.

At the same time, I realized that I was still triggered when my wife asked me a why-question and had an epiphany.
Every piece of relationship advice goes full circle: You change how you express yourself AND you change your perception. From

this insight stem the reversals you read in this book. "Why is it always *me*???" "Why do *I* always have to make the change???" These are questions victims ask who don't want to take responsibility. A victor is keen to gain leverage to create a change in her favor. Notice how the opposite of a victim is not a victimizer. Those go hand in hand, and you find people meandering from one to the other. The opposite of both is the victor.

So, I took the charge off the word "why" for my wife, and everybody else for that matter. How do you take the charge off a word? You can go through the forgiveness process, you can go through the Mental and Emotional Release process, but sometimes it's a lot easier than that. You consciously allow the trigger to trigger something new and experience the positive result, repeat it, and rewire the trigger to elicit a new behavior. In this case, instead of triggering anger, trigger a genuine response to the question.

Chapter 21

REPAIRING CONFLICTS

"Healing begins when we choose to repair rather than retaliate."

If you're reading this book slowly and putting the tools into practice, then the dynamics of your relationship conflicts have probably already started to change.

In this chapter, I want to focus on a few things that have already been mentioned.

In Chapter Two, we already discussed how conflicts are normal in relationships and how it is a delusion to believe they would magically disappear if you were with Mr. or Mrs. Right.

Here's the good news: conflicts are a good thing. Just as you have conflicts with yourself all the time, you can't stop having conflicts with your partners.

Repairing a conflict means moving an emotional conversation back to common and amicable ground by acknowledging your love, appreciation, and respect for your partner, and most importantly, your part in the conflict.

As you make a repair attempt and set expectations for yourself, you set your partner and yourself up for success and prevent the repair attempt from having a negative impact.

How can a repair attempt have a negative impact? By evoking disappointment if it fails to succeed. Know that the repair attempt may be rejected, and that rejection is then an expression of frustration (sarcasm, cynicism, judgment, suggesting ulterior motives...) and even helps your partner release negative emotions.

Do not take a failed repair attempt personally but recognize that you showed the courage to give it a try and stay ready for the next attempt, while listening carefully, expressing empathy and compassion, showing acts of kindness, and demonstrating that you're open and hearing them.

Master Your Emotions

1. Become conscious of your feelings and acknowledge them to yourself to release them (e.g., he/she makes me sad/afraid/angry).
2. Reframe your partner's behavior.
   a) What other meaning could it have? (e.g., Maybe s/he is not yelling to disrespect me but is not feeling heard).
   b) Is there a context where you can appreciate that behavior? (e.g., If s/he were out with the kids and someone would come at them, that's how I'd like him/her to respond).
   c) Recognize an *expression of frustration* as such: Notice that their behavior is not a sniper shot in your direction but you're just "too close to an explosion."

Actions that can repair an argument (during or after)

- Hug.
- Kiss.
- Touch slightly.
- Show an act of kindness (bring a glass of their favorite beverage, clean kitchen, cook/buy dinner, offer a massage...).
- Buy a small gift (flowers, snack) to show that the negative emotions you displayed were isolated to the argument and not meant personally. Hate the play, not the player.
- Breathe together (synchronize breath).
- Engage in a common activity during conflict, like taking a walk.
- Engage in a common activity after the conflict, like watching a movie, taking a bath together, going to the gym.

Words that can repair a conflict

Most conflicts will not escalate from zero to 60 in three seconds; rather, they tend to build up slowly as one partner inadvertently sets the blame carousel in motion and the other partner jumps on it.

Unfortunately, there isn't much you can do about accidentally setting it in motion. However, you can enhance your sensory acuity and attunement with your partner during conversations while still remaining authentic, without walking around on eggshells.

If you avoid walking on eggshells, there may be times when the blame carousel starts moving, and that's okay. The truth is, even when you try to be cautious, you might unintentionally set it in motion.

In that spirit, there are two types of conflict situations you can anticipate and shift, not to benefit yourself, but in favor of the relationship:

1. When you unintentionally set the blame carousel in motion and your partner joins in, but now you want to hit the brakes.
2. When your partner accidentally or deliberately triggers the blame carousel, and although you feel blamed or triggered, you don't want it to start spinning.

Help your partner feel heard, seen, and felt

- It looks like you feel...
- It sounds like you feel...
- It seems like you feel...
- I can only imagine how that must have felt.
- When you said [exact words they said], did you mean [how you understood it]?
- That you said [exact words they said] sounded to me like [your version]. Am I wrong?
- I see how that made you feel like...
- I see how I made you feel like...
- I can only imagine how that must have felt...
- What you are saying is...

- Your feelings are true and valid to me.
- I'm sorry that I made you feel XY/this way (If they say, "Why did you do it?" – "I did not mean to. What I meant was...")
- I am sorry that I disrespected you (If they say, "Why did you do it?" – "I did not mean to. What I meant was...")
- I am sorry that I disregarded your feelings (If they say, "Why did you do it?" – "I did not mean to. What I meant was...")
- I see how what I did made things difficult for you.
- I see what you mean.
- I hear you.
- I understand.
- That makes a lot of sense.
- That's a different perspective. Let me think about that.
- That's a different perspective. Can I ask you a question about that?
- I never looked at it from this angle.
- I never thought of it this way.
- What you say makes a lot of sense.
- I don't agree, but I see where you're coming from.
- Thank you for saying that.
- I think I missed that part.
- That's a great point!

Express your own feelings

- When you said [exact words they said], it made me feel [feeling]. Then ask them to help make it right: "Do you think you could [what would fix it for you]?"
- If their hurtful behavior towards you is clearly connected to something that happened to them in the past that you are aware of and is not based on something you actually did: "I can only imagine how that must have felt when XY did this to you, but I must say that it is a bit hurtful to get accused of something I did not do."
- Her to him: "That felt unloving – did I come across as disrespectful?"

- Him to her: "That felt disrespectful – did I come across as unloving?"

To help your partner hear you

- Do you realize that what you heard is not what I said, and what you think I said is not what I meant?
- May I clarify what I meant?
- I don't feel heard/understood right now. May I try to explain what I meant?
- Can I have your support?
- Are you with me?
- I just need to share what's on my mind. Is it okay if I do that?
- I feel a bit disconnected right now. What did you hear me say?
- This is really important to me. Is it okay if I finish what I would like to say?
- I think I did not express this well. Can I try again?
- Can we pretend this conversation never happened and start over?
- Can you stay present with me? This is so important to me.
- Would it be possible to agree to disagree?

Shift the energy of the conversation

- Can I have a kiss/hug?
- I love you. (If your partner doesn't reciprocate, ask "Can you say it, too?")
- Sorry, I think I reacted too strongly.
- I know we're not currently happy with each other, but I want to emphasize that I love you.
- I acknowledge the part I played in this situation.
- How can I make things better?
- I think I was a bit harsh. Can I try again?
- I'm sorry. Please forgive me.
- I apologize.
- Are we still on track?

- Thank you for being open and clear about this.
- I know it's not your fault.
- Here's the part I played in this...
- Thank you for understanding.
- This is our problem, not yours, okay?
- I want to help you fix this.
- It sounds like we both want...
- Can I do something for you?
- What can I do for you right now in this moment?
- I am here for you. How would you like me to show it?
- I hear and understand you, but I don't agree. I want to be honest with you. Does that make sense?

If you need to pause the conversation

- Can we pause for a moment?
- I really need to go to the bathroom. I'll be back in a minute.
- Can we change the topic for now?
- I have said everything I can say about this topic.
- I am not open to continuing this conversation right now. Can we revisit it at a later time?
- I've expressed my thoughts on the matter. (Repeat instead of engaging or going off on tangents)
- Maybe you're right. Let me think about this.
- I don't think we can find a common understanding in our current state. Can we take a break and discuss it again in [exact time, e.g., 30 minutes]?

A few specific situations

If your partner accuses you of cheating:

- I love you (and the kids and this family) so much! I would never do that!
- I know you've been cheated on in the past, and I can only imagine how that must have felt. However, it also hurts a little to be accused of something I didn't do.

- I know you've been cheated on in the past, and as someone who has experienced that too, I understand the pain. But it also hurts a little to be accused of something I didn't do.

If you suspect your partner is cheating:

- Understand that if they want to keep it a secret, they may find a way to do so, unless you discover it accidentally. There's no way to find out without openly expressing distrust or violating a boundary, except by using an undercover investigator. Accusing someone who is innocent can cause significant damage to the relationship.
- Consider their unmet needs and try to fulfill them while honoring your boundaries. No one ever had their needs met by depriving others of their needs. Express your love and appreciation for them daily.
- Tell them how much you appreciate their honesty and that you can trust them blindly. It means so much to you.
- If they are not cheating, love you, and are a person of basic goodwill, you will strengthen your relationship this way, and they will reciprocate. You won't dwell on the possibility of cheating anymore (unless you have trauma in that area, in which case it's important to work with a coach or therapist and not let it cast a shadow on your relationship).
- If they are cheating, they will eventually come forward and confess because mistreating a person like you will become unbearable to them.

S/he says, "You have done NOTHING for me all day!" (Although you can remember at least three things that you did specifically for them.)

- If those are undeniable things that served exclusively your partner, list them. ("I let you sleep in, made waffles and took the kids to the playground so you could have a morning to yourself, didn't I?")
- Say, "I see that you can't remember any of the things I did for you today (this week). That hurts. We can continue this conver-

sation when you can at least remember a few things that I did." This may move their attention to positive things. If they don't say anything you can say, "As you haven't recognized anything that I did, I see no basis to continue the conversation. From experience I know that anything I say will be labeled an outlier or you may create a narrative of how it actually served me and not you and that is very hurtful/disrespectful."

There is a reward even if you don't see your partner reciprocating. When you respond to a conflict in an empowered way, your partner may still be stuck in it, stuck in their feelings of frustration, their state of stress, their trauma. If you use the tools in this book and you just don't see any reciprocation on your partner's end, that can be a very frustrating experience.

Being in and maintaining a relationship is a daily choice. In times of online dating, a new relationship is always just around the corner. My wife and I make that choice daily, and so do you and your spouse.

Change takes time. For example, it took me four years in the relationship with my wife and almost 40 years of my life to understand apologies.

You can decide at any time that trying to fix this relationship is not worth the effort to you and end it.

One night at a party, Felicia grabs Justin and says, "We're leaving!" Justin is confused, quickly says goodbye to his friends, and they head out. In the car, Felicia tells him, "You ignored me all night long! As if I meant nothing to you. I stood alone in the corner while you were having a good time and didn't care."

Justin wonders... his ex-girlfriend Jessica would not have made such a scene but would have either joined him or found other people to talk to! But then he remembers the time Jessica became so upset about how he was driving that they got into a huge fight and didn't even make it to a party... he continues to ponder... his ex-girlfriend Tina was cool with his driving and fun at parties! But then he remembers the night they got into a huge fight because he didn't respond well when she asked him what dress she should wear, and they didn't even make it into the car...

Mr. or Mrs. Right doesn't exist. Using the tools in this book only changes the likelihood that your partner feels heard, seen, felt, understood, and may reciprocate. It may take time and needs to sink in.

Every day that you stay in the relationship, you are practicing communication with yourself and your partner in a way that makes you grow as a person and will either lead your partner to reciprocate, remove the need for them to reciprocate, or set you up for success in a future – and hopefully – forever relationship.

You are doing this for you, for your family, for your children, and anyone you meet in the future. I am rooting for you.

Reversal

There is no reversal. It doesn't matter who initiated the conflict, as it is often impossible to objectively tell, although both partners may have a firm opinion.

I believe in cause and effect, but in many cases, I am not so sure which comes first.

Chapter 22

DECISION MAKING STYLES

"What makes a decision hard is that you can't tell which choice will get you the best outcome."

Felicia and Justin are getting ready to go to the birthday party of Justin's good friend. As Justin stands in front of the mirror and ties his tie, Felicia comes out of the closet and holds up two dresses: "The green one or the orange one?"

We make decisions every day, and so does our partner. As you and they are different people with different kinds of logic, beliefs, values, convictions, and experiences, you make decisions on a regular basis that your partner would not have made or even frowns upon, dislikes, despises, or blatantly hates.

In this chapter, you will learn how to make better decisions yourself and understand your partner's decisions better. You will become better at catering to their needs or at least you can feel fewer negative emotions around your partner's decisions and maybe even sway a few decisions to be made more in your favor or make a few decisions more in their favor.

There are different ways to look at the process of decision-making, and a big factor of frustration is the level of firmness around decisions. Some people make a decision, and the moment it has been shared, it is set in stone. Others make decisions left and right, overturn their decisions seemingly on a whim, or acting on them is a matter of chance, air temperature, or wind direction. Either decision making style may lead to exorbitant levels of frustration and misunderstanding. It doesn't have to be that way in the future.

Is one decision-making style superior to the other? No. Shock.

Here's the deal. Depending on the firmness of one's decision and the way people work toward their decisions, you can identify five decision-making styles that can also vary a bit based on one's circumstances and state of being. I have met people who say, "I make decisions at work all day long. I just want to come home and not make decisions!"

1. Make decisions on a whim and stick to them.
2. Gather a lot of information, then make a decision and stick with it.
3. Gather a lot of information, then make a decision and maybe overturn it if presented with information that contradicts the initial decision.
4. Gather a lot of information and make a (test) decision with every piece of information they get.
5. Make no decision until action needs to be taken.

Making a decision is always an emotional process. Even rational people who claim their decisions are objective and exclusively based on reason still make their decisions based on emotions. In fact, people with brain injuries or altered brains where the part responsible for processing emotions is disconnected or removed have big trouble making decisions. They reason and reason and come to no conclusion. Benjamin Libet found in his 1983 study *Time of conscious intention to act in relation to onset of cerebral activity (readiness-potential)* that decisions are already unconsciously made and executed before they become conscious. That means the unconscious mind makes the decisions, then the conscious mind rationalizes them. Some people are aware of it, some are not. If you have such a rational partner, you may feel inclined to share this information in hopes it may alter their decision-making process, but it won't. This information can just make you more at ease with what you see and is not meant to change your partner.

Not only the firmness of one's decision is a source of conflict, but how people get to their decision as well.

There are people who need a lot of information and think a lot before they make a decision, and there are people who decide on a whim. These people often despise each other.

When the long thinker makes a right decision, spontaneous man will say, "Sure, after mulling it over for three weeks, I would have made a right decision as well! Also, I would have made a mistake AND fixed it within one week!"

When spontaneous girl makes a right decision, lady long thought will scoff and say, "Pure luck. She had no idea!"

When the long thinker makes a wrong decision, spontaneous man will laugh his head off: "So you thought and thought and thought for three weeks, and that's the best you came up with??"

When spontaneous girl makes a wrong decision, lady long thought will shake her head. "It was so clear from the beginning that you made your decision based on almost no information. I hope you learned your lesson…"

Again, there is no right or wrong. The spontaneous person (unconsciously) trusts their gut, their heart, their unconscious mind, and those are powerful allies when it comes to decision-making. Often your unconscious mind knows and has gathered all the information already, while trusting only the conscious mind and trying to find clarity while stuck in the weeds can be a fallacy. The other way around, our gut can deceive us and find trust in people who only seem trustworthy but are not trustworthy or make us afraid of things that have an aspect of uncertainty while there is no real danger in sight.

It is opportune to use the knowledge above to appreciate and empathize with your partner's decision-making style while becoming more conscious about your own and communicate more effectively around the decisions you make.

Can you improve your decision-making? Scientists have found

that neither decision-making style has a higher success rate. Both are around 30%. This is how you can increase your ratio of good decisions:

Step 1. Gather all information, consider all possibilities, maybe write them down, speak with people who are knowledgeable on the topic, and ponder everything. Consult your grandma regarding cooking and your uncle in finance about stocks, but not the other way around... or your financially literate grandma about stocks and your chef uncle about cooking... You may have a spouse who despises your need to do so and wants you to take her advice about everything. Weather it. Maybe you can pay her or him a bit more attention in other areas.

Step 2. Pause. Occupy your mind with something else. Exercise, watch a movie, play a video game, cook a meal, play with your kids or your dog, take your partner out for lunch.

Step 3. Make a quick gut decision.

Back to Justin and Felicia. Justin smells a trap and says, "I like both."

Felicia: "But which one do you like better?"
Justin: "Okay, maybe the orange one."
Felicia: "Why?"
Justin: "I find it a bit sexier."
Felicia: "So, you think I look fat in the green one? I actually think that I look better in the green one!"
Justin: "Then take the green one!"
Felicia: "But you said I look fat in it!"
Justin: "I did not say that!"
Felicia: "Oh, you did not say that, huh? But you thought it?"
Justin: "That's not what I meant!"
Felicia: "What did you mean then?"
Justin: "I meant that I like the orange one better."
Felicia: "Why?"

Justin: "Because it's shorter."
Felicia: "So, you want everyone to stare at my legs?"
...

Hopefully, Justin will be able to turn this around while Janine presents Frank with two skirts.

Janine: "Blue or red?"
"Blue", says Frank.
Janine: "Why"
Frank: "It's my preference."
Janine: "But why do you prefer it? What if I prefer the red one?"
Frank: "That's great, too. Look, you asked me, and I gave my preference. You look gorgeous either way. I love your taste and you'll pick a fantastic outfit. If you ask me, take the blue one, I think it looks amazing."

Frank accomplished the following things:

1. He used the opportunity to show Janine that he is a confident decision-maker.
2. He used the opportunity to make an honest compliment about a specific trait of hers.
3. He realized that the decision is an emotional one and can't be reasoned.
4. He made it clear that Janine is in charge of the decision, and he is not trying to coerce her into doing something she doesn't want to do.

Felicia asks Justin, "What shall we have for dinner tonight?" Justin replies, "I have no preference, you decide.
Felicia: "Me neither, you pick!"
Justin: "How about Tony's?"
Felicia: "We've been there three times this month. I don't want to go there again."
Justin: "How about Sapporo Sushi?"
Felicia: "I'm not in the mood for sushi."

Justin: "Then you pick a restaurant!"

Felicia: "I don't know, I am fine with whatever you choose. I just didn't like those two..."

Justin: "Okay, let's go to Andy's Steakhouse."

Felicia: "That's too expensive..."

Justin leaves the room, slams the door, and makes himself a peanut butter & jelly sandwich.

In another house, not too far away...

Janine asks Frank, "What shall we have for dinner tonight?"

Frank: "What are you in the mood for?"

Janine: "I don't know..."

Frank: "I know you like sushi and Italian food. Which would you prefer tonight?"

Janine: "Italian, I think..."

Frank: "Is it a Guido's Pizza night, or shall we go to Mario's Pasta House? We haven't been there in a long time."

Janine: "Let's go to Mario's Pasta House!"

Reversal

Janine asks Frank, "Do you have a particular wish for dinner?"

Frank: "No, I'm good. Pick what you like."

Janine: "I'm thinking Chipotle or Olive Garden."

Frank: "Let's go to Chipotle."

As a rule of thumb, the more options available, the more difficult the decision. On the other hand, most people don't like to be told what to do. In most cases, it leads to a quick solution when you offer two alternatives that you know the other person generally appreciates and that you can accept as well. Use language that shows you care about them. Trying to coerce them into a decision doesn't show that you care, even if that's your intention. Asking them what they feel like and offering choices does. Frank did this twice, and although he picked the options, Janine was still included in the decision.

Geshe Michael Roach advises in his book *Karmic Management* that it is not so important what decision you make in the first place. What's important is that you "charge" your decision with effort and energy to make it the right one.

How do you make good decisions quicker?

Making faster good decisions is not the result of making a lot of great slow decisions, and as you get into the habit of making good decisions, you get faster and faster. The opposite is the case: Dare to make faster decisions and fail. Through this practice, your faster decisions become better. It takes courage... Remember that your slow decision may be wrong too, but then you have less time to fix it.

When it comes to making good decisions, it is important to ask yourself the right question. "Should I or should I not" rarely leads to a good decision. When I stand in front of the shower in the morning and ask myself, "Should I take a warm or a cold shower?" The answer is always "a warm shower."

Hard decisions are an opportunity to choose what kind of person you are. When I ask myself, "Who am I?" The answer comes easily: I am a disciplined, health-conscious person who knows and values the positive effect of cold showers."

Another powerful question can be, "How am I going to feel afterward?" That question also makes me choose the cold shower.

Chapter 23

THE 6 STEPS OF COMMUNICATION

"The golden way to find inner piece in misunderstandings."

Felicia comes home, kisses Justin "hello," and goes into the kitchen to throw away some trash that accumulated in her handbag.

"Why didn't you bring the trash out? Didn't I ask you to?"
"No, you didn't!"
Felicia is visibly annoyed. "Yes, I did while you were eating your breakfast, and you said yes! You're so unreliable!"
"I don't remember that. And what's the big deal anyway? You can bring out the trash as well. I'm not your janitor!"
"And I'm not your maid! I asked you, and you said yes. Why are you lying to me?"
"I'm not lying; you didn't ask me. I am sick of your gaslighting!"

The six steps of communication were a game changer for me and are my most important tool to identify and overcome misunderstandings without jumping on the blame carousel.

Conrad Lorenz found in 1963 that communication only has a maximum of six steps:

1. **What you thought is not necessarily what you said.** Have you ever wanted to say something, went to the other person with the intention to say it, and when you reached the person, they started speaking, but in your mind, you checked the box already? Sometimes you can become conscious of it, but sometimes you could swear you did say it... but you didn't. Or you open the message app to text somebody, but you find a new text from someone else, read it, respond to

that person, and forget about the text that made you open the app in the first place.

2. **What you said was not necessarily heard.** Sometimes you talk to another person who is in normal hearing distance, but they don't hear you. Be it that they are standing next to a running faucet, or they have headphones on and are listening to an audiobook, or they are watching TV and the soundwaves reach their ears, but they don't hear them as their attention is directed at something else.

   Or you start writing a text or email, get interrupted, open another application on your phone or computer...

   And the next time you open the message thread with that person, you find that message you started typing a few days ago... or my favorite: Wanting to write someone a Christmas message or Birthday message and finding last year's message that was half-written.

3. **What was heard was not necessarily understood.** Someone shares something with you, and you want to ask a question to comprehend it better, but the other person is still talking, and you don't want to interrupt. By the time they are finished that original question you had is now forgotten.

   The same applies via email; you read an email, but as you want to reply, you get interrupted and then forget about it.

4. **What was understood was not necessarily agreed upon.** In a nutshell: If you ask someone to do something, and you don't get a clear "Yes" or "Yes, I will do XY," then you likely did not receive an agreement. You have just received confirmation that what you said was understood... or even only heard. Or just an acknowledgment of your presence. Especially when the response is only a "mmmh."

5. **What's agreed upon is not done yet.** There is a possibility that you receive a firm "Yes," and the person you asked had the honest intention to follow through, but life happened, and they were not able to or forgot.

6. **That someone did something once doesn't mean it is a habit yet.** Have you ever tried to make something a habit of yours that you really, really wanted to establish but fell

off it again and again? Now imagine you want someone else to do something for you habitually, like your husband bringing out the trash. He does it that day, he does it next week, he does it the week after... and forgets. You're disappointed and may even feel slighted, think he's testing you and trying to get away with it... or you even notice that he did it three times in a row, appreciate that, cut him slack, bring the trash out yourself... and then he forgets the next week again... We will talk about this in depth in the chapter on building habits.

Back to Felicia and Justin. Where did their communication go wrong? Did anyone gaslight?

Did Felicia think she told him but actually didn't? This could look like this:

Justin: "When did you tell me?"
Felicia: "When you were eating your breakfast, as I said! I walked over to you and..."
Justin: "...and I looked up and asked you if you had heard of the rocket launch yesterday."
Felicia: "You're right... I wanted to tell you in that moment, but then we talked about the rocket launch, and I headed out..."

Did Felicia tell him, but he didn't hear it?

Justin: "When did you tell me?"
Felicia: "You were eating your cereal, and I asked you to take the trash out as I was walking out the door!"
Justin: "I am sorry, I had already dialed into a zoom meeting and was listening in on my headset; I must have missed it."

Did Felicia tell him, but he didn't understand?

Justin: "I did empty the overflowing trash can in the bathroom! The one in the kitchen still had space this morning when I did!"

Felicia: "I knew it would fill up over the course of the day, and as trash gets picked up tomorrow, I thought it made sense to take it out even half full."

Did Felicia tell him, and he understood but disagreed?

Justin: "I remember you telling me, but it didn't make sense to me to take out a half-full trash bag."

When you and your partner are in conflict about a past reality, it's easy to accuse each other of gaslighting. Gaslighting is purposefully altering or denying the partner's perception of reality to a point where they question it themselves. The purpose of gaslighting is to gain control over the partner. Gaslighting exists, and it is a horrible behavior that wreaks havoc on a relationship. Most relationships don't experience gaslighting.

In most relationships, two people of basic goodwill love each other, and even when the relationship turns sour (momentarily in a conflict or permanently), many partners still love each other and intend no harm. This book is written for spouses who believe their partner loves them, respects them, and means well. And in this spirit, the source of a conflict is a difference in perception and/or intention.

The six steps of communication offer a solution to the following situations:

1. Your partner is frustrated about something you didn't do, and you either didn't know you should have done it, or you thought you should have done something else. In this case, it helps you pinpoint the source of the misunderstanding and fix it, while taking responsibility and apologizing for the part you played in the situation.
2. You are frustrated about something you wanted your partner to do, and you relied on them doing it just to find that they didn't do it, and you get presented with reasons instead of results. In this case, it helps you pinpoint the source of the

      misunderstanding and fix it or at least find forgiveness quickly.

3. You would like your partner to do something for you and want to make sure that it happens. In this case you intentionally make sure you receive a real agreement and follow up with love and respect.

The accountability for your partner doing what you need them to do is always yours. <u>You can delegate responsibility but not accountability</u>. Even if your partner agrees with a firm "Yes, I will do XY until time zero," if it's important to you that it happens, follow up and remind them in between. If it's absolutely crucial and you know that your partner is not reliable about doing it, you must do it yourself. Otherwise you're just setting yourself, your partner, and the relationship up for failure and frustration. You can't make a fish fly. If your partner's concept of time doesn't permit them to be punctual, they won't be punctual unless you tell them the time every 30 minutes and/or plan with a buffer. If you set the buffer too generously and they find out about it, they may start relying on the buffer or calculate it in.

"But as an adult, they should..."

As an adult, you need to know what you can expect from your partner and acknowledge you have weaknesses as well that don't seem like weaknesses to you but to them. If both of you were relaxed about being on time, it would be no source of conflict. If both of you were anal about being on time, it would be no source of conflict either. It's the difference in beliefs and values that makes it one.

There are whole countries and peoples that operate very well without exercising or expecting punctuality. Spend a few weeks in Spain or India, for example. As there are whole countries and peoples that operate very well being on time. In Switzerland, for example, they announce if a train is even one minute late.

TOOL: THE SIX STEPS OF COMMUNICATION

1. What you thought is not necessarily what you said.
2. What you said was not necessarily heard.
3. What was heard was not necessarily understood.
4. What was understood was not necessarily agreed upon.
5. What was agreed upon is not done yet.
6. That someone did something once, doesn't mean it is a habit yet.

Reversal

1. That you didn't hear it doesn't mean it wasn't said.
2. What you heard is not necessarily what was said.
3. What was understood was not necessarily what was meant.
4. Your acknowledgement of understanding may have been taken as an agreement and meets frustration.
5. That you didn't do something that you agreed to do may be understood as disrespectful, unloving, or impaired trust and can be met with frustration.
6. That you agreed to make something a habit but you're struggling to implement it, is understandably frustrating for your partner or even both of you.

It may be appropriate to apologize to your partner to respect their experience and the part you played in it.

Chapter 24

CREATING THE HAPPY RELATIONSHIP

"Relationships are not about happiness, but about authenticity."

Improving a relationship is not only about reducing conflict or improving your conflict-solving skills. If you were in an unhappy relationship and only improved your conflict handling, you'd still be in a miserable relationship – just with better fights. That sounds neither fun nor sustainable.

So, it's also about making the non-conflict moments happier. And you can make your partner happy, as mentioned in the chapter on apologies. Not when they are flooded with cortisol and adrenaline, but you can make the normal everyday moments happy moments by injecting a little bit of happiness and showing appreciation and gratitude where you didn't in the past.

As mentioned earlier, love can be understood as "unconditional appreciation." The more appreciation you show, the more loved your partner feels. Interestingly, the more appreciation you show, the more loved *you* feel as well. Coincidentally, the author of the book *The Five Love Languages*, wrote another book called *The Five Languages of Appreciation in the Workplace*.

Love can die. How does love die? How is love born?
Besides a general attraction, one person signals an openness to connect. Traditionally, the man is expected to make that approach. What is sometimes overlooked is that a man is only supposed to do so after receiving a respective signal of openness. In ancient times, a woman would "accidentally" drop her handkerchief in front of a man and thus invite him to pick it up and hand it back to her to

initiate a conversation.

Then, the two people carefully explore their compatibility and express their appreciation for each other and plan a date, introduce each other to their parents.

When one date leads to another date and finally to a relationship, appreciation and gratitude form the foundation. Appreciation not only for things the other person does but first and foremost for the other person's *existence*. That's where the five ways to express appreciation from the book *The Five Love Languages* by Gary Chapman can serve as a great model. Not everyone understands and enjoys giving appreciation the same way. These are the five ways to express appreciation and help your partner feel loved:

1. Words of affirmation
2. Quality time
3. Acts of service
4. Touch
5. Gifts

In 2018, I went on a road trip with my parents, and on the long drive, I thought it would be fun to speak with them about the five love languages, a concept they had not heard of. I explained the love languages, asked them to guess the order of importance of the other person's love languages, and let the other person solve their order of love languages. I am not sure if the experience was more enlightening for me or for them, but it turned out that my mother's #1 love language was gifts, and her lowest value love language was touch. My father's #1 love language was touch, while it didn't make sense to him to even have gifts on the list.

In fact, he suggested gifts should be removed. Gifts were way too materialistic and had nothing to do with love. I turned the rear-view mirror so that I could see my mom in the back seat and asked what she thought about the existence of touch on the list, and she said she wouldn't notice it missing. In case you wonder how they made it through over 48 years of marriage (and counting), both their second most important love language is quality time.

I have come to understand a few pitfalls that people can fall into when it comes to the five love languages:

Pitfall #1: After I told my partner my love language, it is now known, and they must speak it if they love me.

Pitfall #2: As my love language is not my partner's, I don't need to speak it.

Pitfall #3: When people are stressed, I can still expect them to speak my love language.

Pitfall #4: If my partner does not speak my love language after I told them what it is, that means they don't love me.

About Pitfall #1:
A love language can never be a demand. It is an opportunity to elevate the relationship, but any kind of pressure works to its detriment. Talking about the love languages doesn't result in a deal or agreement. It means opening the door for each other to express appreciation more effectively, to elevate the relationship, and maybe even inspire reciprocation. Just like any other door, one can choose not to go through it or go through it at a later point in time. Learning a language takes time and practice, be it French, English, Chinese, gifts, words of affirmation, or quality time.

Reversal

Learning languages and learning to understand each other goes both ways. Besides working on speaking their love languages as fluently as possible, you also want to start understanding theirs as well as an expression of love whenever they speak it. If touch is not your jam by trade, start to reframe your partner's hugs and touches and tell yourself that this shows how much they love you. Hold the embrace until they loosen it. If gifts are not your thing, start appreciating gifts and accepting them. Seeing you appreciating their gifts is just as, or sometimes even more, important than receiving a great gift from you.

About Pitfall #2:

When you don't speak your primary love languages, you are sending a signal to your partner's unconscious mind that it is, in fact, not that important to you. You also make it more difficult for them to learn it.

About Pitfall #3: In moments of stress, we tend to default to the love languages that are our "mother tongue." If your primary love language is touch, for example, you will lean in for a hug when times get tough and offer a hug when both of you are stressed. Over time, the other person's love language may get so ingrained that you even do it when stressed, but understand that when your partner is stressed or frustrated, it is natural to revert to their primary love language. That is not a slight, nor does it show that you have become less important.

About Pitfall #4:

I have experienced a previous partner of mine asking me to do something for her, and as I replied that I am not able to do it in that moment but only later, she replied, "We talked about the love languages, you know mine is acts of service, do you not love me? Shall we forget about those love languages if you don't value them anyway?"

Don't use the love languages as a means to manipulate your partner or try to force your preferences on them. The five love languages are not a boundary or a rule; they are an opportunity to elevate your relationship.

In the beginning of a relationship, we speak all the love languages. We show appreciation in any possible way, we are grateful for the simplest things, we overlook the flaws, we give the benefit of the doubt. We are in *acquisition mode*. We know that our partner or our date is not 100% won over yet, and we still need to "acquire" them.

At some point, that acquisition is complete. We're in a stable relationship, we're maybe engaged, maybe even married, and we feel safe.

In some cases, that is the point where one partner starts to show their true self that they hid well through the acquisition phase. In the worst form, a physical abuser takes a 180° turn and unleashes hell on their partner. That, of course, is a rare occasion and nothing to be expected. But other things may surface. Toilet lids stay up, worn laundry lies around the bedroom, shoes are scattered around the house, farts are heard, and dirty plates pile up. Not all of these things are necessarily game-changers or red flags, and many are compensated, but they are all clues... that the relationship is drifting into *maintenance mode.*

Maintenance mode has one very positive aspect: the partner feels safe and comfortable in the relationship. That can be appreciated. However, when in the next step appreciation and gratitude dwindle, the relationship can enter a vicious cycle, see *Figure 14.*

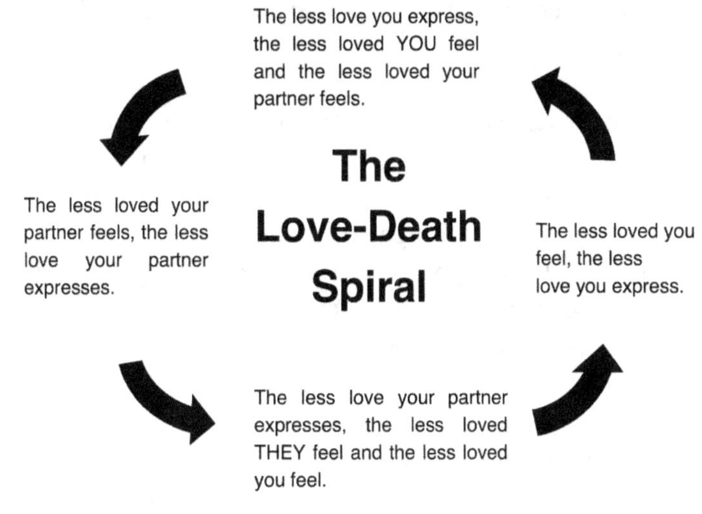

Figure 14

How does that happen? Who does that?

Keeping a relationship alive is a conscious effort. In times where the next relationship is 24 hours away on Tinder, Bumble, or Hinge, putting in the work to make a relationship function appears less and less worthwhile. Ideas like "children are resilient, they'll get over it," "look at Frank, he turned out fine despite his parents' divorce when he was three," or "we're fighting like cats and dogs, it would be much better for the kids to be separate" make it easy to dismiss the responsibility and choose an exciting new lover over working through the issues and one's own toxic contributions.

Relationships experience challenging moments – times of stress like moves, job changes, pregnancies, kids, deaths of family members and friends, and disasters like floods, tornadoes, and fires. In those moments, it is natural to express less love. Heck, you're busy cleaning out the garage before the house is supposed to be put on the market, starting a new job while your stuff is not even unpacked, and the kids are crying for attention when you realize that you forgot to make or order dinner, and as they're adjusting to the new school.

Grief can put a damper on one's mood for weeks or months. In my work, I have experienced how the death of a father can have an especially deep impact on a man, even leading to a shift in his personality.

As you understandably express less love, your partner feels it less. What surprises many people is that when you express your love less, you feel it less too. Expressing love makes YOU feel loved as well; directly through the connection it establishes and indirectly through the appreciation and gratitude you receive in response. As your partner feels it less, they express it less, which makes themselves and you feel it less.

It also makes both of you place more attention on the flaws and shortcomings that we naturally overlook as long as they are compensated with positive things. It's difficult to focus on positive and negative things at the same time. Usually, one dominates. And that's where your power lies. Expressing less love when times are tough is natural and normal. As you still feel it inside, you don't notice it waning by it not being expressed.

You may not notice a weed or two or three, but at some point, you look out of the window into your garden and say to yourself, "I think I need to pull some weeds." Just like that, when you become aware of it, it's not too late.

You can't express love 100% of the time as you need to eat, sleep, work, and so on, so not expressing love while you feel it is naturally accepted and not deemed inauthentic. On the contrary, it may seem as if expressing love when you don't feel it is weird and unnatural. But just as it wasn't inauthentic to not express it in a moment you felt it because you didn't have the capacity, it is also not inauthentic to show love when you don't feel *in love* in that moment.

Have you ever agreed to be intimate with your partner although you didn't feel like it per se? That likely didn't make it a negative experience or weird. More often than not, you probably started enjoying it while you were at it. Have you ever had food although you did not feel hungry, but because you felt it was the right thing to do and good for you? Did that make you an inauthentic eater in that moment?

You can feel love unconsciously, have the hormones of love flow through your body, and act on them… or you can consciously remember how much you love your spouse, how important your relationship is for you, and do the things you used to do when love was young and choose to return to acquisition mode.

It may take an effort, but it may be a (hopefully not so) <u>hard choice for an easy relationship life rather than making an easy choice for a hard relationship life</u> in divorce, sharing children, and ending up with a new partner who turns out to be just the same as every partner was before, just with a new name, face, and hairstyle.

What can you do to make or keep your relationship a happy place? Remember the love languages your partner responds well to. I am placing special emphasis here on how to respond when your partner doesn't speak your love language correctly.

Words of affirmation

- Make compliments to your partner. Every compliment needs to be *specific*.
  - "You look great today" vs. "I love how your hair looks"

> or "You look so handsome with your beard like that."

- "You are a good parent" vs. "I love how patient you are with the kids when you put them to bed" or "I love how dedicated you are when you help the kids with their homework."

- Compliment looks, traits, actions, and what gives them meaning in relation to you. "Good job" vs. "Thanks for emptying the dishwasher, that helped me a lot." Compliment even little things that seem normal or not noteworthy. You can't overdo gratitude.

- Thank your spouse for helping you even if they only did 30% of what they could have. "Shoulding" all over them not only damages the relationship, but it also makes it less likely that they will do it again and you will not even be relieved of those 30%. On the other hand, thanking them for their contribution raises the likelihood that they will go 40% or more next time.

This is especially for the ladies: men play for points. What a man gets points for, he will do again, and better, to score more points next time. Chances are you have no idea what power you hold in your hands. Belittle it as much as you like... Use it or lose it. And remember that the contrary is true as well: If he gets the same or a more intense scolding for doing 30%, you teach his unconscious mind not to do it at all.

Reversal

Man: Go. All. The. Way. Observe how your woman does the job, then model it. You are helping her for the purpose of showing her appreciation, but you make it easier on her if you help her *the way she wants the help* and not the way you think it makes most sense to you. Fill the dishwasher her way and put your ego on the cup rack while you're at it. This is not a man-woman thing, by the way. I know plenty of relationships where he has the specific idea of how the dishwasher needs to be filled, the toothpaste needs to be squeezed out, and towels need to be hung up while it's she who couldn't care less. All these things are opportunities to show your partner appreciation. And that brings us to...

Acts of service

- What things that you (used to) do mean a lot to your spouse?
- Cook, clean, wash, fill up their gas tank, wash the car, take the mail in, get the groceries.
- Ask them if you can help them. Helping a person who doesn't want help is sure to backfire. How often have you enjoyed figuring something out while still swearing at the little hiccups?
- If they want help, <u>help them the way they want to be helped</u>. Don't try to impose your way of helping on them, even if it is objectively better. Chances are, your *objectively* turns out to be quite subjective anyway. If your wife has a special way that she would like to see the dishwasher loaded, you have a golden opportunity to show her how much you love her, how much you listen to her, how important her feelings are to you, and that you are willing to go out of your way for her. Why leave a bitter taste if you can inject a little bit of extra sweetness at zero cost?

Reversal

If your husband loads the dishwasher, celebrate it. There are many ways to skin the cat, and I get that your preference is valid, but so is his. It is an opportunity to inject some sweetness into the relationship, even if using your method makes more dishes fit and would be easier for you to unload or leads to cleaner plates. It's still less effort to unload a dishwasher that he filled than filling AND emptying the dishwasher. Man: GO. ALL. THE. WAY. Them scolding you for doing only 30% is not your ticket to Netflix and chill instead. Show up.

Quality time

What does quality time mean to your partner? Hiking, working out, cooking together, going on a road trip, gardening together, watching TV together, playing video games together... Watching TV together may not mean quality time for some, but it does for others, so do what is meaningful to *them*.

Spending quality time can mean something very different to the masculine and the feminine. For the feminine, spending quality time can involve doing activities together, such as him helping her with chores, going shopping together, working out together, hiking together, watching TV, or enjoying a couple's massage.

To the masculine it often means the feminine simply being present and relaxing while he is engaged in something else. This may be the reason why he takes on the role of the designated driver during road trips or enjoys to work on gardening while she sits outside reading a book or he fixes the car while she keeps him company.

This disparity in perception can explain a stereotypical frustration in many marriages: the moment the husband sits down on the couch, the wife asks him for a favor or to join her in an activity, while he desires to relax in her presence, just as he enjoys to see her relaxation when the roles are reversed.

As a woman, recognize that he may not be the misogynistic, obtuse, unloving individual who relishes the feeling of having a maid around, as you may believe. Understand how loved and respected he feels when he can unwind in your presence.

Reversal

As a man, recognize that she may not be the controlling, disrespectful woman who relishes in controlling you and despises seeing you relaxed. Get up and engage in the activity she needs assistance with, and realize how it makes her feel loved. Then ask if there is anything else you can do or if it would be okay for you to relax on the couch.

In this context, I want to address another common disconnect:

when the couple wants to leave the house, she rushes back and forth to complete tasks that may seem meaningless to him, such as tidying up or sweeping the floors. Many women have shared with me that these unfinished tasks create a sense of unease and occupy their minds if left undone and keep them from deeply relaxing. Your wife is not being neurotic and does not "need to overcome this," but it is a reflection of the fundamentally different experiences and perceptions that men and women can have. Standing there and mansplaining the uselessness of these tasks will only have a negative impact. Roll up your sleeves and offer to help, ask if you can assist, or, at the very least, respect her need to get it done.

Touch

If your partner accuses you of only touching them when you want sex, this is especially important. It doesn't matter that as soon as you touch your partner you get turned on because you find him or her so hot. It matters that getting touched means a lot to them and they need to know that it is something you do because you appreciate them and want to connect and not only a tool to get sex. How do you do it? Touch your partner four times every day. Touching is connecting.

TOOL: 4 TOUCHES

These must be non-sexual touches or, at least, touches that can't be misunderstood as intended to initiate sex. Touch your partner lightly on the arm as you walk past them, hug them, give them a kiss, or a slap on the butt (if that's appreciated – note that not everybody likes it), offer a quick massage as you approach them from behind, or run your fingers through their hair. Avoid transitioning into sexual touches. Complete your touch, and if your partner then initiates sex, that can, of course, be appreciated.

It's perfectly acceptable to set an alarm to remind yourself to touch your partner. If your partner notices it and finds it strange, be open and upfront about it. You're training yourself to develop the habit of meeting their needs.

Reversal

Imagine a relationship with zero touch. We are no longer talking about an intimate relationship. So, the question is not if your partner appreciates being touched, but how. If your partner does not want to be touched at all, there is a deeper issue that needs to be resolved. Or perhaps the relationship has already ended, but neither spouse dares to start the separation process.

Gifts

- A gift doesn't need to be a financial investment. Picked flowers work as well as purchased ones, and a cooked meal or a cake can be a gift as well as an act of service. For some people, it's about the value of the gift, while for others, the value lies in your thoughtfulness and consideration. If the latter is the case, never forget the card!
- Here is a list of possible little daily gifts: Flowers (bought or picked), favorite snacks, energy drinks, books, movies, a freshly warmed blanket, bath bombs, candy, sugar scrub,

gadgets, refills for things related to their hobbies, Starbucks, milkshakes, concert tickets, game tickets, clothes (socks, (personalized) t-shirts, shoes, hats, sweaters...), hidden love notes, cards, sports cards, collectibles, sticky love notes on the mirror...

- An exorbitant birthday or Christmas gift can't substitute the regular little gifts that mean so much to your partner. Just as you can't say, "I told you I love you, now you know, and I will let you know in case it changes!" you can't optimize expressing the gift language to one or two big ones per year.

Reversal

Can gift giving be a mistake? If your partner doesn't like gifts but they are important to you, then you still want to continue giving gifts. But you need to be careful that your partner doesn't feel bribed, "bought," or coerced into doing something for you. A person who dislikes gifts may see them as materialistic and transactional, which makes it understandable that they neither like receiving nor giving them.

Another possibility is that a person who dislikes receiving gifts has low self-worth and believes they don't deserve the gift. Ask them how they feel about gifts, make sure they know that any gift is given unconditionally, or how much they deserve it.

The five love languages are a powerful model for effectively showing love and appreciation, but they are not the only way. To refine your understanding, take an appreciation inventory with your partner.

TOOL: APPRECIATION INVENTORY

Ask your partner, "What things that I do for you do you appreciate the most?"

Depending on the state of your relationship or their state of mind in the moment, they may reply, "I would appreciate it if you…" Be prepared for that response, appreciate it, listen closely, and take mental notes. Thank them for sharing that, ideally ask follow-up questions and then ask, "What things that I do for you do you appreciate?"

This approach accomplishes four things:

1. You learn about the things they like so you can do them more often.
2. By knowing and doing those things, you will feel their appreciation and be less dependent on hearing a "thank you." When you know, you know.
3. By sharing those things, they focus on what you do for them and feel more loved and appreciated in that moment.
4. As they share those things, they will pay more attention and readily notice when you do them, feeling more loved and appreciated, even if the frequency doesn't increase.

Don't expect your partner to ask you back. It's okay if they don't. That's not the purpose of asking them, and if you bring it up, it could make them suspect ulterior motives. You can playfully(!) try asking, "Are you going to ask me too?" If they do, great. If they don't, or even ask if that was the reason you asked in the first place, that's also great because it gives you the chance to show that you offered a *true choice*.

In the chapter on apologies, I wrote about how both masculine and feminine individuals need to hear an apology. The feminine often gets her feelings hurt and feels unloved, while the masculine experiences a form of disrespect. Unconditional love and respect are essential ingredients for a sustainable relationship, especially a happy one.

The book *Love and Respect* by Dr. Emerson Eggerichs explains that a woman needs unconditional love, and a man also needs love, but defines it as respect. In a poll I conducted in several Facebook groups with a total of over 100k members, the results were somewhat sobering. I asked, "What is more important to receive from your partner in your relationship: 1. Love or 2. Respect?" I received 180 responses, and 83% of women and 83% of men stated that respect is more important.

This leads me to believe that love and respect are not the same, nor is respect merely how men understand love. Once again it is more helpful to distinguish between masculine and feminine energy rather than between man and woman. I believe respect is a fundamental pillar of a healthy relationship, and without it, the equilibrium is lost. Love without respect is unsustainable because disrespect causes the masculine energy to wither and dry out and it leads to behaviors that feel unloving.

The bottom line is that we need both love and respect unconditionally. If you say, "My partner needs to earn my respect!" what does that mean? How much respect does he or she need to earn? What qualifies them to be treated with respect? A certain income level? Subjective perceptions like better control of emotions, better performance in household chores, or planning date nights?

Offering love and respect conditionally is unloving and disrespectful in and of itself. The key takeaway for you future conflicts is to ask your partner if your actions came across as unloving or disrespectful, which can lead to a swift return to common ground.

In a 1968 study, Robert Rosenthal and Lenore Jacobson administered a disguised IQ test to all students at a California elementary school. The teachers were not informed of the results. Later, the teachers were told that a selected group of students, about 20% of the school chosen at random and independent of their actual IQ, were expected to be "intellectual bloomers" that year and would likely outperform their classmates. The teachers were given the names of these supposed bloomers. At the end of the school year, the same IQ test was administered to all students again. Both the experimental and control groups in all six grades showed an increase in mean IQ scores from before to after the test. However, first and second graders demonstrated statistically significant improvements favoring the experimental group of "intellectual bloomers." This led to the conclusion that teacher expectations can affect student progress, especially in younger students. Rosenthal believed that even attitude or mood could have a positive impact on the children when the teachers were made aware of the "bloomers." When a student is struggling, the teacher may pay closer attention and treat them differently. This effect was later named the "Pygmalion effect" and was confirmed in various social settings.

What does this mean for your relationship? As mentioned earlier, in moments of high stress, you don't rise to the level of your own expectations but fall to the level of your training. However, over time, humans tend to rise and fall to the level of expectations or assumptions that others make about themselves.

If you treat your partner as someone who doesn't deserve love or respect "yet," you are essentially treating them as someone who doesn't deserve it now. They are more likely to fulfill that assumption than find the motivation to overcome it.

The Pygmalion effect suggests that you can indeed help your partner change or become a better person by treating them genuinely and authentically as if they were already the way you want them to be. Create an environment of love, respect, and faith in them that makes it easy and safe for them to thrive and grow. Your role as a spouse is not to improve your partner but to accept, appreciate, respect, trust, and love them as they are right now, providing a safe space for them to recover from life's lessons and expand on them. Not doing so is the seed of contempt and leads the relationship down a dark path, either towards a power-based relationship where loving and respectful behaviors and their absence are used as rewards or punishments, or a fear-based relationship where your partner walks on eggshells to avoid your expressions of frustration when their actions don't meet your expectations.

Of course, this doesn't mean allowing them to violate your boundaries.

In his over four decades of scientific research, John Gottman identified what he calls the four horsemen of the apocalypse – four behaviors that, when expressed regularly, predict a divorce with staggering accuracy:

1. Criticism
2. Defensiveness
3. Blame
4. Contempt

I mention these in the chapter on happiness because they can arise in normal or even happy situations and turn them sour. The following four sections provide guidelines on what to do instead.

Criticism

I believe criticism is important and sometimes necessary and it can't always be avoided. Even if unintended, things like feedback, setting boundaries, or expressing differing opinions can easily be interpreted as criticism and sour a situation. When you need to criticize, it's essential to follow certain guidelines to ensure it is constructive or to address it when you realize your partner perceived it negatively.

1. Before criticizing, ask yourself: "Is it true that their action needs to be criticized, or are we simply following different philosophies?" "Am I criticizing a behavior that can be changed, or a personal trait my partner identifies with?" "Is it true, necessary, and is there a chance for change?"
2. Ask for permission. Your partner dislikes unsolicited advice

as much as you do, and even if they offer unsolicited advice, reciprocating doesn't "show them how it feels." Instead, it validates their behavior. By asking for permission, you can gauge their openness to receive criticism. Offer them a *true choice*, and if they are not open, acknowledge and appreciate their decision. Criticism will only be perceived as an attack if they are not open.

3. What if your partner *never* gives you permission? As you begin offering true choices, your partner needs time to understand that these choices are authentic and not a trap or temporary phenomenon. Give them the necessary time, which may take a few months depending on the length of your relationship.

4. Instead of criticizing, explore other tools in your language repertoire that can be more effective:

- Ask: Request what you would like your partner to do instead before the undesired behavior occurs.
- Appreciate: Show gratitude when your partner deviates (even accidentally) from their usual unwelcome behavior. Thank them for doing something new and express how much it means to you. Imagine if you told a puppy to sit and hit it when it didn't, or when it lied down or shook a paw instead. It sounds absurd. With a puppy, you say "sit," and when it sits, it receives a treat. That's the power of appreciation versus the ineffectiveness of criticism.

Defensiveness

Responding to your partner by defending yourself can set the blame carousel in motion. You may say that their criticism did, but it takes two to spin the carousel. Defending yourself is your part in the carousel's initiation energy. Here are alternative ways to respond effectively and keep the situation happy:

1. Win the mind game: Become aware of the emotions that

your partner's criticism brought up and reframe. Notice that their criticism is not an instrument to get the best of you, to control you, or to manipulate your behavior, even if it seems that way or they admit it. Criticism comes from a place of pain, unmet needs, and anxiety. Now, <u>do the right thing with compassion instead of the wrong thing out of compassion</u> (or out of your pain).

2. Thank them for their feedback. "Thank you for letting me know" or "Maybe you're right, I will think about that."

3. Sometimes a positive response is too difficult or inappropriate: "I hear what you're saying, and I can imagine where you're coming from. I must say though, that it hurts a bit to hear that."

4. If you're about to get defensive about them defending themselves and the blame carousel is slowly starting to turn, instead, apologize for how you made them feel. Not for the (valid) point you brought up but for the fact that you were not able to express it in a way that they could appreciate. "It seems like what I said frustrated you and I am sorry that I did. Please forgive me."

It's not about being right here. It's about accepting and taking responsibility for the part you played in making them feel negative emotions. It's also not about acknowledging their victimhood. The existence of a feeling does not make one a victim.

Blame

Blame stifles effective or constructive communication. A person who feels blamed sinks back into the couch and sits in it. There is not much to do because now you have it, and you can't undo the past. Blame is different from feeling responsible because responsibility leads to action. Blame leads to feeling like a lesser person. If your partner feels like a lesser person, it turns the relationship into a lesser relationship and comes full circle back to you. Do not blame, reframe blame. Here's how:

1. If you're being blamed, win the mind game: Notice how it makes you feel and label your emotions. Reframe what your partner said as an expression of disappointment in you (or themselves) and notice what part your partner played in the situation. Acknowledge and take responsibility for the part you played.

   Janine: "You didn't take out the trash yesterday, and the trash truck just came by!"
   Frank: "Oh, shoot, I totally forgot! I am so sorry. Can you help me and remind me next Wednesday evening?"
   Janine: "I can try, but I may forget it as well. How about you make a reminder for yourself in your calendar?"
   Frank: "That's a good idea. Let me do that real quick."
   Janine: "We're late! It's your fault!"
   Frank: "Is there anything you could have done differently that would have helped us leave the house sooner?"
   Janine: "No, but you could have helped me get my stuff done!"
   Frank: "I see, I'm sorry."

2. If you're about to blame, rephrase it as an actionable item for the future. "We are late again; I am wondering what we could do to get out of the house on time in the future?"

3. Prevent blame: You can't always prevent blame, but you can reduce its occurrence by phrasing things as a matter of perception rather than existence.

   Felicia: "Can you give me a can of crushed tomatoes from the pantry?"
   Justin walks over to the pantry, opens the door: "We're out of crushed tomatoes!"
   Felicia walks over, points at the can of crushed tomatoes right in front of Justin's face: "Why do you lie to me?"

   Janine: "Can you give me a can of crushed tomatoes from the pantry?" Frank walks over to the pantry, opens the door:

"I don't see them!" Janine walks over, points at the can of crushed tomatoes right in front of Frank's face: "I am sorry, I bought a different brand this time, you were probably looking for a red can."

Janine could have snapped just as much as Felicia, but by Frank talking about his perception, he left the possibility open that there may be an issue on his end, thus making it more likely to find understanding.

Contempt

Contempt targets the masculine in his weakest spot: the need to be acknowledged and respected. It insinuates that the other person is a lesser person and puts you on a high horse, making you one of the horsemen of the apocalypse. It turns the relationship, at least for a moment, into a power-based relationship.

If you feel contempt towards your partner, notice how your contempt is a smokescreen for the true feelings that lie beneath it. Is it a fear of the future? A sadness about feeling unloved? Anger over the consequences of a curveball that your partner threw you, and you must absorb?

Contemptuous or condescending behavior intends to make the other person *finally* see how they need to show up better and put more effort into living up to your expectations, expectations that are basic and nothing special. It disregards their life experience, their value as a person to you, your respect and love for them, and the fact that you care for their well-being. That is probably not your intention, but that is likely how it will be understood. Being contemptuous is justifiable and reasonable, but it can't ever yield positive results. And if it does, those results come at the expense of the relationship. You win, they lose, so the relationship loses, so you lose.

The real intention is to make the partner change their behavior, but you can't *make* them change. You can only inspire change.

Felicia comes home late; Justin sits on the couch and doesn't even look up. Felicia: "Is everything okay?"

Justin: "iS eVErYThinG oKAy? You wanted to be home at 8, what time is it now? You're always mad when I come home late, look what you're doing!"

Felicia: "Exactly! You're late ALL THE TIME, and now me being late ONCE is a big deal, is it?"

How to communicate effectively instead of contemptuous:

1. Win the mind game: Sense the feelings that were brought up by your partner's behavior and label your emotions. Reframe their behavior. Your partner is not acting like a stupid little child who needs to grow up. Your partner is an adult whom you love and respect and who is making their choices based on their beliefs, values, and life experiences. If you had lived the exact same life they had, you'd make the same decisions. At least they managed to get to where they are in life and won your love.

2. Share how their behavior made you feel. Your partner loves you and respects you. The last thing they want is to make you feel bad. Telling your partner how you feel is the most powerful way to release your negative feelings amicably and inspire change.

   Janine comes home at nine instead of eight.
   Frank kisses Janine hello: "Hey, I am happy to see you. It made me a bit uneasy and sad that you were not home at eight already, but I am glad you made it, and we have a little bit of time left together tonight." Janine: "I am sorry, Bettina was telling me about her son's car accident, and I didn't want to cut her off. I should have texted you." (Notice how Janine doesn't give an excuse but uses her circumstance to communicate deeper insight and intention to change moving forward)

3. Ask about the behavior you would like to see in the future:

Frank: "Hey, I was a bit nervous when you were not home at eight like you said and had hoped to see you earlier. I know how that can happen, but would you be so kind as to send me a text next time?"

Two weeks later.

Frank: "Have fun with Bettina, please send me a text in case you run late or leave your phone on so I can reach you if anything comes up. Would that be okay for you?"

Janine: "Oh, sure, thank you for reminding me."

Reversal

How to Respond to a Contemptuous Partner

1. Win the mind game: Sense the feelings brought up by your partner's behavior and label your emotions. Reframe their behavior. Your partner is not trying to disrespect you or prove that they don't love you. Instead, they love and respect you but may be hurt or feeling disrespected themselves. They are making choices based on their beliefs, values, and life experiences. If you had lived the exact same life they had, you would make the same decisions. At least they managed to get to where they are in life and won your love.

2. Ask them about their feelings to go beyond the smokescreen of contempt. "How did it make you feel?" By doing this, the contempt is taken off the table, and you can acknowledge the part you played in making them feel a certain way.

3. Acknowledge how their behavior seemed, looked, or sounded to you and share how it made you feel.

Frank: "Hey, you're an hour late!"

Janine: "Can't you be alone for an evening for once, like an adult?" Frank: "It seems like it frustrates you that I am saying that? I was okay here, had dinner and did some laundry, but it made me feel a bit uneasy and sad when you were not home at eight. I must say that I find your reaction a bit disrespectful."

Janine: "I'm sorry, Bettina told me an awful story about

her ex that really got me into a bad mood. I apologize for not giving you a heads up."

Effective communication is not a magic trick. Janine could still have responded negatively. It's about expressing empathy and then sharing your point. If the response is negative, you can stop the blame carousel before it starts and leave it at that. The last thing they heard is how it made you feel.

Criticism, defensiveness, blame, and contempt can happen in any relationship to some extent. They are all expressions of frustration, and you can never stop frustration with counter-frustration. That just sets the blame carousel in motion. Thinking about how you express your frustration and mastering your state of being with the tools in Part Three of this book, and using Love-Based Language, can stop the blame carousel. It doesn't matter if it's the initial frustration or the frustration that arises as a response to an expression of frustration. The blame carousel needs two energy sources to keep spinning. When you experience the expression of frustration, look through the "how" and make an effort to see the "what" and the "why." <u>Your partner can be right and wrong in how they express it</u>.

If you have been asked to do something and you agreed but did not do it, and your partner misses the tone, it would be wrong to dismiss your commitment just because they did not contain their frustration. Go and do the thing. Then you can say, "I'm sorry that I forgot to do X, but the way you reminded me was a bit hurtful."

Gratitude

Gratitude can be a supercharger for creating happiness in your relationship. I learned this lesson from my wife, and it took me about four years to understand it.

She would thank me for emptying the dishwasher, and I would frown and reply, "Why? My dishes are in there too, and you empty it as well all the time. What's the big deal?" I am very grateful that my mansplanations fell on deaf ears, and she just continued to thank me for the most banal things until I got it. Every expression of gratitude is an opportunity to elevate your relationship with minimal effort, showing your partner love and respect as you go about your day.

Humans play for points, with men possibly doing so more than women. That's why more men than women play computer games, and why people steer their Super Mario cart a little further to the right to collect a few stars for a better score. You can shake your head over this behavior, or you can become aware of the power that's at your fingertips. You can understand every expression of gratitude as a point you give your partner. When they become consciously or unconsciously aware of what scores them points, they will express that behavior more often. Why isn't everyone doing it then? Because you can score points and commit a transgression at the same time.

When your partner cleans 30% of the kitchen, how do you feel?

1. Part of you will be happy because you need to clean less.
2. Part of you is furious because you f***ing clean 100% of the kitchen ALL. THE. TIME. Heck, you may not even notice #1.

Felicia: "You did NOTHING!"
Justin: "I took the trash out, I just forgot to put a new bag in!"
Felicia: "You did NOTHING!"

The emotions you feel are real and undeniably exist inside you. They are justifiable and explainable, and so is your response, but what result does it get?

Justin enters the kitchen after Felicia put the dishes in the dishwasher, washed the pots and pans, and put the cooking ingredients in the fridge. The counter is still smudgy. "Can't you clean up after yourself?"
Felicia: "I put our dishes away, cleaned the pots, and put the food

away!"

Justin: "Does that look like a clean kitchen to you? Do you want me to demonstrate what cleaning a kitchen looks like, or can you figure it out yourself?"

Felicia: "I am not having this conversation; I'm going to bed."

Janine enters the kitchen after Frank put the dirty dishes into the dishwasher. Pots and pans are still on the stove, cooking ingredients are still out, and the counter is smudgy. "Thank you for putting our dishes in the dishwasher."

Frank: "Of course!"

Janine: "Do you have a moment to help me clean the counter and put away the ingredients?"

Frank: "Sure..."

What did each of the four people think that night?

Felicia: "I'll never live up to Justin's OCD. He doesn't see me. That was very unloving."

Justin: "Felicia is such a pig. I wonder why her parents didn't teach her to clean up properly. How angry do I need to get until she gets it?"

Frank: "Damnit, I missed it again. Next time, I'll put the dishes away as well and clean the counter."

Janine: "Frank is trying so hard. He is so sweet!"

When is it too much?

Can you overdo appreciation and gratitude? A client once asked me, "If I just shower my partner with appreciation and gratitude no matter what she does, doesn't that make me her bitch?"

No, it does not. Going above and beyond with appreciation and gratitude, as long as it is honest and authentic, can never have a negative effect on your relationship. But if you combine it with not setting and enforcing your boundaries, then your relationship will suffer because resentment will accumulate on your end. Then you're not showing love, but you are people-pleasing.

Connecting

Sometimes I am asked, "My partner says they feel disconnected. How do I *connect*? What does '*connecting*' mean?" As you come to the end of this book, you may already have an idea, but here are a few general principles:

- When your eyes meet, you're visually connected.
- When you touch, you're kinesthetically connected.
- When your partner feels listened to, you're auditorily connected.
- When you smell each other, you're olfactory connected.
- When you think of each other and express understanding and empathy, you're mentally/spiritually connected.

Ask your partner what it means to them, then explore the respective chapter of this book.

Reversal

There is no reversal. Relationships are built on reciprocity, and it is always up to you to inject happiness into the relationship. Why? Because you can. How do you feel when your partner has the chance to make you happy and passes on that opportunity?

A *victim* feels helpless, is passive, passes on opportunities to take action, but criticizes, defends, blames, expresses contempt, and hopes for a change in the other person.

A *victor* appreciates every bit of leverage she gets to take action and shift the odds in her favor. Your partner may even exercise this fallacy at times, but contrary to many people's beliefs and actions, <u>you will never get your needs met by holding back to fulfill your partner's needs</u>.

Chapter 25

THE FOUR SIDES OF A MESSAGE

"The meaning anything has, is the meaning you give it."

It's a random Sunday afternoon, and Janine and Frank are sitting on opposite ends of the couch, reading.

Janine: "It's a bit chilly, isn't it?"
Frank gets up and closes the window.

At the same time, Justin and Felicia are on their way to visit Felicia's parents and stop at a traffic light.

Felicia: "The light is green."
Justin: "I'm not blind. You're not happy when you don't find an opportunity to tell me what to do, are you?"

A message has a sender and a recipient, sometimes multiple recipients. German psychologist Friedemann Schulz von Thun noticed that every message has at least one and up to four sides to it:

- Factual information.
- A request: The sender would like the recipient to do something.
- A self-revelation: The sender discloses information about him/herself.
- Relationship: Information regarding the relationship between the sender and recipient.

Depending on the state and situation of the sender and recipient, the same sentence can have a different meaning, and the recipient may misinterpret the message, or the sender may miss the tone. You see, the sender speaks with their sender-mouth, and the recipient listens with their listener-ear.

"It's 68 degrees (20°C) in here" entails factual information. But depending on their preference, the sender may feel colder than they are comfortable with. How much colder? While person one may say this sentence when visibly shivering, person two may say "I'm freezing to death" as one toe sticks out under the thick blanket. Person three may sit in the room in shorts and a t-shirt and feel just fine. The longer you know your partner, the more you have an idea about their state of comfort when hearing the words, but they may still vary depending on their emotional or physical state.

"It's 68 degrees (20°C) in here" can also entail a request. There are **inferential speakers** and **direct speakers**. And if that wasn't complicated enough, there are inferential listeners and direct listeners as well and either can be different in different situations. Does that sound like a recipe for conflict? You bet.

If an inferential speaker says: "It's 68 degrees (20°C) in here," chances are they mean "Could you please close the window?"
If an inferential listener hears that, they'll go ahead and close the window, while a direct listener may respond: "Oh yeah, I would have expected warmer weather in July, too."

If a direct speaker says: "It's 68 degrees (20°C) in here," it's likely just a statement to, for example, express surprise about the weather conditions outside but nothing to act on. Or a self-revelation. An inferential listener acting on it may be off.

A direct listener needs an explicit request to jump into action, while an inferential listener may even be offended by a direct request like "Can you please close the window?" and consider it rude.

The bottom line is, people have their preferences, and there is no right or wrong. If everybody heard and spoke inferentially, then things would be just as good as if everyone heard and spoke directly.

Then again, it can even depend on the situation or environment where someone prefers one or the other.

Sounds confusing? It sure is as long as you don't know, as long as you're not self-aware, and as long as you haven't practiced it. The more you practice, the more you recognize how a misunderstanding can be based on a statement being misunderstood as a request or the other way around.

One of the biggest sources of conflict is the area of support. Someone asking for help but not receiving it may feel let down and alone. That can be just as frustrating as sharing a challenge you're facing, and the other person trying to solve the "problem" that you enjoy figuring out yourself.

Janine is putting together an IKEA cabinet and complains: "I have a hard time getting this screw in!"
Frank jumps up and finishes the cabinet for her.
Janine is happy.

Felicia is also putting together an IKEA cabinet and complains: "I have a hard time getting this screw in!"
Justin jumps up, and as he reaches for the screwdriver, Felicia pulls it back. "It's okay, I got it."
Justin: "I thought you wanted help?"
Felicia: "No, I was just saying that it's difficult, but I am enjoying the process and looking forward to seeing and using the cabinet that I built myself."

Many people generally enjoy challenges and don't like being deprived of the chance to solve them. Unsolicited help can be a source of conflict from many angles:

- If you need help and don't get it, you may feel alone.

- If you ask for help and get it, but the helper imposes "their way of helping" on you, you may feel belittled and disrespected.
- If you ask for help and don't get it NOW, you may feel unimportant.
- If you ask for help, and the helper only relieves you of 30% of your problem, but you had expected 100%, you may be unhappier than if you had received no help at all.
- If you don't need help, and a "helper" takes stuff off your plate, you may feel deprived of your autonomy.
- If you're struggling and don't want help, but someone offers it and you decline, they may feel hurt, rejected, and unappreciated.

General guidelines:

- Ask for permission to help.
- Keep your ego out of the equation and don't take things personally (even things that are meant personally).
- Appreciate *expressions of frustration* and don't let them keep you from doing the right thing:

Justin: "Do you need help?"
Felicia: "Of course, captain obvious, come already and hold this!"

Justin: "Don't you see that I need help?"
Felicia: "Sorry, I did not. I'm coming."

"It's a bit chilly, isn't it?" can also have a meaning regarding the relationship. "I am always cold, while you are always hot." In that case, Frank may say: "Let me put my feet on yours so I can warm you and cool myself."

Let's look at Justin and Felicia on their drive. "It's green."

Speaker:

- Request: "It's green, please drive now!"
- Self-revelation: "I noticed that it's green, and I am afraid we might be late."
- Relationship: "Why don't you drive? Don't you see it's green? I wonder how you drive when you're alone in the car as it seems you always need my help with everything..."
- Fact: "The light turned green" (you can drive when you're ready.)

Listener:

- Request: Hits the gas pedal.
- Self-revelation: "I didn't see it, I was looking at the storefront over there."
- Relationship: "Stop telling me what to do!"
- Fact: Checks light, drives eventually.

While it's easy to understand a sentence as a request or interpret information about the relationship into it, we often overlook the self-revelation aspect.

A person who is labeled as a "control freak" rarely just finds joy in remote controlling another person. The underlying motive is often fear or anxiety and the desire to create a sense of certainty.

Anger is often a smokescreen to protect vulnerability. A scared dog may bite out of fear and is quickly labeled aggressive while it really tried to leave but couldn't get out of the corner. Despite the protective intent that lies beneath anger, it is often interpreted by the listener as a smokescreen to hide bad behavior or bad intentions. Anger about being accused of cheating is often interpreted as an attempt to hide guilt. In that case, the message that is really about the relationship—anger about being wrongfully accused—is misinterpreted by the recipient as a self-revelation. At the same time, the latter is of course possible and it may be a self-revelation of guilt.

If you face an unjustified accusation, and need to send a response, being vulnerable about the feelings it brings up in you is much more powerful than a forceful response. At the same time, if you are the recipient of a forceful response, it is still unclear if the sender of that message is hiding guilt or emphasizing innocence.

In other words, when you are on the receiving end and your partner's behavior or words hurt or disrespect you, and you feel the impulse to lash out, think about the other person's underlying emotions. Acknowledge their expression of frustration and address the real problem instead, or ask questions to figure it out.

Reversal

There is no reversal. You are either the sender of the message, then identify or ask how your partner understood it and clarify with empathy, or you are the recipient of the message and empathetically ask for clarification.

Chapter 26

CHANGING YOUR WAYS

"Shift happens."

Change is hard. You can't make your partner change. Yet, we change every day. You have changed. You are not the same person you were ten years ago, neither am I, neither is your partner. None of those changes were forced on us by another person; we chose each little one. As nobody can force a change on you, you can't force a change on anyone else, at least not without damaging the relationship.

You can do two things that will increase the likelihood of a positive change in your partner:

1. Change yourself.
2. Inspire change.

Most of our behaviors are responses to our environment. When it gets too cold, you turn on the heat. When it gets too hot, you turn on the air conditioning. When a dog gets a treat, he will likely repeat the behavior that got him the treat. Sometimes he will have to experience it a few times before he gets it. When I taught Obi to play dead, it took me two months of regular practice before he would do it just by me pointing at him and saying, "Bang, you're dead!" When a behavior of yours gets a positive result, you're likely to repeat it. How likely? Maybe 50%, maybe 0.001%.

As most of your behaviors are responses to *your* environment, most of your partner's behaviors are responses to *their* environment. You are a part of their environment. When their environment changes, the old behavior doesn't make sense anymore, and a new behavior must happen. <u>When you change, your partner's environ-</u>

<u>ment changes – and they will change</u>. For example, if you set and enforce a boundary with love, and your partner loves you and is a person of basic goodwill, they won't be happy in the moment, but it will lead to a positive change that elevates the relationship.

You may also be able to *inspire* change. Inspiration is exclusively positive. Any negativity in connection with the behavior that you would like to see deters from that behavior.

If you want your dog to come to you when you call him, and he comes after the fourth call, and you hit him because he only came after call number four instead of call number one, what does he learn? He learns that when he comes, he may get hit. But "NO, NO!" you say, "It's only if he doesn't come *right away*!" That may be the intention, but it's not the experience of the dog. I love dog metaphors... dogs are like simple humans in so many ways...

It's Tuesday, and Justin's boss told him that he needs to come in for work on Saturday. Felicia and Justin wanted to tour stores that day to look for a new kitchen. Felicia is excited about it, and Justin knows that she will be very disappointed when she hears the bad news.

As he comes home, Felicia made dinner and shares that she would like to watch the new episode of their favorite show that came out today. Justin reminds her that they didn't get to watch last week's episode, and a cozy evening awaits. As they cuddle on the couch and the episode intro plays, Justin remembers his boss's request. He knows that if he shares that news now, the cozy evening will turn not so cozy, and he focuses back on the show. It won't change a thing to tell her tomorrow morning...

The next morning, Justin not only breaks fast but also breaks the news:

"Hey babe, my boss told me that he needs me in the office on Saturday because the project is not where it needs to be, and the deadline is on Tuesday."

Felicia: "Why didn't you tell me yesterday?! You knew that yesterday already! Why can't you be honest for once!"

Justin: "I am sorry, I didn't think of it yesterday."

Felicia: "That's a lie! Of course, you knew it yesterday! You want to tell me that it didn't cross your mind the entire evening?"

Justin: "It didn't, but even if it had, we would not have had such a nice evening."

Felicia: "See, I KNEW you were lying! You just wanted to have sex with me! And no, sir, if you had told me yesterday, everything would have been fine. I am just upset because you didn't tell me RIGHT AWAY and lied to me about it!"

Justin: "But I didn't lie..."

And so, the blame carousel spins...

While Justin thinks, "Thank God I prevented yesterday evening from going this way... I hope she doesn't keep that mood for too long. Maybe I should have told her Friday..."

It's Tuesday, and Frank's boss told him that he needs to come in for work on Saturday. Janine and Frank wanted to tour stores that day to look for a new kitchen. Janine is excited about it, and Frank knows that she will be very disappointed when she hears the bad news. As he comes home, Janine made dinner and shares that she would like to watch the new episode of their favorite show that came out today. Frank reminds her that they didn't get to watch last week's episode, and a cozy evening awaits. As they cuddle up on the couch and the episode intro plays, Frank remembers his boss's request.

"Hey Babe, my boss came to me with a really upsetting request today."

Janine (sits up): "What is it?"

Frank: "I told you about the project not going as planned, and with the deadline coming up on Tuesday, I need to go into work on Saturday. I know we wanted to look for a new kitchen that day, I am so sorry."

Janine: "That's a bummer. I was really excited about it."

Frank: "I know, I was looking forward to it as well."

Janine (cuddles up again): "I guess it's no big deal to wait a week."

Would that have been Felicia's response as well if Justin had conveyed the news earlier? Maybe, Felicia believes so. Justin's expectation looks like this:

Felicia: "Why didn't you call me right after your boss talked to you! I don't want to watch anymore. I'm taking the puppy for a walk. I wish I could walk her off leash, but someone hasn't trained her yet."

How could Felicia and Justin change the dynamics of such situations?

The first step for each, or at least for one of them, is to make the decision that they want to change. They need to be personally motivated to make a shift within themselves. To get to that point, one of two things, or even both things, must happen:

1. The desire to get away from the painful situation needs to reach a threshold where it becomes unbearable.
2. The desire to find a way to create a satisfactory outcome for situations like this needs to become strong enough.

When one of those or both of those states are reached, then the motivation exists to create change.

When the motivation is there, **the second step** is to create the ability to solve the problem. That can mean to acquire the skills to be able to perform the task. It can also mean to practice the behavior so that it comes to mind automatically when needed. Practice makes permanent.

Like when you want to create a habit of flossing your teeth, you don't need to acquire the skill to floss but the challenge is to make it an automatic thing to reach for the floss upon putting down the toothbrush. To do that, you can go into the bathroom, put the toothbrush in your mouth, put it down, reach for a floss pick and floss a tooth, put the floss pick down, take the toothbrush, and repeat the back and forth 30 times. Chances are, you'll now automatically reach for the floss after brushing your teeth and you collapsed 30 days of practice into one hour.

In Justin's case, he needs to overcome the fear of ruining the situation and develop the habit (and skill) to communicate bad news using language that makes it as likely as possible to receive a positive response. He could try Frank's approach. Or he could say, "Hey my love, I know how much it upsets you when I don't share bad news right away, and I have something really awful to tell you."

Maybe Felicia is just a person who has a hard time mastering her emotions, so he needs to give her some space to digest the news. So, he could call her as he leaves the office so she has the rest of his drive home to digest, and he could even stop at the store to get her something nice.

Felicia may notice that she is a bit of a hothead and realize that part of Justin not sharing bad news as early as he could is that he doesn't feel safe doing so. She can work through Part Three of this book and practice reframing situations. To practice, she can train in her *mental gym*.

TOOL: MENTAL GYM
Choose a relaxed moment in which you have some time and space for yourself. Close your eyes and remember a perpetually stressful situation in which you want to respond differently in the future. In your mind's eye, see what you saw, hear what you heard, and feel what you felt at the time. Employ those virtual senses we discussed in part one of this book. Acknowledge and name the feelings that you experienced.

Now, imagine displaying the behavior that you desire to express in similar situations in the future. Repeat this process a few times. Why repeat? Because chances are that you repeat negative situations in your mind anyway. Now you can use that pattern in a positive and productive way.

By doing this, you create a (fake) memory of how you acted in a desired way. The next time a challenging situation occurs, you won't need to invent a desired reaction on the spot, but rather repeat what you've already envisioned in fantasy.

The third step to changing the habit is to get your partner to help you change the habit and share your commitment to change.

In Justin's case, he says, "Fel, I know how important it is for you that I share bad news as timely as possible, and I really want to do that. As I promise to try really hard, I was wondering if you can help me a little by asking me when I come home, how my day was, or if anything happened that I think you would like to know."

In Felicia's case, she can go into her mental gym, remember the last three situations where Justin shared information later than she would have wanted to know it, and practice a calm response.

Asking your partner to help you implement a new habit can be a delicate task. For example, if you want help losing weight and ask your partner to remind you not to eat certain foods or to work out, you need to master your frustration when your partner provides that help and you feel unhappy about yourself. It is easy to then project that unhappiness onto your partner and find inadequacies in their tone of voice. If you know that this may happen, I recommend skipping this step.

Step number four is doing it together. If Justin and Felicia come to the conclusion that they are both contributing to this perpetual problem, they may do it together, talk about their intentions, and empathize with each other when they fall off their new habits. The key is acknowledging the partner's honest effort and goodwill with a loving and forgiving attitude towards them.

The fifth step is implementing rewards and repercussions. As Felicia and Justin's situation shows, repercussions are not likely to work. Why? Because you can avoid a repercussion in multiple ways, but you can only reap a reward for doing one *specific* thing.

Fido can avoid the punishment by coming after the first call, but he can also delay it by coming after the tenth call or avoid it completely by running away and coming home after two days to find his owner ecstatic that he's still alive.

For example, Justin could reward himself with a milkshake every time he conveys bad news immediately, even if Felicia throws a fit. Felicia could do the same every time she keeps her cool when confronted with bad news. Both could implement a habit tracker on which they put a green check mark for every time they follow through with their intention and a red cross if they slip into the old pattern. Just measuring your progress and making it visible is intrinsically rewarding.

If they are in it together, they can create a shared habit tracker where they want to see two green check marks for every bad news situation.

Addressing a new identity is more powerful than a new behavior. So you can further improve the habit tracker by giving it a title that describes your new identity: "I am an athlete" instead of "workout tracker," "I am an honest person" instead of "honesty tracker," "I am a healthy eater" instead of "diet tracker," or "I am a loving husband/wife" for a habit tracker that tracks how often you speak your spouse's love language.

Step number six is changing the environment so that it becomes as *unlikely* as possible to slip into the old pattern and as *likely* as possible to exercise the new behavior.

Justin could put a post-it that says "bad news?" on his steering wheel so that he remembers to call Felicia on his drive home if something comes up. Would that be appropriate? That's Justin's call to make.

This step is especially important to implement physical habits like flossing teeth: Put the floss next to the toothbrush or put the next floss pick out and ready after using the last one.

Most people overestimate one factor when it comes to building a habit: willpower or discipline. How often have you said to yourself or others, or at least thought, "I just need to be more disciplined!"

Many people believe that discipline means exercising willpower over an extended amount of time. That's not discipline. That's setting yourself up for failure.

For example, if you sit down in the living room, put a bag of chips on the living room table, and say, "I will now practice discipline and not eat these chips," chances are, one of two things will happen.

1. At some point, you'll notice that the chips are gone, and you can't even tell how.
2. You leave them there for a while and then decide, "I was so good and disciplined for such a long time, I'm going to reward myself with this bag of chips!" and eat them anyway.

Discipline is not exercising willpower over an extended amount of time. <u>Discipline is a decision to choose what you really want over what you want in the moment</u>. Like:

- As you push your cart through the chips aisle, choosing not to put chips in the cart but pushing through and putting berries and (unsalted) nuts in the cart instead, so you don't have to constantly choose at home.

- Choose to make the bed as you get out of it because you know your partner will notice and appreciate it.
- Choose to bring the trash out when you put an item in and need to push the whole pile into the can to make it fit.
- Choose to fill the dishwasher as you put your dish in the sink, which is already full. (And empty the dishwasher if it's clean)
- Throw some flowers or your spouse's favorite snack in the supermarket cart.
- Touch your partner as you walk past them, and if you don't remember to do that, set a reminder for yourself to create those "accidental" moments.
- Choose to agree to have sex even when you are really tired because you know how important it is to drive connection.

As you do these things and alter your environment to make them more likely, by doing them, you alter your partner's environment too. They now live in a more loving, appreciative, more grateful environment and are more likely to contribute to it as well. If you join a house with five millionaires, you'll be the sixth. If you join a house with five homeless people, you'll be the sixth. If you create a loving, respectful environment, your partner will become more loving and respectful as well.

The problem with discipline is that you may not feel like doing it in the moment, and the devil on your shoulder (a.k.a. your ego) whispers in your ear, "If you show love, respect, and trust when you don't feel it, you are a hypocrite."

The truth is that doing what is right despite not feeling like it does not make you a hypocrite. Kind of like getting up in the morning although you are still tired is not hypocritical. It makes you a responsible, mature person. Showing love, showing respect, showing trust to your partner although you don't feel it in that moment makes you a responsible, mature spouse. Treating your partner with respect despite disrespectful behavior on their end hits the brakes on the blame carousel and is the responsible, mature thing to do with compassion for yourself and them. And setting boundaries, of course.

<u>A strong new habit can be built when you use at least four of the six steps</u>.

Part of building a habit is falling off it. Falling off habits is connected to habit building like the moon is connected to the night sky. You don't always see it, but it comes up eventually. There can be different reasons that you may or may not consider legitimate, like an illness that keeps you from working out or a business trip that keeps you from making your partner a coffee in the morning, or you just forget. What does your self-talk sound like when you fall off a habit? How do you talk to your partner when they fall off a habit that's important to you?

We used to have a gardener who left the garden gate open. That is not a problem in most gardens that he works in, but we have chickens and a dog, and the thought of chasing a chicken down the road or even finding it in a car accident was reason enough to ask the gardener to keep the gate closed while working in our garden. <u>You can't delegate accountability; you can only delegate responsibility</u>. If a chicken escapes and gets run over by a car, I am accountable. I have one less chicken. I can then cause pain for my gardener by firing him, but that doesn't resurrect my chicken. It's gone, and I am accountable. I can make my gardener responsible for taking measures that ensure the chickens don't escape and communicate with him effectively so that it becomes as likely as possible that he will handle this responsibility in a way that I can trust.

As I entered the garden, I saw the chickens running around, avoiding the noisy mower while the gardener had his ear protection on and went about his business.

My impulse was to just close the gate – what's the big deal? – but I knew that would make me the designated gate closer moving forward, and if I'm not at home, the chicken or dog may escape. I also knew that just telling the gardener to close the gate next time would leave it to chance if he would remember or not. The chance that he remembered would be pretty low, as I would have contradicted my words by doing it myself. I did feel a bit bossy about myself, telling him to close the gate a few feet away from us, but despite my feeling of uneasiness, I knew it needed to happen so he would build the habit that I desired for him to develop.

I walked up to him and tapped him on the shoulder.

He switched off the mower, lifted his ear protection, and looked at me.

I said, "Would you be so kind as to close the gate? It is important so the chickens or the dog can't run out."

He nodded with a friendly, agreeing smile, put his ear protection back on, and restarted the mower.

I tapped him on the shoulder again; he switched off the mower, lifted his ear protection, and looked at me. "Could you please close the gate right now?"

He nodded, walked over to the gate, and closed it.

I thanked him profusely and went back inside.

The next week, the gardener mowed, and the gate was open, chickens running around like, well, scared chickens.

I walked up to him and tapped him on the shoulder.

He switched off the mower, lifted his ear protection, and looked at me.

I said, "Could you please close the gate? I don't want the chickens or the dog to run out."

He nodded with a friendly, agreeing smile, put his ear protection back on, and restarted the mower.

Yes, you read that already on the previous page.

I tapped him on the shoulder again; he switched off the mower, lifted his ear protection, and looked at me. "Could you please close the gate right now?"

He nodded, walked over to the gate, and closed it. I thanked him profusely and went back inside.

For the next three weeks, the gate was closed while he worked in the garden.

Then it was open again.
What thoughts may have crossed my mind?

1. "Is he an idiot? I think he needs to understand my frustration, so I'll let him feel it."
2. "He did so well the last three weeks, I'll cut him some slack and close it for him."

What result would those responses have?

Number one would connect negative emotions with the action I'd like to see him perform. Negative emotions deter from the thing they are connected to, so I may have programmed his unconscious mind to *not* close the gate, as thinking of closing the gate would make him feel negatively about it.

Number two would be a generous approach, but what if the gate was open again the week after? I may feel slighted, disregarded, disrespected, taken for granted, taken advantage of, feel not taken seriously, and revert to choice number one. Doing it for him would demonstrate to his unconscious mind that him closing the gate is actually not that important for me, that there is a possibility that I will do it if he doesn't. It would remove the sense of importance. That would not be my intention, but it may be the resulting effect of my action on his unconscious mind.

I picked option number three. Knowing about the process of habit building and that falling off a habit is an integral part of creating it, I walked up to the gardener, tapped him on the shoulder, and after he switched off the mower and took off his ear protection, I asked him again kindly to please close the gate. His body language showed him remembering, and he immediately went and closed the gate.
From then on, it was shut for the rest of the time that we lived at

that place.

How often have you been in a similar situation with your spouse? They agreed to do something habitually, and they fell off it. How did you respond?

The most powerful thing you can do is remind them kindly and motivate them to do it. At the same time, absorb any expression of frustration they may show for different reasons.

Maybe they feel guilty or not good enough for having forgotten it and letting you down. Maybe they feel sad for disappointing you. Maybe they feel belittled or understand you as condescending for asking them to do it right in front of them. Reframe it with compassion and stay off the blame carousel.

A possible answer could be: "I am sorry; it just means so much to me that you're doing this for me." Then thank them afterward.

It also helps to notice and thank them when they do it without being reminded.

Especially if they tell you that they did it, don't respond with a sarcastic "You want a medal for that? Do you want me to run to you with every chore I do?"

You could call that self-sabotage, as instead of using the opportunity to inject love, respect, appreciation, and gratitude into the relationship, you'd do the opposite.

	Motivation	**Ability**
Personal	**1: Make the undesirable desirable** What will happen if you continue doing the old habit? What will happen if you start the new, empowering habit? ⇨ See it, hear it feel it	**2: Surpass your limits** • Practice. Practice even tiny, little, ridiculous things. Find a way to repeat the new habit and engrain the pattern in relaxed situations so you have them at your disposal when the going gets tough. Start small but religiously: One minute a day. • Change the approach: If you have tried to change the habit in the past, you MUST do something DIFFERENT now! • Hook a new habit to a habit that you already follow (Hug/kiss your partner when you come home.)
Social	**3: Harness peer pressure** Commit openly to people (your spouse, friends, a coach or therapist) whose opinion is important to you. Allow them to remind or encourage you. If your spouse wants to change, ask them if they want you to remind them but accept a "no" (Offer a true choice.).	**4: Find Strength in numbers** Find other people who want to change with you. Changing your environment is the most powerful lever you can utilize. It is so strong that it changes you even if you don't intend to change. E.g., start a new habit together with your spouse/ coworker. Introduce the 4-eye principle.
Structural	**5: Design rewards and demand accountability** Remember: A baby does not need a system of rewards and punishments to start walking and talking. Experiencing its own personal growth is sufficient. Make the change visible and acknowledge the progress, for example with a habit tracker. But there is no harm in treating yourself to a Starbucks coffee when you reached a milestone.	**6: Change the physical environment** • Put up signs or other visual reminders like a habit tracker. • Raise the hurdles to exercise the old habit – move things out of reach. • Lower the hurdles to exercise the new habit – put things in reach.

Reversal

If you forget to do something you had committed to, and your partner responds frustrated, take it easy. Most people don't know the concept I just shared. You won't reap any benefits from mansplaining or womansplaining this concept to them.

Instead, it's up to you to find compassion for their frustration. If you agreed to do something, you forgot, and your spouse misses the tone as they remind you, reframe their expression of frustration and kindly do the task, ideally immediately.

<u>Their expression of frustration is not a valid excuse to withdraw a commitment</u>. They may be right but wrong in how they express it. If appropriate in your situation and you see a possibility of a positive response, you can do the task, and then you may say something along the lines of, "I am sorry that I forgot. The way you reminded me was a bit hurtful, though."

Chapter 27

INTIMACY

"You will never get your needs fulfilled by withholding what fulfills your partner's needs."

If you feel the need for more intimacy in your relationship or want to reignite the passion, you are empowered to do something about it. Hint: it's not nagging.

Missing intimacy is not a gender-specific thing. It's not that men always want more sex than women, nor is it the other way around. The truth is that two people will usually have different sex drives, maybe not so much in the beginning of a relationship but certainly as the relationship matures.

It's kind of like two individuals always having different preferences regarding cleanliness, tidiness, and organization. There are people who are great at organizing, so it's important for them that things have their place. But they may be okay if things are not in that place for a while. It also doesn't mean that they need everything sparkling clean all the time. They may be okay with a layer of dust. Maybe even both partners are okay with a layer of dust. But every person has a threshold at which they think cleaning must commence, and the person with the lower threshold may think that the other person is a pig.

As two people have different sex drives, what influences sex drive, and what can you do about it? How can you inspire your partner to fulfill your needs? There is no magic trick, no magic word, no magic action. It's kind of like inside your own body; you can make a fist and hold it up in front of your eyes, decide to stretch your index finger, and do it instantly. You can't instantly have an orgasm. You can just do things that will then lead to an orgasm. You have only indirect control over this bodily function.

Just like that, if your relationship is in a state where your need for intimacy is not met and you want to rekindle the passion, you have no direct control over your partner's sex drive and openness to sex. You have only indirect control to create an environment that makes it as likely as possible to experience intimacy and fire up the passion. You have two angles to approach this:

1.   Stop suppressing the sex drive.
2.   Court and entice them to want intimacy.

Here's the primary reason that stifles most people's sex drive: stress. The hormones of stress direct the blood flow away from those bodily systems that are not needed during your fight with a wolf. Obviously, your sexual organs are part of that. If you want to have or want to want more sex, take care of your stress levels. Part Three of this book can help you with that, and here are a couple more things:

- Make sure you get the amount of sleep that you need.
- In men, a drop in testosterone can lead to a low sex drive. Eating healthy, getting enough vitamin D, avoiding excessive alcohol consumption, working out regularly, and managing stress to increase testosterone production, and maybe even seeing a healthcare professional if you have concerns about your testosterone level.
- Touch your partner at least four times every day. A touch is a touch, no matter who initiates it, and it drives connection.
- If you have gained weight over time to a point where it is unhealthy, or you believe it may turn your partner off, then do something about it. If you had a different physique when you met, chances are, that is the kind of physique that turns your partner on. They love you, they appreciate you, they are grateful for you and for all you do for them, but their unconscious mind is not attracted to you as much

anymore. I know it can be triggering to hear this, but when you lose weight, then you would like your partner to notice, appreciate it, and pay attention to it. They can't notice and appreciate a weight loss if they didn't notice or even slightly dislike your prior weight gain.

Reversal

If your partner gained weight and you nodded through the last sentences, take a deep breath. Criticizing your partner's weight will in no way, shape, or form serve the relationship or inspire your partner to lose weight. Show the affection you've always shown or have shown in the past. You're not asked to compliment on things you don't appreciate; it would not be genuine, and your partner would see through it anyway. Instead, compliment every sign of weight loss that you recognize. Inspire healthy eating by not being the one who buys the chips and ice cream and certainly not the one who produces the snacks as you sit down by the TV. "Why do I have to cut my freedom of choice to solve my partner's problem?"
You are not solving it. You create a supportive environment that makes it as likely as possible for your partner to achieve the change they desire, and you do so because you exercise your freedom of choice and choose partnership over your own comfort. And it's not like you're not benefiting as well...

- Have sex anyway. We start having sex by feeling it and then doing it, but the other way around works just as well if it comes from a place of exercising a true choice and from a place of love. Sex sets certain biological and chemical processes in motion that deepen your connection and desire for more sex.

If you want more sex but your partner doesn't, you can do what's in your control to reduce their stress levels. Mastering your state of being and keeping your expressions of frustration amicable by speaking Love-Based Language will contribute.

Scripture says that sex is your marital duty, and that has pros and cons. If it motivates you to engage in sexual activities to fulfill your partner's needs and commit to always agreeing to have sex when they want it, this is an empowering belief and will elevate your marriage.

If you use this belief to try to get your partner to do something that they are not open to doing, then you may feel absolutely righteous and good about yourself, but it will either not result in more sex, or if so, your partner's agreement comes from a place of guilt or fear and undermines the core of a Love-Based Relationship.

As you see it as their duty, chances are you may not even reciprocate and not express yourself in a loving or appreciative way afterward. If you can find that kind of behavior in your recent past, this is a good time to reflect on it and think about alternatives that meet your partner's needs as well.

Other things you can do to relieve your partner from stress:

- Offer massages (and don't cut them short).
- Take over as many household chores as possible or join in when they do them.
- Connect and listen to your partner.
- Touch your partner at least four times every day in a non-sexual way.
- Show as much appreciation as possible (five love languages).
- Show as much gratitude as possible.
- Offer to go on walks with your partner.
- For women only: Join your partner in silence. The result of just sitting by your partner while he is doing something like reading, working on a hobby, working in the garden, and bringing him a glass of his favorite beverage can be almost miraculous. (You may wonder, "Oh, THIS is why he is so annoyed when I immediately ask him for a favor when he sits down).

- Tell your spouse (especially husband) how much you respect him. Hearing those words can have a profound effect.
- Tell your partner how beautiful/handsome they are.
- Tell your spouse (especially wife) every day that you love her.
- For men only: Helping your wife with chores around the house has been seen to increase their sex drive… If the help comes from a place of love and not from a place of apparent sexual desire. Some experts say, "Sex starts at breakfast."

As you consume relationship advice books, you will discover a shared opinion on how sexuality works with men and women.

In his "Tale of the Two Brains," which I recommend watching on YouTube, Mark Gungor puts it like this:

"To get to have sex with a woman, a man needs to go through her heart."
"To get to a man's heart, a woman needs to have sex with him."

How does that make sense?

Many single men may be open to having sex with a lot of attractive women, but only for a few will they invest the effort to court her, get to know her and her family, introduce her to his family, spend time with her, understand and fulfill her needs, and stay present with her when she feels frustrated. A woman who is looking for a long-term, possibly forever relationship needs to look for a man who does just that to make sure that he will stay with her in case of a pregnancy and times of crisis.

When a man puts in the effort, he still needs to manage his expectations because his efforts may still end in rejection. A man who attaches himself too early may find himself in the painful state of needing to detach, express inappropriate behaviors like stalking or find himself in the "friendzone", hoping the woman may reciprocate his feelings one day.

In case the courting is successful the agreement of the woman to have sex indicates that attaching himself to her is now warranted. The act of sex then sets biological and chemical processes in motion that corroborate the bond.

This may all happen unconsciously, but the societal shift to "free sex" is too recent for biology to adapt. Our biology developed and got hardwired over millions of years. I believe that following those biological principles increases the chances of creating marriages that last.

As sex solidifies the bond and provides the biological and chemical glue to keep the partners together, stopping sexual activities sets the relationship up for failure. Committing to agreeing to sex whenever the partner initiates it in that spirit seems to be a principle that serves each partner, the relationship and the family. Maybe the Bible was onto something there after all.

Inside a long-term relationship you can say that if a woman craves connection, initiating intimacy with her man can be an effective way to foster it.

You can also say that if a man craves intimacy, then connecting, listening, showing appreciation, and gratitude is the most effective way to have that need fulfilled by providing what the partner needs.

What about women who crave more intimacy and men who crave more connection? In that case, I would go back to the feminine and masculine analogy. It *can* be reversed.

That begs the question, what do you *know* about your partner's need for intimacy? Here are a few questions for your next pillow talk:

- What does sex mean to you? What does sex provide for you?
- What do you believe sex provides for me? If they are off or if there is more: "May I share what it really means/provides for me?"
- What words or things that I do really turn you on?

- How would you like me to initiate sex?
- How do you signal when you want or are open to sex?
- How long in advance do you want me to initiate sex? Do you want to prepare in the morning for an evening session or a few minutes before?
- What do you need right after sex or even in the following days to feel appreciated and excited for the next time?

Asking those questions offers a *true choice* to your partner. If your question is not welcome in the moment, shelve it. The best time to ask those questions is a relaxed moment, for example, right after sex when there is no possible ulterior motive of an underlying frustration.

What holds true either way is: You can never get what you want by keeping from your partner what they want. In other words, you will never get your needs fulfilled by withholding what fulfills your partner's needs.

In a nutshell, you lay the groundwork for a healthy relationship and a fulfilling quality and quantity of intimacy and passion by offering unconditional love, unconditional respect, unconditional trust, and unconditional agreement to sex on your end, and reducing your own and your partner's stress levels to the best of your abilities.

PART FIVE

THE EDGES OF RELATIONSHIPS

"An end is a new beginning."

Chapter 28

NAVIGATING A DIFFICULT BREAKUP

"Clarity of thought leads to clarity of action." - Thomas Leonard

Breakups are always painful, whether in the moment, immediately after, or beforehand. In the best-case scenario, a breakup is swift, like ripping off a band-aid, and partners go their separate ways. However, sometimes things are not that easy. Couples break up and get back together, or one partner struggles to accept the breakup, leading to a confusing emotional mess.

This chapter aims to provide clarity if you and your partner are currently separated, stuck in a cycle of breaking up and getting back together, or questioning whether it's time to break up in a fear-based relationship. Your situation may resemble one of the following:

1. A loves B, but B no longer loves A. A is trapped in the *belief* that B is the one and only, unable to let go.
2. A loves B but sends mixed signals, engaging in a toxic back-and-forth that pushes B away.
3. A loves B and is certain that B loves them back, but B sends mixed signals, creating a toxic back-and-forth and pushing A away.
4. A doesn't love B and initiates a breakup, but B still loves A and refuses to accept or respect the breakup.

If you find yourself in any of those situations you may wonder if what you feel is truly love?

Apart from the love we experience in a happy, loving relationship, we have an "attachment system" that gets triggered when we fear losing our beloved or when we desire closer connection with someone who reciprocates. Conversely, we employ "distancing strategies" to detach inappropriate emotions of love and connection when we feel we're becoming too close to someone, or when someone has wronged us in an unforgivable way, left us for another partner, or even passed away.

For instance, if you're in a healthy, loving relationship but find yourself developing feelings for a cute colleague or a friend, you would use distancing strategies to restore the previous distance and remain faithful to your partner.

Not cheating isn't about dramatically pushing a naked person away and declaring, "I can't do this!" Rather—in case you ever find yourself in a situation of feeling inappropriately attracted to a person of the other gender—it involves acting on your body's biological signals of closeness and promptly creating distance.

The attachment system helps us maintain or strengthen love in a happy, loving relationship when we sense growing distance or face physical separation, such as during work travel or when the hunter left to cave to feed the family.

Love is: unconditional appreciation, freedom to be your authentic self, love hormones (Oxytocin, Vasopressin), and peace of mind. It thrives in a committed relationship through unconditional respect, trust, and a healthy sexual bond.

The expression of love and the expression of an activated attachment system can appear similar and be easily confused:

Love: When you're in love, the other person is on your mind a lot. Thoughts of others don't arise at all or fade quickly. There's an urge to see and touch your loved one. Your thoughts are respectful, focusing on positive qualities, intimacy, trust, and future possibilities. This strengthens your self-confidence and empowers you.

Activated attachment system: When you're not in love but experience an activated attachment system, you find hope in small gestures, rationalize dismissive behavior as "not their authentic self," and find ways to explain and reason such behavior. The other person also occupies your mind, but in the form of preoccupation and obsession with ways to win them back. Instead of trust, anxiety and fear prevail, and creating closeness may involve disrespecting their desire for distance to achieve physical closeness.

Every attempt to distract yourself from thinking about that person or to entertain thoughts of someone else feels like "giving the other person up" or "neglecting them." It's because you don't want them to experience the same detested behavior you're suffering from.

The preoccupation, obsession, desire for closeness and intimacy, and the highs that follow even the smallest doses of attention bear similarities to the thought patterns experienced when in love. However, it's not love; it's mistaken for love.

The difference lies in the thoughts themselves, which revolve around negativity, impossibilities, undermine self-esteem, and disempower.

Questionnaire

How can you determine if you are in love or just suffering from an activated attachment system?

Question	Love	Activated Attachment System
When you think of the other person you feel...	Anticipation (positive Expectation)	Insecurities and anxiety that you may not see the other person soon, that they will ignore you or you fear to lose them completely if you make a tiny mistake (negative Expectation)
Thoughts of the other person...	Create a feeling of inner peace	Create a feeling of unrest
The result of interactions is	Mostly satisfaction	Mostly disappointment with rare sparks of hope
Thoughts of the other person...	...raise your energy level, increase your performance and spirits	...lower your energy level, performance, and spirits
You would love for the other person to...	...stay the way they are: Unconditional appreciation	...change and start to express love desire/allow intimacy give up something else (e.g., another relationship)
Your self-confidence...	...becomes stronger	...becomes weaker, thoughts of self-recrimination are present

In the presence of the other person, you can...	...be your authentic self	...not be your authentic self. You fear that the tiniest mistake can end all hopes. You believe that your mistakes lead to them not being able to love you anymore and once you change and are able to convey that change to them, they must inevitably fall in love with you again.
You spend most of your time...	...with feelings of gratitude and beautiful feelings regarding their affection.	...self-recriminating about having pushed the other person away, trying to overcome your "misbehaviors" and break the wall around their heart so you become lovable again.
The person/ partner...	...makes you be your best self	...makes you scramble to become enough
Negative behaviors of the other person...	...are the exception and are dwarfed by positive behaviors	...are the norm and you justify and trivialize them

Small gestures OF the other person...	...are being recognized, met with appropriate gratitude, and reciprocated	...are overvalued as signs that the relationship is growing stronger again or as PROOF that the other person still feels love
Small gestures TOWARDS the other person...	...are being recognized, met with appropriate gratitude, and reciprocated	...get ignored or labeled as "pushy" and rejected. When a gesture gets reciprocated that will be overvalued as a sign that the relationship is growing stronger again or as PROOF that the other person still feels love
You know that the other person loves you...	...because you are being loved with words and actions	...because you interpret small friendly gestures and words as proof of love
The other person...	...says "I love you" and wants to be close to you	...doesn't say "I love you" or says "I love you" but stays distanced. Words and actions contradict each other. They send "Mixed signals"

Authenticity Check:

1. Do you have more answers in the right column, but you trivialize those points by giving questions where your answer is in the left column more weight?
2. Did you revisit the answers in the right column and tried to switch them over to the left?

Which column received more results? (If an answer in both the left and right columns is true, it has to be counted for the right column.)

If you have five or more answers in the right column, then you are probably not experiencing love but an activated attachment system that you are mistaking for love.

I have an activated attachment system; how do I switch it off?

You broke up, and you believe that was the right decision to make. Yet, you're in pain, and it's hard to let go emotionally. You fear that if your ex-partner approaches you and finds the right words, you may give in and give him/her another chance, although you *know* that you can never be happy in a relationship with that person.

Or your partner broke up, and you have made your peace with it consciously but not emotionally.

Either way, you want to cut the ties and move on. You can use the following distancing strategies:

- Delete pictures and remove memorabilia.
- Stop contact.
  - How NOT to stop contact:
    - Write "Last message," communicating that you will stop contact now.
    - Arrange a "last goodbye meeting" (If you are not in a relationship or your partner is even in a new relationship, then a breakup talk is not appropriate

anymore.)
- ◆ In short, MAKING contact to communicate END-ING contact is a contradiction or mixed signal.
  - How to DO stop contact:
    - ◆ The last outgoing message/call was the last one.
    - ◆ Leave incoming messages/calls unanswered. If they don't stop, block the person to keep them from entering your environment.
    - ◆ Take measures that make it as difficult as possible for the other person to sneak back into your life (block all social media accounts).
- In moments of doubt:
  - Remember the questionnaire and read it again.
  - Remember their flaws and write them down.
  - Write a letter and put EVERYTHING in it. Work on that letter until it is complete. Keep it. When thoughts come up, then give yourself a choice: "Shall I pull out the letter and continue working on it, or can I be more productive with my time?" Then follow your answer. One day, in a few months or years, you may stumble across that letter, chuckle, and toss it.
  - When thoughts come up about how great things were with that person, like sex or long talks, notice how those things were not that great anymore right before the last breakup. THAT is your point of reference, not the rainbows and unicorns from the past in-love phase.
  - Do things you like to do but they didn't like to do with you.
  - Listen to music you like to listen to, but they didn't.
  - Watch movies you like to watch but they didn't.
  - Eat things you enjoy but they didn't.
- Spend more time with friends/family and pets.
- Meditate.
- Chant a mantra.
- Spend time outdoors.
- Date (I don't mean screwing around but having coffee with members of the other gender and get used to talking and

getting to know other people.)
- Go to places where you will meet people of all genders (take dance lessons, try a new martial art, take art classes, cooking classes, visit seminars, go to concerts, join meetups, toastmasters, ...).
- Go through the Ho'oponopono forgiveness process! (Disrupt the energetic connection)

The attachment system and the deactivation strategies live off the attention they receive. As soon as they don't get attention, they dry out and die. You can't "withdraw attention" just as you can't not think of a pink elephant. You can just direct your attention somewhere else. Remember the Marshmallow test.

Why is there an attachment system but no detachment system? Because detachment is just the absence of attachment. You'd be pretty busy if you had to run everything out there that gets your attention for a minute through a detachment system. There are only deactivation strategies to deactivate your attachment system if it tries to connect you to someone whose presence in your life doesn't serve you anymore.

Too much love scares me. What if I notice that I have trouble allowing closeness?

You are in a relationship with a caring and loving partner, and you love them as well. Still, you catch yourself running deactivation strategies to manage your emotions when you are in distress to try to get back to a "safe" place.

So, at times you express love and the desire for closeness, but at other times, your behavior seems like you would prefer to be alone. You send "mixed signals."

You may have a belief that a partnership, marriage, or having kids limits your freedom. Or you may think that you could be exploited by your partner or pressured into things you don't want. In general, relationships or certain relationship situations have an aspect of uncertainty, and when it's triggered, you pull away to a "safer place."

It can also mean that while your relationship runs smoothly, you tend to inject some chaos into the relationship to – consciously or unconsciously – test if your partner still really, really loves you. But by doing so, you present yourself as unreliable, not trustworthy, not loving, disrespectful, not meeting your partner's needs.

How it can manifest:

- You can feel uncomfortable or even unsafe when your partner shares their feelings.
- You sometimes rationalize their feelings or disregard emotional cues.
- You sometimes suppress loving feelings and emotions instead of showing them.
- You believe you are not responsible for your partner's happiness but believe only they alone are responsible for their happiness.
- You catch yourself sometimes not being courageous and honest in your actions.
- Your partner complains that you need too much alone time.
- At times you find your partner needy.
- When things don't go well you fantasize about how great an ex-relationship was or how much better a different, new relationship could be.
- You were hurt in the past, and now you'd rather play it safe than be hurt again.
- You saw how one of your parents hurt the other parent, and you don't want that to happen to you.
- When your partner does something that bothers you, then you sit on it for days before bringing it up, or you just become unfriendly, sarcastic, and/or distant... a bad mood can last for days.
- You sometimes obsess over your partner's flaws and question if the relationship is "meant to be."
- You think independence equals self-reliance.
- You sometimes assume malicious intent in your partner's

actions.

- You sometimes focus your attention only on the negative traits of your partner and downplay the positive ones, thus convincing yourself (temporarily) that you don't love them and numb loving feelings.
- You sometimes inflate yourself by putting them down (verbally or in your thoughts) and don't act encouraging.
- You withdraw/stonewall when your partner does something that hurts you or made you sad or angry (stop physical contact, reject sex, sleep curled up as far away from the other person as possible in bed or even in a different room).
- In fights, you may leave and only come back at an uncertain time in the future, leaving your partner guessing.
- You have a hard time naming your feelings.

My partner loves me, and I love my partner, but I have an urge to pull away sometimes. What can I do to overcome it and make my relationship a safer place for both of us?

- Make a list of their positive traits and reasons why you trust them.
- Visualize and possibly write down beautiful moments you have shared.
- Remember things they have done that you are grateful for.
- Make a list of ways you can express love and then take action (love is not only a noun but also a verb).
- What is their primary love language, and how can you better speak it?
  - Say more kind words and give specific compliments.
  - Give small gifts (See chapter on love language gifts)
  - Do small things like preparing their favorite drink or cleaning their stuff, or filling up their car with gas.
  - Touch them four or more times every day, such as hugging more often, giving massages, and greeting with hugs or kisses.
  - Be present with them by putting your phone away and turning off the TV, and go for walks together.

- Accept opportunities to get closer to their friends and family. Find the interesting stories in everyone you meet, build rapport, and compliment people on things you appreciate about them.
- Spend time imagining and envisioning a shared future with your partner.
- Find creative ways to be close while also allowing for personal space when needed.
  - Consider moving into a place where you share a bedroom but also have separate spaces like an office, library, meditation room, man cave, shed, or art room.
  - Get a pet that you can care for together.
  - Join a gym, take dance lessons, or engage in martial arts together with your partner.
  - Go camping as a way to bond and spend quality time together.
  - Practice being "vulnerable with confidence." Differentiate between sharing feelings and playing the victim by blaming the other person. Express your specific feelings using "Istatements" and reflect on the response. Discuss your feelings and the response with trusted friends or family members.
  - Example: "When you did XY, it made me feel loved, grateful, anxious, sad..." instead of "You disrespect me/don't love me because you did XY."
- Create an environment that encourages openness. For example, have crucial conversations during activities like walks or cooking, as it can make it easier to open up and share feelings when focused on something together, rather than feeling confrontational by solely looking at each other. If that's what you're doing already and it's not working, try sitting opposite of each other or at a 90° angle.
- When you need to take a break from an argument, communicate how long you'll be away and where you're going. Return within the specified time to avoid leaving your partner guessing.

My partner sends mixed signals. How can I make it stop? How can I help them express love and other feelings?

While reading the previous section, you gained insight into the mindset of an avoidant person.

It's unlikely that they would be open to reading this, so it's best not to expect it. However, if they do, consider it as an amazing surprise.

Evaluate whether an avoidant person can fulfill your relationship needs. Letting go may be painful but can be the right choice to honor your relationship values, self-love, and self-care.

However, people can change. By implementing the following strategies, you may see them expressing love in new ways:

- For crucial conversations, create an environment that distracts them slightly, which may make it easier for your partner to open up and share their feelings and recognize yours. For example, have crucial conversations on walks or while cooking together.
- When expressing empathy and compassion, begin sentences with phrases like "It seems like," "It looks like," or "It sounds like." This approach avoids putting them on the spot and lets them know it's okay for you to be wrong in your assessment of their feelings. For example, instead of asking, "Why are you angry?" ask, "What made you angry?"
- Avoid using the word "why" in your questions. Instead, start with "how" or "what" or "do." This may require practice, but it can lead to better communication. For instance, replace "Why are you angry?" with "What is frustrating you?" or "How are you feeling right now?"
- When they point out your negative traits or criticize your actions, ask them to identify your positive traits or what you're doing right. Avoid falling into the trap of defending yourself, as they might find something negative or belittle your positive actions. Respond with, "If you can't remember

a single positive thing, then it seems like you're not being honest with me right now." This can shift their focus back to positive aspects and their love for you.

- Inquire about the things you do for them that they appreciate the most. Even if they initially mention what you don't do, listen carefully without engaging, and then repeat your question. It's alright if they don't ask the same question in return.
- Speak their love languages to communicate affection in ways that resonate with them.
- Anticipate their fears and help them feel secure. For example, suggest moving into a place with a home office space to respect their need for personal space.
- Instead of scolding or belittling them when conflicts arise and they tend to run away, find creative solutions. For instance, when you can predict their impulse to leave, say, "I'm feeling a bit stressed right now and need to catch a breather. I'll go for a walk and be back in 30 minutes." Return within the specified time, demonstrating a healthy way to take a break while building trust.
- Ask them how they feel. Even if the initial answers are unsatisfying, the more frequently you ask, the more they will reflect on their feelings and become better at assessing and managing them.

Someone loves you who you don't love (anymore) but they just won't give up

While going through the following steps, you may discover lingering feelings that prevent you from fully implementing them. In such cases, reevaluate your emotions carefully. Perhaps you still love them?

- Ask them how they feel about you. Then inquire if they want to know your feelings about them.
- Express your emotions, set boundaries, and ask them, "Can you respect that?"

- If they respond negatively, ask them how they envision a functional relationship where mutual respect is lacking.
- Ask them how they think you (really) feel.
- Ask them how they would feel if someone they didn't love refused to respect their decision for no contact.
- Inquire what actions you would need to take for them to stop contacting you.
- Ask them how much money it would take for them to leave you alone or move out. This approach may seem unusual, but it redirects their focus towards the possibility of distance and prompts them to consider it as an option. It also attaches a tangible value on the importance for you to be apart from them. This realization can be sobering. Even if they provide a value, it doesn't mean you have to pay it or that they will accept it. Respond with, "Okay, let me think about that."
- If you're comfortable with it, you can even compensate them or cover expenses (like hiring movers) to demonstrate that it's worth money to you for them to leave.
- Cease engagement and refrain from responding at all. It's not about responding differently; it's about not responding at all. If necessary, block them on all communication channels.
- Do something exceptionally kind for them, but don't allow them to reciprocate. If they send gifts or flowers, leave them outside your door (if they notice them still there after a few days, it sends a strong message). If they send a letter, return it to the sender. This approach may seem harsh, but it's less harsh than keeping them in suspense or sending mixed signals that might mislead them into thinking you're still interested.
- Have conversations with their friends and parents about how you genuinely care for them but no longer wish to be in a relationship, seeking advice on how to help them understand.
- When in their presence, speak to someone on the phone or in person about your efforts to make them understand that the relationship is over or that there will be no relationship. Make sure they can hear this conversation.
- If they become angry in response to any of these steps, allow

them to experience and process their anger. Giving in to their anger and trying to calm them down sends mixed signals, reinstates suspense, and encourages them to continue pursuing you. This only works if there is no risk of abusive behavior. Your safety must be your priority.

If you haven't gained clarity yet, then the question remains: When is it time to break up? There is no set of boxes that, when checked, imply a breakup. Breaking up is a decision beyond logic, just like creating a relationship. It boils down to the question:

What do you want?

But if your partner shows abusive behavior, then I believe you need to get to a safe place and ask yourself that question when you have reached it.

I am aware that this chapter may have ruffled some feathers. A breakup is a highly emotional situation, and it is often not as black and white as I may have made it seem. Breakups can bring out shadows from the past and surface traumatic experiences from past relationships and baggage that was created in the early stages of childhood beyond our conscious memory. As much guidance as this chapter provides, if you find yourself dealing with emotions that keep you stuck, then working with a therapist or coach is advised.

— Chapter 29 —

DATING

"The most important four-letter word in dating is NEXT."

If you are reading this book as you're coming out of a bad break-up and preparing for the next relationship to come, this chapter is especially for you.

If you're interested in witty pickup lines and tricks to lure a potential partner into your bed or into marriage, I must disappoint you. I even warn you against consuming such content. If you do things that are outside of your usual behavioral spectrum, you must either keep doing them (which is hard to sustain) or you will eventually stop those things, potentially disappointing or confusing your partner and making them wonder if you stopped loving them.

The best thing you can do is show up as your authentic self. That way, you'll attract a partner who can appreciate you just the way you are. At the same time, practice empathizing and effectively communicating with yourself and others, and value and set boundaries with your date, friends, coworkers, and family.

Manifest Mr. or Mrs. Right:
Take a letter-size or A4-size sheet of paper and split the page into four quadrants, see *Figure 15*. Label each quadrant: physical, emotional, mental, and spiritual. Then fill out each quadrant in as much detail as possible. The quadrant to which you find the fewest things to add is the most important one because in this area, you are driven by your unconscious mind and default to traits that you probably have unconsciously modeled after people from your childhood.

<table>
<tr><td>Physical</td><td>Emotional</td></tr>
<tr><td>Mental</td><td>Spiritual</td></tr>
</table>

Figure 15

Then reflect on your own personality and consider whether someone with the traits you listed on your paper will be attracted to you. Do you need to make changes to the paper? Do you need to change? This is not meant to challenge your confidence but to take an honest inventory and understand if there is a mismatch.

When it comes to a successful long-term relationship, the most accurate yet very simple predictor is kindness. Observe your date closely and don't accept uncouth behavior towards others. How does he or she treat the people they meet? How does he or she treat waiters and store clerks? How does he or she treat their family members? Chances are, that's how you're going to be treated when he or she feels safe around you. I don't think road rage is an acceptable behavior. It is up to you to decide at what level of expressed frustration it becomes road rage. The principle "how you do something is how you do everything" has served me well. If you find yourself road-raging once in a while, the tools in Part Three of this book will serve you well.

Identify your date's love language as quickly as possible. Relationships can last forever despite having opposite primary love languages, but having a relationship with a person who shares the same primary or even secondary love language makes things so much easier.

Remember that the extra effort required to speak someone else's (foreign) love language can be too much to sustain in times of stress, which then adds stress to the relationship. If both of you have the same love language, such as touch, for example, when you get stressed, you will lean in for a hug, making your partner feel loved at the same time.

Set and enforce your boundaries, with love, early. Letting your partner violate a boundary and only starting to enforce it a few months or even years later may make them feel unloved. Authenticity is a foundation for a happily-ever-after relationship.

Reversal: This may be a reason why many women "fall for the bad guys". They believe they see authenticity while they are really experiencing rude and unloving behavior. Don't mistake rudeness with setting and enforcing boundaries.

Find out as much as you can about your date, not as an investigative journalist, but from a place of genuine curiosity and interest in the person in front of you. Find out what their values are, their beliefs in areas that are important to you and their beliefs in areas that are important to them. Test their sense of humor. Find out what sex means to them. Find out what marriage means to them.

In 1990 a team of researchers led by Arthur Aron, Ph.D. and Elaine Aron, Ph.D., conducted a study called *The Experimental Generation of Interpersonal Closeness: A Procedure and Some Preliminary Findings* or better known as the list of "36 questions to fall in love." The researchers developed a list of 36 questions that create closeness and, if answered authentically, can help partners explore aspects of their being that help open up to each other and identify if their personalities match.

You can find them with a quick Google search. They provide a great basis for many deep conversations. I fondly remember talking about those questions with my wife as we were dating, for example, during dinner in a little restaurant in Carmel.

The paper you created earlier in this chapter can help as well to derive questions that reveal how well you and your date match.

Sex connects. A large portion of the feeling of love is a chemical/biological response inside you and your (sex) partner. I believe a lot of relationships end in marriage and then divorce because people have sex before they really know each other and create that biological bond before understanding if they match in other aspects of their lives. It's never "just sex." Sex sets a bonding process in motion, activates the attachment system, that is painful to undo.

On the contrary, when you have dated and become intimate, many people wonder how quickly they should move in together. Personally, I believe you can't move in together too soon if both of you feel like this could be the forever relationship. What's the worst that can happen? You separate after a month. And in that case, it has saved you a lot of time, your most valuable asset.

When it comes to marriage, I believe a couple should wait at least a year and go through all four seasons together, learn to know each other's families and friends, and progress through the fleeting "in love" phase.

Is marriage necessary at all? Technically, no, but there is value in celebrating the choice to stay together forever and involving each other's friends and families in this celebration. However, scientists have found a reverse connection between the money invested in wedding celebrations and engagement rings and the length of a marriage. The more expensive the ring and celebration, the shorter the marriage. There are, of course, plenty of exceptions, so this may just be an interesting side note and certainly not a means to deprive the woman of your dreams of having the wedding she's been dreaming of since she was a little girl.

I believe it is not advisable to go into debt or suffer financial hardship to realize a big engagement ring or wedding celebration. The stress and resentment that may come from that will likely outweigh any benefit. Planning a wedding together, getting creative with it, and doing a lot yourself can be a fun bonding experience that you will look back on forever. Set your expectations:

Men: If there are specific boxes that need to be checked, check them, don't mansplain. I had to learn, for example, about the importance of Chiavari chairs for my wife. Disclosure: I had no idea how to spell Chiavari and looked it up just now, but I sat on one during our wedding.

Women: He may not get it. Understand this during the dating phase and don't think you'll be able to fix it later.

I have talked with a few people who were in distress about their relationship, complained about their partner, tried in vain to make their partner open up emotionally and connect, or wondered if they should break up. As I realized that something was off and asked deeper questions, it turned out that those people were in a relationship with their partner for months, and some even for years, without ever having met their partner. Coincidentally, all the people I talked to were women. If that is you, read this very carefully:

- You are not in a relationship. There is nothing to break up. Having met, felt, smelled, tasted, and spent time with a partner outside of select phone or video calls is the prerequisite to calling a relationship an intimate relationship.
- A man who wants you will move mountains to get to you. He will fly, book a hotel close to where you live, agree to meet at a safe location, and you can take it from there. If he doesn't, then he is not into you. Don't believe the excuses about no time, no money, a stressful job, or a wife that they are "about to leave." Stop speaking with that person if it takes longer than a couple of months. Do not fly to him. DO NOT SEND HIM MONEY. If you have already sent him money, cut your losses and the connection. This is the only situation in relationships where I believe setting an ultimatum is the right thing to do.

More mystery, less history

It is important to understand your partner's beliefs, values, sense of humor, manners, preferences, and boundaries. You do not need to know anything about your partner's past relationships. You do not need to know anything about the conflicts your partner had with their ex-partners, what issues their ex-partners had with them, how many sex partners they had, or even anything about their sexual experiences.

Imagine you had a POV video of your life, and your partner had one of their life, and you made each other watch the whole thing. I don't think there are a lot of relationships out there that would survive it. And probably not even because of the bad moments, but because of the good moments. The *very* good moments.

Here's why more mystery, less history is the better choice for the relationship:

1. Every positive moment with an ex that you share creates a mind movie in the mind of your partner. The worst case would be sharing specifics about a sexual encounter. As their mind movie is created in that very moment, it's seems to their unconscious mind as if you were cheating in that moment. You're setting your relationship up for distrust.
2. Sharing a problem an ex had with you or a problem you had with an ex makes your partner try on their hat/perspective as well and opens/sensitizes their perception filters for the part you played in that conflict. You may find your partner mansplaining/womansplaining to you a few weeks, months, or years later how your ex was right.

As much as it is important to understand each other as well as possible, it is up to you to find out how your partner presents themselves in the relationship with you. This will be different than in any past relationship as it will entail the learnings from those relationships. And since you are a different person with unique values, beliefs, preferences, and boundaries, you're not doing yourself a favor by comparing your partner to how they acted towards an ex.

How do you know if a man is open to being kissed? This question is not relevant. If it's important to you to find a guy with a minimum level of confidence, empathy, sensory acuity, and courage, someone who may one day ask you to marry him and who will show up for you and your family, then let him make the first move and kiss you.

How do you know if she is open to being kissed? If you're open to being kissed but guys never get the hint, what can you do? Typical signals include flicking her hair over your shoulder and exposing her neck, biting her lips, having her feet pointed towards him, allowing or initiating physical touch like holding hands, or accidentally touching his hands too frequently to be a coincidence.

If she doesn't exhibit any signs or if her feet are even pointed away from you, the best course of action is to ask for the check. Remember, the guy is the one expected to make the move, but only with a clear invitation. She shouldn't even have to say "no" because if she does, either you didn't read the signs or she's sending mixed signals. In that case, it's best to move on and avoid a life of confusion.

How does she know if a guy wants a real relationship? This is a difficult question because there are guys who genuinely want a real relationship, some who pretend to want one but just want sex, and others who solely seek physical intimacy and are upfront about it. The challenge lies with the second type of guy who will adapt his behavior to convince the girl, regardless of what advice is given. Some guys even enjoy the pursuit and have no qualms about pursuing a girl for weeks or months, only to lose interest after achieving their goal.

If you are seeking the right man to marry, following the advice below increases your chances of finding someone genuinely interested in spending their life with you:

- Wait for at least a few dates before engaging in intimacy.
- Clearly communicate your intentions for the relationship and observe his response while maintaining eye contact.
- Inquire about his preferences and don't allow him to deflect the question back to you before he answered, so that you make sure he communicates authentically with you.
- Watch out for red flags such as "love bombing" (intense and excessive expressions of affection, attention and flattery in early stages of a relationship going back and forth between ignoring and love bombing), discussing children together early on, or any signs of impatience, pushiness, or anger during the initial weeks of dating. Remember, his behavior at the start is likely his best behavior, so don't expect improvement or think you can change him.
- Pay attention to basic good manners:
  - If he doesn't make an effort to pay for your drinks or food, it may indicate a lack of interest or self-centeredness. Remember to offer to pay for your own tab, and if he allows it, take it as a clue.
  - According to etiquette, a man is expected to walk up the stairs behind a woman and down the stairs in front of her. Opening the door for the woman is also a common courtesy. Give him the opportunity to do so by slowing your pace, but be ready to grab the door handle to avoid awkwardness. It's not about setting him up; it's a test of basic manners.
  - Does he use "please" and "thank you" in his interactions?

If I were to boil dating advice down to one sentence, it would be: show up authentically.

If you show up as yourself and your date is not interested, that's a great thing. If you pretend to be someone different to win someone over, you have to keep up the façade or hope for understanding and appreciation when it inevitably falls apart. Don't take that gamble.

EPILOGUE

Thank you for taking the time to read this book. I hope it served you well. Relationships can be hard work, and being in a relationship is a process of constant growth and learning. I am learning every day as I go.

Every relationship book I read revealed a few nuggets that I was unaware of or added a perspective to my own view, expanding my horizon and enhancing my ability to understand a client, and often myself, better. Every client adds perspectives and clarity to my work.

I hope when you read the following list, tools and ideas come to mind that will elevate your relationship:

- Love-Based Language
- True choices.
- Mansplaining/ Womansplaining
- Master your state of being.
- Accept expressions of frustration.
- The blame carousel.
- Do the right thing with compassion instead of the wrong thing out of compassion.
- Every Relationship challenge has two sides to it.
- A victim blames others and feels like "Why always me?!", while a victor appreciates every leverage and opportunity he finds to take action and sway the situation in her favor.
- Avoid criticism, defensiveness, blame and contempt.
- You can't overdo appreciation and gratitude.
- When you express love, your partner feels it more and you feel it more.
- It seems like/it looks like/ it sounds like

I would love to hear your feedback and questions and have the opportunity to make this book even better. Email me at service@ imagine-evolution.com.

Thank you.

ACKNOWLEDGEMENTS

Writing this book has been on my heart for many years, but if I had written it upon my first inspiration to do so, it would not have been a fraction of what it has become.

I am deeply grateful for my beautiful wife and best friend, Morenike – the kindest soul I have ever met and an inspiration for me to become my kindest, most loving, and courageous self. Our relationship experiences have shaped me, this book, and my work with my clients. Thank you for seeing my soul through my flaws, mistakes, and shortcomings. Your lessons in kindness, gratitude, and appreciation continue to make me a better person, father, and husband every day. I married up.

I thank my children, Felix and Lara, for being my greatest mentors. They show me the darkest and brightest corners of my soul, and I am excited to learn from them and with them every day. They were my main inspiration to write this book, as I hope it will help guide them to relationship happiness. This book is for them.

I thank my parents, for setting me up for success to become the human I am today and for their uncompromising support. The negative childhood experiences I shared in this book, for the purpose of inspiring change in others, do not do justice to the love and dedication they invested in raising my siblings and me. I look back on an extraordinarily happy childhood that I would not have wanted to be any different. Despite the ups and downs life took them through, my parents have been married for over 48 years and counting, overcoming struggles that few couples have to endure.

I thank my sister, Astrid, who is also my best friend and the beacon I can turn to in celebration as well as in distress. I am deeply humbled and grateful for the lessons in forgiveness that I receive from her every day, which I may not even deserve.

I thank my brother, Bruno, for his patience, for helping me overcome my self-consciousness, and for teaching me to acknowledge and appreciate the inherent value and beauty of all human beings.

I am deeply humbled by my clients turning to me for mentorship and guidance, allowing me to facilitate the changes they want to see in themselves and their relationships. I am forever grateful for their help in teaching me so much about myself and relationships, as well as pointing me to additional literature that has elevated my own relationship, will elevate relationships of future clients, and yours. Much of what I learned from them has found its way into this book.

RELATIONSHIP-TRANSFORMING BOOKS

Alison Armstrong, *Celebrating Partnership* (Audio book, 2012)

Gary Chapman, *The Five Love Languages* (1992)

Gary Chapman, Paul White, *The Five Languages of Appreciation in the Workplace* (2011)

Stephen R. Covey, *The 7 Habits of Highly Effective People* (1989)

Dr. Joe Dispenza, *Becoming Supernatural* (2017)

Emerson Eggerichs, *Love and Respect* (2016)

Daniel Goleman, *Emotional Intelligence* (1997)

Joseph Grenny, Kerry Patterson, David Maxfield, Ron McMillan, Al Switzler, *Influencer* (2013)

John Gottman, *The 7 Principles for Making Marriage Work* (1999)

Gay Hendricks, *The Big Leap* (2009)

Dr. Matt James, Tris Thorp, *Mental and Emotional Release* (2017)

Harvey Karp, *The Happiest Toddler on the Block* (2004)

Oren Klaff, *Pitch Anything* (2011)

Amir Levine, Rachel S.F. Heller, *Attached* (2010)

Leonard Mlodinow, *Subliminial* (2012)

Geshe Michael Roach, *Karmic Management* (2009)

Marshall B. Rosenberg, *Nonviolent Communication* (2015)

Simon Sinek, *Leaders Eat Last* (2014)

Chris Voss, *Never Split the difference* (2016)

ABOUT THE AUTHOR

Following an international corporate career as an engineer in Germany, Product Manager in Switzerland and in Corporate Development in California, Arno became a professional business coach in 2018.

Coincidentally, his first business clients were struggling in their relationships, which began to thrive again over the course of his coaching programs, with the added benefit of helping clients overcome bulimia, phobias, and trauma. Recognizing this pattern and considering his own transformation, Arno began to focus on elevating and healing relationships as a relationship coach and has remained passionate about it ever since.

He also teaches intentional relationship-based leadership as an executive coach and corporate trainer.

Another book by Arno Koch:

EmpowerZen: Planner and Life Coach in a book.
ISBN 9780578317267